THE ANC BILLIONAIRES

Big Capital's Gambit and the Rise of the Few

Praise for *The Stellenbosch Mafia*

'The book offers something quite different: a thoughtful account of how a few big-hitting Afrikaner businessmen came to make Stellenbosch their base, and an analysis of whether there is any merit to the suggestion that they have acted in concert to pull the levers of politics and governance behind the scenes ... The Stellenbosch that comes through most vividly from Du Toit's book is not so much the town awash with money and influence – though yes, that too – but the town seething with gossip, rivalry, and social snobbishness ...'

– Daily Maverick

'Du Toit walks readers through the book with a keen understanding of how socio-economic divisions further exacerbate hostility towards the elite.'

– Fin24

'Woven together with the goings-on and opinions held in boardrooms and at dinner tables around town, the story quite lives up to its tantalising title.'

– Country Life

THE ANC
BILLIONAIRES

Big Capital's Gambit and the Rise of the Few

PIETER DU TOIT

JONATHAN BALL PUBLISHERS
JOHANNESBURG · CAPE TOWN · LONDON

First published in South Africa in 2022 by
JONATHAN BALL PUBLISHERS
A division of Media24 (Pty) Ltd
PO Box 33977
Jeppestown
2043

ISBN 978-1-77619-134-5
ebook ISBN 978-1-77619-135-2

Every effort has been made to trace the copyright holders
and to obtain their permission for the use of copyright material.
The publishers apologise for any errors or omissions and would
be grateful to be notified of any corrections that should be
incorporated in future editions of this book.

www.jonathanball.co.za
www.twitter.com/JonathanBallPub
www.facebook.com/JonathanBallPublishers

Cover by Sean Robertson
Design and typesetting by Martine Barker
Printed and bound by CTP Printers, Cape Town
Set in Garamond and Gibbs

To my family

CONTENTS

Cast of characters

Sir Ernest
Oppenheimer

Harry
Oppenheimer

Gavin
Relly

Michael Spicer

Clem Sunter

Bobby Godsell

Doug Band

Anton Rupert

Mike Rosholt

Theuns Eloff

Martin Kingston

Chris Ball

THE LIBERATION MOVEMENT

Oliver
Tambo

Thabo
Mbeki

Nelson
Mandela

Trevor Manuel

Jay Naidoo

Jeremy Cronin

Vella Pillay

NEW MONEY

Cyril
Ramaphosa

Saki
Macozoma

Patrice
Motsepe

Tokyo
Sexwale

Mzi
Khumalo

Nthato
Motlana

Vusi
Khanyile

THE POLITICIANS

PW Botha   FW de Klerk

THE FIXERS

Jürgen Kögl   Frederik van   Douw Steyn
                Zyl Slabbert

Timeline of events

1983   • United Democratic Front (UDF) established, consisting of a range of local, community-based organisations.

1984   • Tricameral parliamentary system introduced, excluding black representation.
           • Widespread township violence commences and spreads across South Africa.

1985   • Oliver Tambo declares the ANC's intention to make South Africa ungovernable.
           • International banks call in South African loans after apartheid president PW Botha's 'Rubicon' speech.
           • Botha declares state of emergency, which will last until the release of Nelson Mandela.
           • Business delegation under Anglo's Gavin Relly meets Tambo and the ANC in Lusaka.
           • Congress of South African Trade Unions (Cosatu) established in Durban.

1986   • Anglo's internal 'high road, low road' scenarios for South Africa gain national prominence.
           • Big capital meets PW Botha at the Carlton Hotel.
           • Secret meetings between apartheid justice minister Kobie Coetsee and Mandela start.

1987   • Afrikaner dissidents meet the ANC in Dakar, Senegal.
           • First meeting of the Mells Park group between Afrikaner intellectuals and ANC leaders.
           • Standard Chartered, Barclays Bank and Citibank quit South Africa.

1988   • Apartheid spy boss Niël Barnard starts dialogue with Mandela in prison.
           • Consultative Business Movement (CBM) is established to facilitate contact between business and Mass Democratic Movement (MDM) leaders.

1989 • South African Communist Party (SACP) conference held in
Cuba, chaired by Thabo Mbeki.
• Paris conference about future of South Africa arranged by
French first lady Danielle Mitterand.
• FW de Klerk replaces Botha as apartheid head of state.
• The Berlin Wall comes down and socialism collapses in
Eastern Europe.

1990 • Namibia formally gains independence from South Africa.
• De Klerk announces the release of Mandela, unbans ANC
and other liberation movements.
• First official contact between the apartheid government and
the ANC as exiles return.
• First meetings of the Brenthurst Group between big capital
and the ANC are held.

1991 • ANC holds its first elective (national) conference in South
Africa for more than 30 years.
• National Peace Accord is signed, paving the way for
constitutional negotiations.
• Codesa I is held at the World Trade Centre in Kempton Park
in December.

1992 • Mandela visits Davos, and an ANC delegation visits the
World Bank and the International Monetary Fund (IMF) in
the US.
• Codesa II is held in May, but suspended after the Boipatong
massacre.
• ANC adopts 'Ready to Govern' policy document, starts
formulating the Reconstruction and Development
Programme (RDP).
• Thebe Investment Corporation, a black-owned firm, is
established with the ANC's support.

1993 • Multiparty Negotiating Forum (MPNF) meets to negotiate
an interim constitution.

- Chris Hani is murdered; Mandela goes on national television to ask for calm.
- Macro-Economic Research Group (MERG) economic policy proposal is rejected by ANC.
- First big empowerment deal, between Sanlam and New Africa Investments Limited (NAIL), is concluded.

1994
- ANC wins the first democratic elections.
- RDP becomes the democratic government's broad policy and economic framework.
- Patrice Motsepe, a young lawyer, starts his own mining business, Future Mining.

1995
- A small technical team starts designing a new macroeconomic policy for South Africa.
- Mandela tells Trevor Manuel to closely shadow then finance minister, Chris Liebenberg.
- Second significant empowerment deal, the unbundling of JCI by Anglo, is announced.

1996
- The rand comes under attack after rumours circulate that Mandela is dying.
- RDP office in the presidency is closed by Mandela.
- Manuel is appointed minister of finance, and Cyril Ramaphosa leaves politics.
- The government adopts Growth, Employment and Redistribution strategy (GEAR) as its macroeconomic policy.

1997
- Motsepe establishes African Rainbow Minerals (ARM) and takes ownership of seven AngloGold shafts.
- Saki Macozoma, Transnet CEO since 1996, is appointed to the board of Standard Bank.
- Truth and Reconciliation Commission holds hearings on the role of business during apartheid.

1998
- Ramaphosa is appointed chairperson of a commission to consider black economic empowerment (BEE) legislation.
- Tokyo Sexwale establishes Mvelaphanda Holdings.

2000 • New legislation vests mineral rights in the state, causing a
        collapse of mining shares.
2001 • Ramaphosa establishes Millennium Consolidated
        Investments.
      • Macozoma becomes chairman of the board at NAIL, the
        iconic black investment firm.
2002 • Motsepe's ARM lists on the Johannesburg Stock Exchange
        (JSE).
2004 • Motsepe leads a consortium to become Sanlam's black
        empowerment partner.
      • Sexwale leads a consortium to become Absa's empowerment
        partner.
      • Macozoma and Ramaphosa become Standard Bank's
        empowerment partners.
2006 • Ramaphosa leaves Johnnic after a bitter boardroom fight with
        former struggle comrades.
2007 • South Africa runs a budget surplus for the first time in
        democratic history.
      • Thabo Mbeki is removed as ANC leader and replaced by
        Jacob Zuma.
      • Manuel resigns as finance minister, rattling the markets, but is
        later reappointed.
2008 • The global financial crisis hits, but South Africa navigates it
        thanks to strong reserves.
2009 • Sexwale resigns as chairman of Mvelaphanda Holdings to go
        into Zuma's cabinet.
2010 • Motsepe donates R10 million to the Jacob Zuma Foundation.
2011 • The China Investment Corporation acquires a stake in
        Ramaphosa's Shanduka.
2012 • Ramaphosa is elected ANC deputy president; Motsepe
        becomes a significant ANC donor.
      • Thebe Investment Corporation takes a stake in Shell South
        Africa and Capitec Bank.

2013 • Sexwale is axed by Zuma in a cabinet reshuffle.

2014 • Ramaphosa becomes deputy president of the country and Manuel leaves politics.
• Macozoma leaves the board of Standard Bank and Liberty after 17 years.

2015 • After becoming deputy president of the country, Ramaphosa exits all his business interests.
• Motsepe signs deal with Sanlam to remain a 'core shareholder' until 2025.
• Zuma fires his minister of finance, costing the country billions of rands in four days.

2016 • Motsepe establishes finance and investment house African Rainbow Capital.

2017 • Ramaphosa is elected ANC president.

2018 • Zuma is ousted as head of state and replaced by Ramaphosa.

2020 • Macozoma is appointed chairman of the board at Vodacom.
• Motsepe, Nicky Oppenheimer and Johann Rupert each pledge R1 billion for pandemic relief.
• Burglars allegedly steal $600 000 from Ramaphosa's game farm Phala Phala.

2021 • Motsepe is appointed president of the Confederation of African Football (CAF).

Acronyms and abbreviations

ANC	African National Congress
BEE	Black economic empowerment
CAF	Confederation of African Football
CBM	Consultative Business Movement
Codesa	Convention for a Democratic South Africa
Cosatu	Congress of South African Trade Unions
Fabcos	Foundation of African Business and Consumer Services
GDP	gross domestic product
GEAR	Growth, Employment and Redistribution strategy
Idasa	Institute for Democratic Alternatives for South Africa
IFP	Inkatha Freedom Party
IMF	International Monetary Fund
JCI	Johannesburg Consolidated Investments
JSE	Johannesburg Securities/Stock Exchange
MDM	Mass Democratic Movement
MERG	Macro-Economic Research Group
MK	uMkhonto weSizwe
MPNF	Multiparty Negotiating Forum
Nafcoc	National African Federated Chamber of Commerce and Industry
NAIL	New Africa Investments Limited
NBI	National Business Initiative
NEC	national executive committee
NIS	National Intelligence Service
NUM	National Union of Mineworkers

Numsa	National Union of Metalworkers of South Africa
PAC	Pan Africanist Congress
RDP	Reconstruction and Development Programme
SACP	South African Communist Party
SARB	South African Reserve Bank
Swapo	South West Africa People's Liberation Organisation
UDF	United Democratic Front
USSR	Union of Soviet Socialist Republics
VAT	value-added tax

Introduction

The winter of 2022 was a difficult one. Eskom, the parastatal that has the monopoly on the provision of electricity, was in an advanced state of failure as loadshedding crippled the economy and further depressed South Africans' standard of living. Unemployment was at crisis levels, with the expanded definition closing in on 50 per cent, and continued tepid economic growth, high inflation and the rising cost of living meant that the country wasn't about to exit the stagnation and regression of the previous decade and more. And South Africans were increasingly starting to question the country's underlying social compact, querying what undergirds our society and challenging the agreements and covenants we entered into during the political transition from apartheid to democracy.

There are very few achievements in this country's tumultuous history that rank alongside the political transition between 1990, when the African National Congress (ANC) was unbanned, and 1996, when the final Constitution was adopted. In the space of six short years, South Africa went from exclusionary white minority rule to a democracy under a black majority government. This wasn't achieved easily, nor without bloodshed, but the country avoided a civil war and protracted strife because the main actors on all sides of the divide were able to look beyond the horizon. And it was these main actors – principally the National Party (NP) government and the ANC – who were able to agree on the main tenets of what was achievable and what wasn't.

Of course, there were many factors that contributed to decisions about the interim constitution, the final election date and the government of national unity. But it was the elite pacts – the agreements between those groups in society that possess political and economic power – that ensured stability and breakthroughs.

While the political compromises have been investigated, documented and analysed, the economic compromises and agreements that took place among the elite have had similar, if not more consequential, repercussions for South Africa. Almost 30 years after political freedom was achieved, the country is still searching for agreement on how to change the structure of the economy, how to ensure that more people are included, and what needs to be done to achieve faster, efficient growth. And while the ANC government, in power for 28 years in June 2022, remains engaged in its internecine wars of power and succession, and while big capital retreats from investment just enough to remain profitable while hedging its bets on South Africa's future, ordinary South Africans stagger on, trying to remain afloat in an increasingly hostile economic environment in which living costs are shooting up and wages remain behind.

The rise of a few well-connected and very wealthy billionaires and millionaires after 1994, all of them connected to the ANC, is testament to the opportunism of some individuals who very early on identified the rich seam of economic opportunity that freedom brought, and who believed that their alignment with the post-apartheid political elite could be a very profitable bargaining chip. It is also testament to big capital's solutions to the existential crisis it went through in the 1980s and 1990s. By the early 1990s these conglomerates – Anglo, Rembrandt, Sanlam, Old Mutual, Liberty Life, AngloVaal – controlled 86 per cent of the Johannesburg Stock Exchange (JSE) and had been producing rich profits for decades.[1] They had to find a way to survive.

But the ANC did not really believe in the free market, and it most certainly did not believe in apartheid capitalism. So the conundrums during the transition years were, for big capital, how to protect its interests while embracing the new regime, which historically had been antagonistic towards it; and, for the ANC and liberation movement, how to implement its stated policies in a rapidly changing global environment antagonistic towards its ideological foundation.

The repercussions of the decisions made by big capital and the ANC to account for those challenges are still being felt today. Big capital is operating in a market-friendly global environment, with capital flowing freely from hospitable to inhospitable climes to ensure the best returns for investors, while the ANC remains in government and in charge of policy and other governance levers able to influence the shape of wealth accumulation and redistribution.

Michael Spicer, an executive at Anglo American during the transition years and someone who played a central role in big capital's attempts to move closer to the ANC – and in attempts to help move the ANC closer towards business – remained adamant that early empowerment was 'absolutely necessary'. After establishing contact with the ANC during a period in which the apartheid government seemed to be resolutely unwilling to do so, big business moved to create structures and relationships to help it understand the ANC – but also to ensure that the ANC understood that they were now in a different environment than 1980s exile. 'It was very, very difficult to navigate that space during that time,' Spicer, who died suddenly in March 2022, said in an interview for this book. 'The movement spanned Stalinism to free marketeers, and it tried to provide some coherence, but in general it wasn't market friendly. And then throw into the pot race, apartheid and the history of the country ...'[2]

But big business had no option other than to navigate that space if it wanted to continue operating in South Africa, and what followed were thousands of hours and hundreds of days of influencing, cajoling, meeting and convincing the liberation movement of the value of South African big capital – with some of its leaders even providing logistical and organisational support for the political negotiations process. Spicer said that after individuals like Gavin Relly, Anglo

American's boss who succeeded Harry Oppenheimer, and Mike Rosholt, at the top of the Barlow Rand empire, agreed what had to be done, there was a largely coherent view that big business, too, 'needed to make changes'.[3] He recalled 'a flurry of activity' in big business, trying to massage and persuade the presumptive new political leaders of their bona fides and what was needed to ensure future success. 'Business was taking a hands-on, coordinated and coherent approach.'[4]

One of the 'many streams' that came together to ensure a peaceful transition was the country's strong civil society. 'Churches, universities, the judiciary, a strong business community and a vibrant NGO sector – all of these managed to pull together,' Spicer said. 'And business played quite an important role in that it had relationships – personal relationships – with all the leadership. The relationships built up in the discussions, both in exile and when [the ANC] came back, were one of the reasons we had a successful transition.'

Business was quite clear about its intent; the ANC less so. The movement arrived back in South Africa uncertain of its exact economic policy positions, save to proclaim allegiance to its 1955 Freedom Charter, a document which by then had become moribund as a guideline for modern economic theory, opaquely advocating for the nationalisation of banks, mines and monopoly industry. Saki Macozoma, one of post-1994 South Africa's most successful black businessmen, says he was involved in long discussions at the highest levels in the ANC about keeping the party in line with the main policy positions of the Freedom Charter, but that implementing them as was envisaged in 1955 wasn't possible. 'When those of us in the ANC's economic transformation committee were putting together the Ready to Govern document in 1992, we tried to keep it aligned with the Freedom Charter. But applying it to the economy largely did not make sense; it was not going to work, irrespective of the conditions we found,' he said.[5]

Trevor Manuel, who was finance minister between 1996, when he was appointed by Nelson Mandela, and 2009, when he was shifted to another portfolio by Jacob Zuma, says there was a singular determination to run the country efficiently and to gain the trust of the global community. 'We wanted to demonstrate that we weren't two-bit players just out of nappies; we were serious about running the country,' Manuel said.[6]

And what did this in effect mean? South Africa had to become a credible investment destination, and it had to play by the rules. So it meant the adoption of pro-market, conservative economic policies that had as their goal the consolidation of state expenditure, the reduction of debt and, crucially, the redistribution of wealth and social development through economic growth.

It also meant bringing formerly excluded black businessmen into the rosewood-panelled salons of big capitalism. And some of them became fabulously wealthy.

Almost thirty years later, amid high levels of poverty and deprivation, and the deterioration of social services, the question is being asked ever more urgently: did the ANC sell out the ideals of the liberation struggle? Could the political transition have been concluded in such a way as to ensure a just and sustainable economic transition?

Bobby Godsell, who once headed Anglo American's gold division and who distinguished himself as Cyril Ramaphosa's sparring partner in the 1980s at the Chamber of Mines' negotiating table, is strident in his beliefs that there hasn't yet been an economic transition. 'The problem is that the focus in the 1980s was on political transition and avoiding a race-based civil war, and, let's be clear, that was a good thing to focus on. But we've had black inclusion in the economy now for almost thirty years, and if you want to look at the economic transition, what new business can you think of? What new technology? What significant expansion of a business, other than cellular phones?' he asked.[7]

The ANC, on its return, exuded a sense of entitlement, Godsell said. 'I think right from the beginning, there was the sense that

political office, political power, entitles you to economic benefit; it entitles you personally to benefit.' And he noted that they didn't like
'the white guys' and were 'looking for new partners' – 'Remember who
introduced the Guptas to South Africa – not Jacob Zuma but Thabo
Mbeki.' He continued, 'For the last twenty years, the ANC has been
more open to influence from foreigners than from white South
Africans. So race has corrupted our concept of power and accountability, in politics and in economics, and particularly in the link
between the two. And we haven't done a good job of separating those.'[8]

Jay Naidoo, Cosatu's first general-secretary, a minister in Mandela's cabinet and still a significant voice on the left, concurred that the
economic transition – and ensuring a more equal, caring society – has
not worked. 'We failed completely. The statistics show us that. You
don't have to be a rocket scientist to see it.' He cited high levels of poverty and unemployability among black youth as the most significant
failure of democracy. 'The question then becomes, why did we fail?
And how do we ensure we don't repeat the same mistake, because we
have an opportunity to put things right, but now we're headed down
the same road.'[9]

He had a view of how it should have been done. 'If we wanted
to build a black business sector, we should have taken our traditional
allies, who were Nafcoc [the National African Federated Chamber
of Commerce and Industry], Fabcos [the Foundation of African
Business and Consumer Services], the taxi associations, and sat down
in a room with them and said, "How do we help you guys, who were
already building businesses under apartheid, grow into medium and
large enterprises?"'[10]

As for black economic empowerment and 'the way it morphed
into a transfer of assets to a politically elected elite: there was never a
discussion of that,' he said.

But did the ANC sell out to big capital? Did it betray what it
set out to do, which was not only deliver political freedom for
the oppressed, but also restore them as significant players in the

country's economy? Said Naidoo, 'Were there agendas and sub-agendas? Absolutely, probably hundreds. Maybe there were elements that did sell out, but you can't take Mandela and that generation across the arc of their life and say, "This is the generation that sold us out," because their generation was here to deliver us political freedom. One person, one vote was the ANC legacy, and they created a constitutional democracy that gave us the levers of power to address the legacy, be that economic, the land issue or issues of exclusion. If we failed to do that, we can't blame the Mandela generation. That's where we take responsibility and I'm very happy to take responsibility for my role in fucking up.' But, he reiterated, 'It wasn't like the entire MDM colluded with big capital in order to sell out the people. It didn't happen like that.'[11]

Spicer was clear about what big capital's agenda was: ensuring that the ANC adhered to market liberalism. And how big capital went about ensuring this by drawing in the new political elite in the ANC makes up a large portion of this book. Business wanted to survive, and in order to do so, it had to make the black elite owners of capital, even though they couldn't afford it. The black elite had to own a chunk of the country's wealth so that the system could survive; and the transfer of assets to a politically connected elite was enormously profitable for big capital.

When the mines and the banks and the conglomerates went about shopping for empowerment partners, for the first decade at least, it found the same partners every time. Cyril Ramaphosa became extraordinarily wealthy not because he was a shrewd businessman with a knack for turning around flailing companies, or because he was an industrialist who created a new service, market or product. He, like many others, was favoured because of his links to the governing ANC.

Of course, this wasn't new in the world of capitalism, where the moneyed class move, if not in lockstep with, very close to the holders of political power. Under apartheid, Afrikaner capital exploited its proximity to the NP government, with the establishment of business empires such as Anton Rupert's Rembrandt considered a project of Afrikaner nationalism. But it now seems as if the project is starting to consume itself. The ANC government remains unable to create an environment for capital to thrive, and capital seems to be at the end of its tether with the political class. Neither has much more to offer the other. And poverty and unemployment are worse than in 1994.

'The trouble is that the ANC has turned out to be no different from many other liberation movements,' said Spicer. 'It has never progressed, and it's essentially stuffed with people who have a nationalist view, and behind that there's a sort of neo-patrimonial, pre-capital type of behaviour.'

Not only is there a deep distrust of how business works, said Spicer, but there's also a lack of understanding. 'Zuma epitomised that [type of behaviour]: it's jobs for cadres and family and chiefs, not constrained by the law, and someone like Zuma was puzzled [by adverse reactions to it] because he thinks it's natural. Many think it just happens, and the notion of profit remains an illegitimate concept.'[12]

This book attempts to explain the rise of ANC-connected billionaires and millionaires by tracking attempts by big capital to influence and direct the political transition, and the ANC's progression from an organisation with socialist leanings and communist sympathies to a government that reluctantly embraced the free market. It is by no means an exhaustive history of the period, nor is it a definitive account of someone like Patrice Motsepe's remarkable ascension to the top table of South African business and wealth. It does, however, attempt to weave together the machinations of the political economy of the pre- and post-transition period, with the establishment of the first class of super-rich black and empowered businessmen.

From my analysis of events, both in my nearly 20 years of reporting on this country's politics and history, and researching this and a previous book (*The Stellenbosch Mafia: Inside the billionaires' club*), it is clear that big capital has always held enormous sway in the halls of political power. Business does not make money without the acquiescence of politics, and politics doesn't deliver if business doesn't thrive. It has always been, and will continue to be, a fraught relationship beset at every turn with the danger of corruption and patronage. If the years of state capture have taught us anything, it should be that.

South Africa is at a dangerous inflection point. Naidoo listed the country's woes: 'One in three people are dependent on a grant, the same and worse go hungry, half the population is mired in poverty and 45 per cent of people are unemployed. How did we get here?' It could have been different, he believes, if big capital, the then-government and the ANC had risen above their constituencies. 'Politically, we got the National Party to rise above its constituency and find common ground with us. Couldn't we have done that on the economy? It would have made absolute sense, rather than us sitting now with these high walls, electric fences, armed responses and too terrified to even leave our homes.'[13]

Spicer expressed his frustration with billionaire Ramaphosa's reluctance to make difficult decisions as head of state, saying that his style of social compacting, where politics trumps everything, inevitably ends up with decisions made based on the lowest common denominator. 'We're unstrategic and unfocused, and this at a time when the global environment is very challenging. Even in Africa, South Africa is falling behind, where countries like Rwanda and Kenya are making difficult choices.' Describing Ramaphosa as 'not a conviction politician,' Spicer added, 'The trouble with him is that he believes in leading from behind, and our problems don't allow for a gradualist approach. But that's the guy's nature; he's not a get-out-ahead, decisive sort of guy.'[14]

South Africa's political transition was a remarkable feat of tolerance and pragmatism. Big capital's desire for survival meant it had to cross boundaries and co-opt its erstwhile enemies. And the new ruling political class saw, and exploited, the opportunities this rapprochement presented. But years of destructive politics now means that the brittle pact reached between economic and political elites almost 30 years ago is under extreme pressure. We may have seen some new billionaires join the establishment class of the Oppenheimers and the Ruperts, but this country will have to make tough decisions, and make them soon, to ensure that it isn't only the few that are lifted out of deprivation.

This book attempts to shed light on how we came to this point, and how difficult decisions were made in the 1990s. 'These weren't easy; they weren't namby-pamby discussions. They were often loud and angry, but we worked through them, and we had to ensure that the objectives that we had set were attained,' said Manuel.[15]

And we're going to have to do it again.

PART I

TURBULENCE

1985–1990

1

The long road to Lusaka

'South Africa in the 1980s was a dramatically different
place [to the 1950s]. We were talking about the rise of
Japan, about Ronald Reagan's Star Wars project and
how it was going to break the Soviet Union ... And they
were still banging on about the Freedom Charter.'

– Michael Spicer, special assistant to
Anglo American's chief executive in 1985.[1]

Gavin Relly had been at the helm of Anglo American for more than
two years when he led a small group of South African businessmen
and journalists to a lodge in Zambia for a meeting with the banned
ANC on 13 September 1985.

Anglo was a giant organisation, and increasingly felt change was
coming – and that nothing should be left to chance, said Michael
Spicer, Relly's special assistant. 'So the idea behind the mission
to Zambia was not only to go and make contact with fellow South
Africans, but to talk to them about how the world was changing and
how the ANC needed to get their thinking up to speed.'

With Relly were Tony Bloom, chief executive of Premier Milling,
Zach de Beer from Anglo, Peter Sorour, director of the South Africa
Foundation, Tertius Myburgh, editor of the *Sunday Times*, Harald

Pakendorf, editor of *Die Vaderland*, and Hugh Murray, editor of *Leadership* magazine. Among the ANC luminaries were Oliver Tambo, Thabo Mbeki, Chris Hani, Pallo Jordan and Mac Maharaj. The meeting was brokered by Zambia's president Kenneth Kaunda.

The businessmen were clearly pleasantly surprised by the ANC delegation and noted that while they themselves wore informal safari suits, Tambo's team was dressed in suits and ties – evidence, Bloom said, of how seriously the ANC was taking the meeting. 'It was difficult to view the group as hardline Marxists, bloodthirsty terrorists who were interested in reducing South Africa to anarchy and seizing power with a hatred of whites …'[2]

The two parties had animated but friendly discussions at the Mfuwe Game Lodge in the east of the country, under the shade of a tree on the banks of the Luangwa River.[3] Zambia had become the ANC's main refuge, with 'KK', as Kaunda was affectionately known in liberation circles, providing resources and protection to the organisation, which ran their global anti-apartheid campaign from both Zambia and London. And Lusaka, the country's capital, became synonymous with the ANC.

Kaunda held a unique position among the leaders of frontline states[4] in that he maintained a relationship with apartheid South Africa's white leaders and historically had a measure of influence with them; he and PW Botha's predecessor, BJ Vorster, had met on more than one occasion, and cooperated to help bring the Rhodesian war to a close.[5]

And Kaunda had a relationship with the Oppenheimers, whose family empire included both Anglo and diamond miner De Beers, and with Relly. 'Anglo had developed the copper mines in Zambia that were later nationalised by the government, and Gavin had a spell up there and many of his close associates also spent time up there,' said Spicer.[6]

Even though Kaunda opened the meeting with the statement that there was more that united the two groups than divided them, both parties – the ANC and the South African businessmen – held strong convictions. For the Anglo people, politically, it was about ending the armed struggle and the accompanying violence, while economically they were at pains to stress the importance of a growing economy to any future reforms. For the exiled ANC group, it was about explaining that it wasn't the liberation movement who were the aggressors, and that bringing an end to the armed struggle and violence was up to the Pretoria regime. And as far the economy was concerned, the ANC wasn't about to be dissuaded from following every prescript contained in the Freedom Charter of 1955.[7]

So there was a gulf between the two sides, with the Relly group, despite its constructive intentions, believing themselves to live in a normal society, albeit one with deep structural issues. The businessmen gave an analysis of how they viewed present-day South Africa and explained why they believed president PW Botha was serious about reforms. They also believed that Botha's tentative steps could be accelerated if the ANC renounced violence and suspended the armed struggle.

Relly added that steps needed to be taken to put the question of universal franchise – essentially 'one man, one vote', that well-worn phrase used to scare white South Africa – on the agenda, because he didn't believe it was attainable at that time. (Interestingly, three-quarters of a century before, Relly's grandfather, Sir Walter Stanford, had argued unsuccessfully for black franchise at the 1909 national convention that led to the South Africa Act being adopted later that year.[8])

Both Mac Maharaj and Pallo Jordan strongly rejected the businessmen's points of view, giving a completely alternative analysis of the South African situation. Maharaj said the Botha government hadn't only lost legitimacy, but that it was 'fumbling and rudderless' and clearly at a loss for ideas. He agreed that change was in the air, but said that it was because of ordinary South Africans starting to resist the regime. Then Jordan 'in a passionate fashion' and Mbeki 'forcibly'

5

explained that the problem in the conflict lay on the side of the apartheid government: 'There is a right side and a wrong side. The problem is being created by one side and that side is not the ANC,' Jordan said.[9]

The business delegation argued that belligerent statements from the ANC had forced white people into hardened positions, while the ANC delegation emphasised that violence was the last option.[10]

After a lunch break, during which the businessmen and ANC delegates 'mixed very easily', and seating was informal and conversation relaxed, the discussion turned to the economy. Tambo said the struggle was not about capitalism versus communism, but about freedom. Mbeki then denounced the concentration of wealth 'in the hands of only three companies' [presumably referring to Anglo, Rembrandt, Sanlam or Old Mutual] and said that an ANC government would have to start spreading wealth immediately should it come to power.

Relly countered Mbeki by saying that things were 'infinitely more complex', and detailed the need for investment by capital to alleviate poverty and hunger, and to account for the needs of a growing population. Bloom backed Relly up, saying that an ANC government 'should be very careful about formulating any policies which in any way would have the effect of killing initiative'. This was essential for the maintenance of growth and was missing elsewhere in Africa.[11] And Bloom rejected the notion of nationalisation, saying that while he agreed that government should be in charge of certain services, it should not run industry 'because, quite frankly, they simply made a terrible job of it'. South African state-run industry was mostly badly managed, he said.[12]

It seemed that the businessmen were struggling to convince the ANC group of the virtues and the necessity of a free market and private enterprise system, even though there was no doubt that Mbeki, who had a master's degree in economics from Sussex University, understood exactly what they meant and what they were saying.

Nonetheless, the meeting closed in a cordial manner, with the group taking photographs for posterity and the ANC delegates joking that their pictures were already on file with the security police. 'The departure was a strangely poignant moment – we were returning to South Africa and they were staying behind, and there was almost an air of sadness,' Bloom said.[13] Indeed, Tambo had told the Anglo delegation how pleased he was to be with 'fellow countrymen', and that he and his comrades 'lived and existed for their dream of returning to South Africa'.[14]

Michael Spicer said later, 'One of the overriding impressions that [Relly] came back with was how magical it was to sit and talk to a bunch of South Africans who were desperately longing to come back. And we discovered how much we had in common, despite the dramatic differences there were due to our past.'[15]

The importance of Relly's safari should not be underestimated, says Trevor Manuel, the later minister of finance who was then playing a leading role in the United Democratic Front (UDF), effectively the ANC's internal wing. 'The overarching situation was that the apartheid government, or the apartheid regime, as we preferred to call it, had lost its ability to govern, and included in that was that the issue of the rooi gevaar had kind of disappeared. And you had, from the mid-1980s, a grouping of well-heeled South Africans making their way initially to Lusaka. The business group that was led by Relly and Bloom was actually quite important in this regard, because part of what it did was to kind of start communicating to the rest that you could talk to the ANC.'[16]

The meeting almost hadn't taken place. PW Botha, the tentative reformer cum hardline nationalist, initially hadn't interfered, but then, once the impending visit became publicly known, had intervened directly to try and prevent the group from leaving South Africa.

The purpose of the meeting, which made 'a dramatic impact', said Spicer, 'was absolutely not to anoint the ANC as heir apparent'. Rather, by mid-1985, Relly had let it be known that Anglo would have to take a leading role in shaping South Africa's uncertain political future, because the country, in the grip of widespread violence, governed by a series of states of emergency, and throttled by wave after wave of sanctions, was reaching breaking point.

As far as Anglo was concerned, Spicer said, it was largely due to Relly's insistence that it should do everything it could to engage the ANC. Relly, Spicer contends, 'was a statesman' who challenged his leadership 'to bend their minds', even though many were wary of the ANC, still considered to be a communist organisation. The Anglo chief 'wanted to influence unfolding events,' Spicer said.[17]

But Botha persuaded 'quite a few of the Afrikaans businesspeople, and the non-Anglo crowd, not to go'.[18] Botha – 'tough, brutal, over-powering and, at times, thuggish, vindictive and petty'[19] – hated being upstaged by anyone, least of all South Africa's capitalist barons, and specifically by representatives of English-speaking capital.

Harry Oppenheimer, informally regarded as the leader of the English-speaking business community in the country, did not want Relly, his successor as Anglo chair, trekking north. (Rembrandt's Anton Rupert was considered to be Harry's counterpart among Afrikaner-owned business; he'd declined an invitation by Relly to accompany him to Lusaka.[20]) This was despite the fact that as far back as the 1970s, Oppenheimer had told his management team to start building relationships with prominent black employees, even while the government of John Vorster was taking the hardest line of any previous apartheid government against the black majority. It is unclear why Oppenheimer was opposed to the trip, but Spicer said despite the Anglo supremo detesting the Nationalists, he also didn't want to antagonise the government unnecessarily.[21]

But Relly was Anglo blue blood, having climbed the corporate rungs to run its coal business, and its Canadian and Zambian mining operations, and eventually being appointed to the executive committee and the corporation's board in 1965. Relly was the Anglo prototype: well educated, well read and well travelled, he was always immaculate in a dress shirt and double-breasted blazer with a pocket square. Schooled at the elite Diocesan College, or Bishops, in

Newlands, Cape Town, he went to Trinity College at Oxford University for his tertiary education, where he obtained a master's degree in politics, philosophy and economics, then fought with the South African forces in Italy during the Second World War.

In his 20s, Relly served as personal assistant to opposition leader Sir De Villiers Graaff, whose United Party had been ousted from government by the National Party in 1948. Relly became private secretary to Sir Ernest Oppenheimer, Anglo's founder, in 1949, and then to his son, Harry, when he took over the chair of Anglo from his father when Ernest died in 1957. 'He had a grounding in business and politics equalled by few,' wrote business journalist Hugh Murray.[22]

Despite Botha's open antagonism and Oppenheimer's private doubts, he was determined to fly to Lusaka and sit down with the ANC. He was already fielding strong and diverse opinions about the political situation in the country on his management committee – Relly was a reformist, but many in his leadership team weren't[23] – and believed a face-to-face meeting with the ANC was necessary.

'He was my mentor and I admired him tremendously because he was, in a slightly different way, a statesman of equal stature to Oppenheimer: very warm-hearted, gregarious and a people person. He thought holistically about South Africa's situation,' said Spicer.[24]

Clem Sunter, another senior Anglo manager at the time, said Relly was 'a pro-reform and get-involved type of guy, as was Harry, who brought with him his whole relationship with the Progressive Party.'[25] Harry, considered a visionary leader by those who worked for him (and who thought himself to be a businessman-politician, and sometimes vice versa), had been elected as the United Party's member of parliament for Kimberley in 1948, when theologian DF Malan became the first apartheid premier. (The Progressive Party had been formed in 1959 by liberal former United Party members who sought a stronger opposition to apartheid, and Oppenheimer maintained close links to it and its successor parties, including the later Democratic Party.)

Relly was under no illusions that grand attempts at national reform would be difficult. 'You can remove every tenet of apartheid, every law which applies to it, and you would still not have dealt with the prejudices and attitudes which 300 years of South African history and 38 years of apartheid have built up in white people, and by association obviously among black people. Apartheid has demoralised the white and degraded the black,' he said at the time.[26]

But Anglo, the backbone of South African industry since the First World War, and a major beneficiary of apartheid's labour policies, was ready to talk to the leaders of the oppressed.

Still, Martin Kingston, who knew the ANC intimately during exile – he was married to OR Tambo's daughter, Thembi, while working in the banking industry in London – cautioned against seeing Anglo as driven by morality and the desire to see social justice done. 'It was hardly an altruistic position they took,'[27] he said.

And Doug Band, who was head of CNA and Gallo Records, both part of Anglo, said that Relly too exhibited some of the contradictions of the time. 'He had, in my view, quite liberal tendencies in one direction, but in other directions he could sometimes shock me by saying things that took me by surprise.'[28]

'There is no modern economic thinking in the ANC,' Gavin Relly said on Anglo's corporate Gulfstream jet on the flight back to South Africa.[29] It was as if the organisation, marinated in Marxism-Leninism after having been in exile for almost 30 years and supported by the Soviet Union, was still stuck in the 1950s.

The Anglo boss was concerned about the state of the ANC, and its lack of insight into and knowledge of a rapidly globalising and modernising world, and its 'fossilised' economic ideas. 'What really bugged Gavin and the people working for him, and the people who were in touch with the ANC, was that they had no modern economic thinking. South Africa in the 1980s was a dramatically different place (to the 1950s). We were talking about the rise of Japan, about Ronald Reagan's Star Wars project and how it was going to break the Soviet

Union … It was the period where globalisation was advancing rapidly, it was about the advance of technology, the demographic changes … All of that was going to change the world. And they were still banging on about the Freedom Charter,' said Spicer.[30]

To Relly, the world as it was seemed beyond the grasp and capabilities of ANC. 'The onset of globalisation had forced governments to be aware of imminent change and align themselves to that. Business did, too. And this was completely beyond the ANC, because their lodestar remained the Freedom Charter of 1955,' Spicer said. 'The Freedom Charter was just not an adequate guide to economics in the 1980s, let alone in the 1990s, as we saw the major trends emerging. Countries had to behave very, very differently, and the sort of old-style statism from circa 1950, 1960 would be appallingly inappropriate.'[31]

The Freedom Charter is the statement of core principles of the South African Congress Alliance, which included the ANC and the South African Indian Congress. It opens, 'We, the People of South Africa, declare for all our country and the world to know: that South Africa belongs to all who live in it, black and white, and that no government can justly claim authority unless it is based on the will of all the people; that our people have been robbed of their birthright to land, liberty and peace by a form of government founded on injustice and inequality; that our country will never be prosperous or free until all our people live in brotherhood, enjoying equal rights and opportunities; that only a democratic state, based on the will of all the people, can secure to all their birthright without distinction of colour, race, sex or belief.'

Specific reference is made to 'the country's wealth' being 'restored to the people': 'The mineral wealth beneath the soil, the banks and monopoly industry shall be transferred to the ownership of the people as a whole' and 'all other industry and trade shall be controlled to assist the wellbeing of the people.'[32]

The contrast between that thinking and the way Anglo American operated couldn't have been starker. Established as a mining com-

11

pany by Sir Ernest Oppenheimer in 1917, Anglo modernised South Africa's gold- and diamond-mining industry and played a significant role in establishing the migrant labour system that was responsible for so much social strife and misery under apartheid. Spicer explained that it was thanks to the ingenuity of Anglo – and other mining companies – that deep-drilling techniques now in common use across the globe were perfected.[33] But mines were also in need of cheap labour, and the Truth and Reconciliation Commission – a statutory body that convened hearings around the country in the late 1990s in order to grant or refuse amnesty from criminal prosecution for anyone who was involved in apartheid-era crimes and atrocities – later found that mining bosses helped the apartheid government devise and design legislation to ensure a consistent supply of mineworkers.[34]

But Oppenheimer and Relly's enterprise wasn't just playing a walk-on part in the war; it was a dominant player in the tightly controlled apartheid economy. It was part of a group of massively diversified conglomerates that controlled the vast majority of the country's economy. Anglo moved beyond its interests in gold and diamond mining even before the National Party came to power in 1948, acquiring chemicals manufacturer AECI in 1929 and Union Steel in 1945. In the 1960s it started competing with parastatal Iscor by establishing Highveld Steel, bought Scaw Metals and established Mondi Paper. In the 1970s it moved into vehicle retail and production, and property, and obtained a large chunk of Barclays Bank. It also possessed a significant share in another giant conglomerate, Barlow Rand. Later, during the 1980s, it took over Ford and the whole of Barclays after their parent companies divested from the country. It also had interests in South African Breweries and sugar giant Tongaat-Hulett, and co-owned Premier Milling with insurance giant Liberty Life.[35]

By 1992 Anglo controlled 34 per cent of the JSE's entire market capitalisation, followed by insurance behemoth Sanlam with 16 per cent, Anton Rupert's Rembrandt with 15 per cent, Old Mutual with

14 per cent (which included Barlow Rand), Liberty Life with 5 per cent and mining company AngloVaal on 3 per cent.[36] Together they controlled 86 per cent of the JSE.

So for the largest part of its existence, Anglo had dominated the country's economic landscape, with most of the stock traded on the JSE in the mid to late 1980s being controlled directly or indirectly by the company.[37] It was a capitalist behemoth, at one stage producing a third of the world's gold output and 80 per cent of all diamonds[38] – a boon for the developing South African state in the twentieth century.

Relly told Spicer what the Zambia delegation had wanted to impress on their exiled compatriots at that September 1985 meeting: 'Guys, wake up! The Freedom Charter is a 1950s document; it's a guide to the world of the 1950s. That world has gone. It's gone definitively. There is a new world.'[39]

2

South Africa burning

'Between 1985 and the release of Mandela was a period of real strife in which the apartheid state smashed anything standing.'

– Jay Naidoo, general-secretary of Cosatu 1985–1993.[1]

On the night of 3 and 4 September 1984, South Africa's new tricameral constitution took effect. It was the result of a national referendum by which coloured and Indian South Africans were granted limited representation in parliament, but with in-built domination by the white chamber. This meant that whatever happened in the houses of representatives (coloured) and delegates (Indians), the white house of assembly would always hold sway.

Black South Africans weren't included in the new system. The apartheid government, however, proceeded to implement black governance structures, along the lines of what HF Verwoerd had wanted to implement, with the establishment of local black councils tasked largely with collecting rent in townships. Critics maintained that these councils, 29 of which were established nationwide in terms of the Black Local Authorities Act, 'did not address the fundamental issues' that had condemned previous attempts to failure: the granting of full political rights.[2]

But on 3 September 1984 – the day of Botha's constitutional triumph – violence erupted in Sharpeville in the Vaal Triangle in protest against an increase of R5.50 in local rent. The deputy mayor of the Lekoa town council was hauled out of his house, stoned, doused with petrol and set alight.[3]

And other townships – Evaton, Tembisa, Sebokeng – were also burning.[4] On the same day, 26 people were killed during a school stay-away and rent protest – four were black members of the apartheid-established councils, and the rest were killed by security forces.[5]

This led to a train of events that put South Africa on edge and refocused the world's attention on the country. Violence escalated on the Witwatersrand, including the East and West Rand, with boycotts and marches leading to injuries and death.

The intensity of the resistance forced authorities to back off, and protests, stayaways and boycotts proliferated throughout the country, including in the western and eastern Cape, with the UDF playing a leading role in organising community action in concert with a range of local organisations.[6] The nationwide 'insurrection'[7] also signified a course correction for the Federation of South African Trade Unions, the largest federation of trade unions at the time, which had started to participate in protest and political action after the position of black trade unions was secured with the passing of the Labour Relations Amendment Act in 1981, and a decision by the Supreme Court in 1983 that prohibited government from refusing to register unions on racial grounds.[8]

The apartheid government responded forcefully, with lessons learnt from the 1976 Soweto Uprising. Early on the morning of 23 October 1984, in what came to be known as Operation Palmiet, a 'seemingly endless column of Ratel armoured personnel carriers, police Casspirs, military trucks, jeeps and police paddy-wagons trundled into three East Rand townships'. Such armoured columns had been seen many times before in the south Angola bush, but this was the first time they'd been deployed in such strength in urban South Africa, and it was a decisive

15

departure from external defence to internal policing. 'More than 7 000 troops entered Sebokeng, Sharpeville and Boipatong townships "to restore law and order".'[9]

In response, on 5 and 6 November 1984, between 300 000 and 500 000 workers stayed away from work in protest against military action in the townships.

From then, and on into 1985, the country was gripped by widespread violence, which saw the vice of Botha's security machinery on the country grow ever tighter. This was also the period in which the state's illegal killing operations were ramped up, with a number of activists murdered, including the Cradock Four of Matthew Goniwe, Fort Calata, Sparrow Mkhonto and Sicelo Mhlauli. On 20 July 1985, the day on which the four were buried, Botha declared a state of emergency.[10]

Just a month before, at the ANC's conference in Kabwe, Zambia, Oliver Tambo had said the 1980s was shaping up to be 'the decade of liberation'. Delivering the ANC's political report, he said that 'this mass offensive is directed at the destruction of the state machinery, at making apartheid inoperative, at making our country ungovernable'.[11]

And indeed 1985 was to see civil insurrection reach a high point. 'During that year, more than 350 000 township residents would take part in rent boycotts which would leave black councils millions of rand in the red. School boycotts continued in the year and in the eastern Cape consumer boycotts of white-owned shops began.'[12]

Jay Naidoo, the firebrand unionist who was elected as the first general-secretary of the Congress of South African Trade Unions (Cosatu) when it was formed that year, said he wondered whether South Africa would simply 'implode', given the levels of violence and the apartheid government's response. 'That period was incredibly dangerous,' he recalled.[13]

Tambo's exhortation to his comrades to make South Africa ungovernable seemed to have found fertile ground. And it looked like South Africa was coming apart at the seams.

For the intellectual elites in the National Party, said Naidoo, 'I think there was the understanding ... that time was running out.'[14]

South Africans were at a loss in the mid-1980s. The armed struggle and violent action in the townships were in direct response to apartheid repression, and the state's counteraction was to introduce stricter security measures and to take a harder line against any criticism about its domestic policies.

Having succeeded Oppenheimer as Anglo chair in 1983, Relly wanted to try and plan for what was then – as in present-day South Africa – an uncertain future. Anglo, Relly felt, had to try and anticipate major domestic and international shocks, and what their impact on its business could be. And although he wanted insight into how the global order was changing, with the Ronald Reagan presidency and the American economy booming, and Soviet leader Mikhail Gorbachev seemingly taking a different approach to the cold war, it was South Africa's domestic situation that bothered him.[15] Botha was firmly entrenched as leader of the NP and there didn't seem to be any debate about a successor, which meant the political environment would continue to be dominated by the national security management system implemented by the government.

Jay Naidoo explained, 'The state security council was the real power in the country; that's where decision-making was exercised. It's important to understand that power didn't sit in the cabinet or the National Party leadership. It was concentrated in the hands of the state president and the military industrial complex. Cabinet, finance was subservient to the state security council.'[16]

It was against this background that Relly put Clem Sunter, who was then secretary to the Anglo executive, in charge of the company's nascent 'scenario planning' team. 'The initial plan was not to write scenarios to convince the South African government or society at large about the need for change. It was purely an internal exercise to help buttress the company against future instability – and to

17

get Anglo's senior staff to start thinking differently,' said Sunter.[17]

The company for many decades maintained an ethos and tradition that its managers would be educated at Oxford, not Cambridge, though the latter was also one of the world's most elite tertiary institutions. 'I mean, for God's sake, let alone anyone from Stellenbosch or Wits!' said Band, who described this tradition as 'really, really bizarre'. 'Julian [Ogilvie Thompson, Anglo's chief executive between 1990 and 2000] once went on record saying, "No, we don't employ fellows from Cambridge."'[18]

This was when Michael Spicer – a graduate of Rhodes University – was recruited. 'I joined Anglo, really, to help write the South African scenarios for Clem Sunter, and to be the first full-time person in Anglo working on what was then called public affairs. I think I was the first full-time person in South Africa who ever occupied a public-affairs-government-international-relations sort of job.'[19]

Initially, the scenario planning 'was designed to flex the minds of management and to make them nimbler to plan for different futures, alternative futures, and not to be caught out by the sort of shocks, like Shell in the 1970s, when oil crises caught them out big time,' Spicer said. 'Anglo decided they must be able to think in a way that provided them with the planning tools to avoid being completely shocked by different outcomes. So originally this was done for internal purposes.'[20]

In late 1985 and early 1986, Sunter's team worked on the now-famous Anglo scenarios for South Africa's future. 'We formed teams in London and Johannesburg, and we had outside experts as part of these teams, and they did scenarios for the 1990s on the global economy. And then our local team, which included [economist] Michael O'Dowd, [executive] Bobby Godsell and Michael Spicer, and one or two of the internationals, took on the topic of political risk,' said Sunter.[21]

Sunter and his team went around at Anglo, presenting the scenarios – via transparent slides on an overhead projector – to the leadership and management of all the Anglo affiliates. 'It wasn't about forecasting the future … What we did was to write different scenarios of fairly extreme outcomes, and sort of weigh them up and give them probabilities.' Their scenarios became a smash hit inside Anglo, and spread like wildfire once introduced in the public domain – in spite of the fact, Spicer said, that Relly was adamant that Anglo 'wasn't going to go around banging on doors and proselytising'.[22] 'We didn't wag a finger at them and say this is the way you have to go,' Sunter confirmed.[23]

In July 1986, Sunter was asked by Mangosuthu Buthelezi, the leader of the Inkatha Freedom Party (IFP), to present his scenarios at a conference in Durban. Relly was enthusiastic for Sunter to give the scenarios a wider audience because he thought they could contribute to the national dialogue about the future. 'And that's because Anglo was politically involved. Oppenheimer was always politically involved,' said Sunter.[24]

The response was overwhelming, and Sunter said almost immediately he received 'about 23' invitations to present at other gatherings – from the government. And before long he was presenting to the chiefs of the South African Defence Force and the police, as well as to members of parliament and the secretive Broederbond, the elite Afrikaner organisation that influenced so much of the government's policy and counted almost every influential Afrikaner among its number. The team crisscrossed the country presenting to everyone from members of book clubs to dinner parties and board meetings of large companies, and everything in between. 'It wasn't planned, but it just exploded,' Sunter said. 'I gave my first public presentation in mid-1986, and then it just went up like a rocket. And I think the reason was that everybody at the time was looking for something different, and this was different, because we put it in a global context.'[25]

The first half of the presentation wasn't challenging people to make up their mind about South Africa; it was looking at the world at large. 'Particularly, we looked at America, Russia and Japan, and indeed the global scenarios hung around the relationship between the three, which shows that scenario planners can get it wrong, because obviously the one big country we missed out on in the 1990s was China.'[26]

19

During the second half of the presentation, on the back of the changing global environment, the South African scenarios were presented. And the Anglo team were surprised how they were received – even among conservatives. 'I never got anybody standing up and saying this is a whole load of rubbish and we've got to hold on, even in the most conservative constituencies that I spoke at. People listened.'[27]

As time went by, Sunter amended the presentation because, he said, people had good ideas. 'I remember [NP cabinet ministers] Roelf Meyer and Wynand Malan offering their opinions on it, and so I kind of did grow the presentation a bit through the comments by members of the audience.'[28]

The Anglo futurama became known as the 'high road, low road' scenarios, which set out how the South African crisis could play out in the following decade. Sunter and his team explained the possible transition from the 'current' or 'old' South Africa to a new dispensation, and one which could go the 'high road' or the 'low road'.

Spicer said the point of departure was 'a classic revolution is not a scenario'. During a conference call with around a hundred international finance journalists about Anglo's financial year in 1986, Spicer rejected their analysis of the country. 'There was an absolute hard line from all of them that if not within three weeks, then within three months, this society was over a cliff and into bloody racial revolution. And you couldn't argue with it because it was just the accepted wisdom at the time, partly because it made for good newspaper copy and also because they wanted their position validated. But based on the South African scenarios that we wrote, we said, "Guys, you're barking up the wrong tree. It's not going to happen. That is not a potential future, because the state is still capable of absolute repression and you can have more of the same, or you can start preparing a negotiated outcome." They didn't believe it,' he said.[29]

But there was general acceptance in the ranks of the liberation movement that a military or violent overthrow of the apartheid state wasn't possible, due to the relative strengths of both the apartheid machinery, and the ANC and its allies. Russian-made T-72 tanks weren't going to roll down Queen Wilhelmina Avenue (today's Florence Ribeiro Avenue) in Pretoria, and strike down the apartheid national flag.

'The high road was a negotiated compromise ... and that was 1985! We were proposing a negotiated compromise in 1985!' said Spicer.[30]

The low road was a deteriorating economy, more and more repression, 'the generals take over, the economy worsens, then they get ejected, there's an attempt to put it together, but so much has been lost that it doesn't work. You have populism for a while, and then the generals take over again. Basically, what Latin America has been through repeatedly,' said Spicer.[31]

'That was obviously the critical difference between the high road and the low road, which at the time was quite revolutionary because, of course, the ANC and the Nats in 1986 and 1987 were still very much on a collision course,' Sunter noted.[32]

Sunter said they argued that political crossroads couldn't be resolved through co-option, but always through 'proper negotiation'. And even if consensus were reached between opposing forces, the country could still end up on the low road and spiral into the 'Latin American tango' described above.

'In a funny way, that's happened,' said Sunter. 'We did take the high road politically, and unfortunately it hasn't been backed up by high economic growth. And so that was probably the most prophetic of all our graphs: that if we wanted to become a developed country like Switzerland, we had to back up all the political advances we made with economic advances, and we didn't.'[33]

Due to the workload in presenting the scenarios, his team expanded at the beginning of 1987, and they subsequently addressed more than 30000 influential South Africans, from the top of the national executive to regional Rotary clubs and even Nelson Mandela, who asked that Sunter present to him at Victor Verster Prison outside Paarl. 'We published a book about the scenarios ... and we even shot a video which went straight to the video stores. I was very happy to be right up there with Michael Jackson's *Thriller*,' he said.[34]

After a presentation arranged by technology firm Altron, Pik Botha asked Sunter to present to the police leadership. 'It was quite weird for me, having been born in England, to be put on a police helicopter and flown out to a place called Mariepskop in the deep Northern Transvaal to give this presentation that you're going to have to negotiate with the ANC – the high-road scenario. And my mother kept saying to me, "You weren't even born in the country, how can you go around telling people about their future?" and I said, "Because they're listening, Mummy."'[35]

It opened the door for Sunter and Anglo to National Party luminaries and the Broederbond. 'I presented to the Broederbond at Rand Afrikaans University. That was an interesting experience in itself.'[36]

In today's world, scenario planning might not look revolutionary, but in the apartheid-gridlocked South Africa of the mid-1980s, the Anglo initiative set tongues wagging. And while the scenarios were originally only for the consumption of Anglo's management, the success they had outside the confines of Anglo American's sprawling head-office complex at 44 Main Street in downtown Johannesburg showed the urgency and need for creative thinking about the country's future.

'One of the key messages of the high-road scenario, that is, what makes a winning nation in the new global economy, is that South Africa must have small government, should allow entrepreneurs to create new businesses, and should have low taxation rates that stimulate the work ethic because people keep their own money. So, it was a pretty liberal economic set of scenarios,' said Sunter.[37]

For Spicer, it was crucial that people of influence were made aware of 'alternative futures'. 'And yes, we remained concerned that there was no sophisticated economic thinking in the ANC at that stage, and we wanted to communicate alternatives,' he said.[38]

Spicer said 'there was quite a significant Anglo influence' on business's attempt in the 1980s and 1990s (as will be explored later) to direct events as they were unfolding, whether it was to provide material support to returning exiles (including Mandela), or to create an enabling environment to keep the negotiations going.

According to Sunter, however, this was not due to a prevailing culture in Anglo of being overtly liberal or the company sprinting down the road to Damascus. He believed it was the role played by Relly and, to an extent, Oppenheimer, who wanted to be involved in whatever change was going to come. 'There were individuals in the boardroom who combined a kind of political sensitivity with their normal responsibility of being a director or a manager inside Anglo. But there were quite a few other directors who basically just did the job, and it was just lucky that at the time that we did the scenario exercise, we had some amazing individuals, and I would single out O'Dowd, who was a sort of resident intellectual at Anglo American, and Godsell, who was pretty political. In a funny way, I call them the sort of John Lennon and Paul McCartney of the whole high-road/low-road exercise because they really wrote the material and I just sort of put it in a way that could make it a popular presentation.

'Ja, we had these amazing individuals. Spicer obviously was another who combined the normal business responsibilities at Anglo with a serious enthusiasm to change the country. So, it was more a set of individuals within Anglo rather than it being an overall company culture, because I think most of our directors were just normal business guys.'[39]

3

Not crossing the Rubicon

'At that time, after the Rubicon, there was a sense of a
massive, massive disillusionment, because there was so much
built-up expectation, that something was going to
change and that we were going to be set on a
path of going somewhere.'

– Doug Band, head of CNA and Gallo Records, 1983–1987.[1]

Michael Spicer, then 32, had been working at Anglo for five months when he was sent to listen to South Africa's belligerent head of state PW Botha deliver what was expected to be a banner speech at the city hall in Durban on the evening of 15 August 1985, a month before the Lusaka meeting. 'It was one of my first assignments at Anglo. I sat in the front row, literally within spitting distance, and listened to Botha's Rubicon speech, which turned out to be the non-Rubicon speech,' he said.[2]

Tension had been building for weeks ahead of the state president's address to his party brethren at the Natal National Party congress, with high expectations that he was to announce fundamental reforms. Roelof 'Pik' Botha, South Africa's long-serving and flamboyant foreign minister, had even travelled to Europe to meet senior officials from the United States, Britain and West Germany to inform them of the impending changes that looked set to lead the increasingly isolated country out of the political impasse in which it found itself.[3]

The backstory to Botha's angry speech remains one of that period's great political mysteries, because two weeks before, on 2 August 1985, at a meeting of senior cabinet ministers, members of the state security apparatus and senior party leaders, various policy reform proposals had been made and seemingly accepted by Botha, who'd instructed ministers to submit draft contributions to his speech.[4] These proposals included black representation at cabinet level, the future of black homelands and the release of Nelson Mandela.[5]

But on stage in Durban, Botha showed no inclination to 'cross the Rubicon', as had been anticipated both locally and abroad. Spicer listened in astonishment as Botha insisted he would not be browbeaten by his cabinet colleagues, the liberation movement or the international community. South Africa would not be forced into an unworkable solution for its unique political problems by those who did not understand the country nor care about its future, the angry president thundered. 'I am not prepared to lead white South Africans and other minority groups on a road to abdication and suicide,' he said. 'Destroy white South Africa and our influence, and this country will drift into faction strife, chaos and poverty.'[6]

Botha clearly felt under siege, pushed by unfolding events to commit to reforms he wasn't prepared to execute, while the security situation in the country became increasingly volatile. Atop the apartheid security apparatus, Botha held the state and party in an iron grip, and it was clear he wouldn't be pushed off course by liberals in his caucus nor vandals in the townships. *The New York Times* called the performance 'combative, bellicose and defiant', and quoted *The Star* in Johannesburg's editorial: 'Instead of rising to the challenge, the nation's leader retreated into an insecure shell.'[7]

The Botha speech was a hammer blow to many who'd hoped that he would at last announce significant reforms, and that it could signal that negotiations, resulting in a democratic political dispensation, were in the offing. Instead, 'in his Rubicon speech ... he resorted to the style he was familiar with: the confrontational and abrasive one suitable for a NP congress but repulsive to Western audiences.'[8]

After the speech, Botha's ministers were aghast, and the country was hit by a new wave of sanctions: the penny dropped in Washington and London that apartheid South Africa, despite ever firmer appeals to embark on actual and adequate political reforms, wasn't going to do so fast enough. And when banks like Chase Manhattan (described as 'a loyal lender to apartheid regimes'[9]) in New York decided not to roll over South African loans in the wake of the speech, the repercussions for the country's economy were enormous.

At the time South African banks borrowed heavily in dollars from abroad to take advantage of exchange-rate fluctuations. The inflow of dollars was encouraged by the South African Reserve Bank (SARB), and was used to finance imports and exports. It also enabled the government to repay its foreign borrowing. And local banks, led by Nedbank, embarked on international forays, establishing international operations, with Nedbank's New York subsidiary the most ambitious of the lot.

But Botha's speech led to a run on the rand, and foreign bankers decided 'almost unanimously' to call in South African loans. The rand suffered enormous losses. British journalist Anthony Sampson went to the JSE the day after the Botha speech, and saw bedlam. 'I went to the stock exchange and watched the hysterical dealing and yelling as the rand collapsed and investors bought gold shares to protect themselves. Politics was now in full collision with business, and most stockbrokers reckoned that the first step to renewing confidence would have to be Mandela's release.'[10]

The Botha government, in the wake of the market's rejection of its intransigence, closed the JSE for five days, froze foreign debt repayments until the end of 1985, and reintroduced the financial rand[11] to staunch the bleeding of money out of the country. And it immediately dispatched the governor of the SARB to London, New York, Frankfurt and Zürich to negotiate a rescheduling of foreign debt repayments.

'South Africa was now in a cash crunch and was steadily being isolated from the international financial system – not because of any action taken by a government in Washington or London, but because bankers saw that the government was unable to quell escalating violence caused by apartheid,' financial journalist Nigel Bruce wrote, explaining that 'the foreign bankers have imposed a capital boycott that in effect places strictures on the South African economy that are far more stringent than any trade embargo was ever likely to be.'[12]

It became difficult – embarrassing, even – to engage in commerce. 'I personally was involved in the music business and the video business, where we depended a lot on licences from overseas people and principally the United States of America,' said Doug Band. 'And as things progressed after the Rubicon, it became a situation where when I went to New York or to Los Angeles, people I'd had long-standing business dealings with would say to me, do you mind if we meet at Joe's Pub? Or do you mind if we have a coffee at such-and-such a place? They didn't want me to go to their offices.'[13]

For the grandees at Anglo's headquarters at 44 Main Street, Botha's speech was a disappointment but not unexpected. Deeply involved for some decades in changing the business and labour environment in a changing world, both Harry Oppenheimer and his successor, Relly, had found that the apartheid government was falling further and further behind domestic societal and global shifts.

Anglo had, in fact, been in conflict with the NP government since it had come to power in 1948 and threatened to nationalise various parts of the economy, followed by Hendrik Verwoerd's refusal to engage with Anton Rupert, and then Vorster and Botha's clear and repeated admonishment to business not to meddle in affairs of state and politics. Band said it was an accepted fact that president PW Botha wasn't only antagonistic towards capital, but downright hostile to 'English' capital.[14]

Relly said in 1985 that he was convinced that business should step up their engagement with government and play a stronger role in national affairs. This represented a departure from organised capital's historical role, with big business extremely reluctant to involve themselves in matters of the day. Those days were over, Relly said. 'I think it is a much better thing for the country in the long term if we listen to what each other is saying. I don't think it is necessary for the linkage (between business and government) to be too close. The politicians have the job of running the country, providing sensible infrastructure, a credible legal system, security and managing our external affairs. From business's point of view, it is entitled to say when it thinks those politics are jeopardising its ability to create wealth.'[15]

And that was now the case, Relly and other senior business leaders believed: they'd been duped by Botha and had been co-opted into his strategy. Relly 'bluntly' put his views forward: 'Piecemeal reform in the current style is now identified clearly in the black mind as tinkering with apartheid and only a visible process of political negotiations that symbolises real intent to share power will end the stonewalling tactics pursued by many black political leaders.'[16]

Government, Relly explained, should accept that business would become more strenuously involved in planning and preparing for the country's future. It was entitled to do so because it was responsible for a vital economy. 'Our attitude should be based on the practical realisation that there is no future for any of us aside from an African quagmire, unless we can express our views and seek to have the government realise the deep concern we feel about the conditions as we find them today.'[17]

Which is why, on 13 September 1985, less than four weeks after Botha's Durban speech, Relly led his delegation to meet ANC leaders in Zambia.

Relly and his colleagues returned to howls of criticism. Botha publicly denounced them as traitors, while Oppenheimer remained unhappy with his protégé's decision, and the conservative members of Anglo's management distanced themselves from their boss's initiatives.

Spicer said there was 'deep concern' at 44 Main Street about the ANC's ideas about a future South African economy. Anglo was 'transcendent' across almost all walks of life in South Africa, its interests were varied and vast, and it formed the backbone of the economy. So Anglo, with Relly leading the charge, was convinced the ANC needed to be brought into the world of modern economic theory. The party, making allowance for its historical proximity to socialism and given the support it had received from the Soviet Union and East Germany, had to understand that the South Africa it could one day inherit was built on a free-market economy, albeit with unique apartheid characteristics. And even though the ANC's leadership might not agree with Anglo's analysis of the domestic and global environment, they had to see that the quaint world of 30 years before no longer existed.

The ANC had 'simply not thought about' economics, Spicer said. 'They had thought consistently about politics, and of course the difficult life of exile – who's blaming them – breeds paranoia; you get into this whole secretive way of living and thinking,' he noted, referring to the ANC's centralised decision-making processes and 'need-to-know' culture. 'It wasn't conducive to think about the future South African economy. And who knew then, in the mid-1980s, that in a couple of years' time they'd have to really start thinking about it. Well, we were encouraging them to get on with it.'[18]

Mbeki was reportedly deeply disappointed with the lack of dividends the Zambia meeting delivered; he'd hoped to get immediate reward from it. But he understood why it was businessmen who'd initiated the first formal contact between the ANC and South Africa's white elite: 'Because businesspeople tend to be more realistic. They don't like to deal with poems and dreams but facts. Relly came because he was sensitive to the depth of the crisis and [understood

29

that he] needed the ANC to get out of it,' he said later.[19]

Both sides – business and the ANC – had their own reasons for having talked to each other. Apartheid had become ruinously expensive to maintain, and business increasingly found that the system was seriously undercutting their ability to expand and deliver returns for their shareholders. For the ANC, it was important to find a way into a constituency with actual power and influence.

And what both business and the ANC knew was that they needed each other. Business wanted to break out of the stranglehold of the apartheid capitalist system and craved global acceptance. The ANC needed as many partners inside South Africa as possible, and hoped that capital could start playing a meaningful role in forcing political change.

So, on Relly's return, Anglo stepped up its efforts to help along history. The chief executive of South Africa's most powerful conglomerate decided that nothing should be left to chance – and Anglo should help to direct events from that point as far as possible. 'What business needs to do most of all is to make the world realise that you can't have sensible reform without economic growth … they need to understand that we are not capable in the long run of creating an even moderately stable society, unless we can develop economically as a nation giving jobs to people and creating new services,' Relly said.[20]

Relly's enterprise, as the dominant player in the tightly controlled apartheid economy, was prepared to expend 'vast resources over an extended period of time' to influence the process of political and economic change, said Spicer.[21] First Relly and then his successor, Julian Ogilvie Thompson, invested much to ensure the company had eyes and ears everywhere. 'They [Anglo] ran massive intelligence operations,' said Trevor Manuel.[22]

Years after the tumult and uncertainty of the unravelling of apartheid, Spicer admitted that business's approaches to the ANC wasn't all about human rights and individual freedoms – but that, by the same token, it was much more complicated than simply accusing business of harbouring only concern for itself. 'Yes, we had to look after our own self-interest, but one would hope it was enlightened self-interest. Of course, it was self-interest in the sense that in order to continue to operate in South Africa, one had got to have at least a degree of market economics, particularly post the fall of the Berlin Wall and the break-up of the Soviet Union, and the delegitimising of out-and-out social-ism. So, an untried, untested group of people who had been nurtured in Soviet thinking and practised it – many of them had lived in the Soviet Union – was to come back to this country and had the Freedom Charter as its guiding document. The Freedom Charter was, at best, a Fabian socialism type of document, and, at worst, could be interpreted as Stalinist. This was not going to cut it.'[23]

Big business in South Africa had nowhere to go. It couldn't take its money out of the country, and it was almost impossible to invest in companies and ventures overseas. 'If business wanted to stay in the country, it would need to have politics that were essentially, and at least, market oriented. And so that was the drive, and if people accuse us of being self-interested, well, what else would we do? Do you think that we would connive in our own destruction by encouraging people to do things that we knew would make it impossible to do business?'[24]

The apartheid economy of the 1980s was the product of a construct in which the state played a central role – much as in the socialist countries that the NP government and their supporters so abhorred. Business was able to expand and grow thanks to policies that ensured a steady supply of cheap labour, while tariffs protected vulnerable industries like agriculture from outside competition.

Although various economic sanctions were in place by 1985, they weren't strong enough to cripple the apartheid state, which was still able to maintain an acceptable balance of payments as well as its ability to service foreign debts, despite a slowing economy. This changed with the Rubicon debacle, when a new wave of sanctions and disin-vestments was unleashed on the country.[25] The Reagan administration instituted a 'mild sanctions package', but the US Congress soon went much further and banned all new investments and loans to the South African government.[26]

The Commonwealth followed the American example, and similarly forbade new loans and investments. Britain's Conservative government remained reluctant to punish the Botha government, although Margaret Thatcher's patience was wearing thin.

'Institutional investors across the world, particularly in the UK and the US, would increasingly not do business with banks if those banks had exposure to South Africa,' said Martin Kingston. 'They wouldn't invest, so the sanctions were implemented in an unsophisticated and rather crude way, and I think that despite their crudity, they were very effective. It starved South Africa of access to capital, both the corporate and the public sector.'[27]

This took an enormous toll on the country, with many international companies quitting in that period, selling their assets on the cheap before fleeing in the face of the rising tide of opprobrium towards apartheid and its overlords. A fifth of British firms operating in South Africa left the country during the 1980s, with British direct investment having halved during the course of the decade.[28]

Band, operating in a business that relied on international links and relationships, was at the 'cutting edge' of where sanctions cleaved the economy. 'The screws were tightening and tightening and tightening, and it was apparent that unless something broke, and unless there was a massive accommodation, we would be driven into being a complete and utter pariah state, and finally the economy would collapse under the weight of it all. There was a gung-ho period where we all, to some extent, actually quite enjoyed being able to try and work out ways to circumvent things ... but then the hard reality started to hit.'[29]

The weakening of the South African rand meant that the government had to spend more on international debt repayments, which in turn led to slow economic growth, high interest rates, high unemployment and increased insolvency – 'an economic recipe for political turmoil'.[30] The skewed, contained and overheated nature of the apartheid economy was described by Trevor Manuel, who was to become South Africa's longest-serving finance minister, as abnormal and unsustainable.[31] The situation 'was completely untenable', said Band.[32]

At the same time, Tambo's ANC, with his chief diplomat Mbeki at the forefront, was singularly focused on corralling a global front to impose a broad suite of sanctions, including the cultural and sports boycott. The focus was to upend the apartheid state, not to spare the economy in favour of an imagined future.

Very often disinvestment led to South African companies acquiring multinational corporations at bargain-basement prices. The big conglomerates, including Anglo, diversified into anything and everything they could, from mining to movies to newspapers and agriculture. For example, Anglo – whose core business was gold and diamonds – bought the local operations of the Ford Motor Company and Barclays Bank (later First National Bank) when their parent companies ditched their South African operations.[33]

And companies like Anglo American ended up with nowhere to go. Sanctions and government policy meant it was extremely difficult, if not completely impossible, to take money out of the country in order to invest elsewhere.

4

Marxist-Leninists and fears about the ANC

'The South African business community was shit-scared of what was coming down the pike, and a lot of them were of the view that they were a bunch of communists and Marxists that were going to walk in and nationalise everything and wreck the economy. In fact, that's how they talked. That's how they thought and that's how they talked: that this was just going to be a wrecking ball ...'

– Banker Martin Kingston, about the ANC pre-1990.[1]

In mid-1985, the South African public generally knew very little of the ANC, apart from the fact that it was a 'terrorist organisation'.

After the party was banned in 1960 under the Suppression of Communism Act, the apartheid government went to extreme lengths to snuff out any traces of the organisation, arresting and banning its leaders, forbidding the publication of pictures of ANC leaders or their words, and making the display of ANC flags punishable by law.

Indeed, fears about communism and socialism were very real. During the visit by Relly's group to Zambia to meet Tambo and his fellow ANC leaders, the ANC's links to the South African Communist Party (SACP) were a significant point of discussion, with the ANC chief refusing to denounce the two organisations' relationship.

34

Spicer and Theuns Eloff (who played a leading role in negotiations between South African business and exiled liberation movement leaders) both cited the prevailing fears around the ANC and communism as very successful in shaping the views and approach of business to the ANC and its allies. And, of course, the National Party government portrayed the 'total onslaught' – the supposed threat to South Africa and indeed to the western world by the Soviet Union's designs on the strategic value of South Africa – as part of a master plan to eventually install a communist regime in Pretoria.

As Stephen Ellis argues in his seminal study of the ANC in exile, all of this was to some degree true.[2] South Africa, Anglo and the ANC all played a role in the larger cold war environment.

The cold war, which lasted roughly from 1947 to 1991, was the global power struggle between the USA and the Soviet Union and their respective allies, and resulted in anti-communist suspicions and international incidents that led the two superpowers to the brink of nuclear disaster. During that period, the ANC received support from the Soviet Union as part of the Soviets' attempts to expand its reach in the third world and to counter its principal enemy, the United States.

The Angolan civil war, which involved another Soviet client state, Cuba, was also a terrain of cold war conflict, where the apartheid state came into direct contact with communism. The South African Defence Force invaded Angola in 1975, and allied with the National Union for the Total Independence of Angola (Unita), which was engaged in a war to overthrow the People's Movement for the Liberation of Angola (MPLA) government of Angola. Cuba sent combat troops in support of the communist-aligned MPLA against the pro-western Unita.

But Moscow's appetite for African adventurism evaporated in the late 1980s as its commitment to African liberation struggles, which it had maintained throughout most of the cold war, weakened. And when the Berlin Wall fell, and the Soviet Union disintegrated two years later, in 1991, the ANC's central ideological plank broke and left the organisation in crisis.[3] And with the demise of communism in Eastern Europe and Russia, the threat of communism also disappeared.

In this age of global interconnectedness, information highways and the rapid, real-time sharing of information and multimedia, it must be borne in mind that in 1985 the world was a much, much different place. The flow of information to and from the South African state by the apartheid authorities was strictly regulated, and it was difficult to gather open-source intelligence about the ANC, its leaders and its policies. The ANC itself, having been forced underground and targeted by the apartheid security machinery, became paranoid, and it was tricky to make contact with and meet leaders and representatives of the organisation.

Business, in an economy in which 80 per cent was dominated by Anglo (the Oppenheimers), Rembrandt (the Ruperts), Liberty (the Gordons) and AngloVaal (the Menells and Hersovs),[4] and all run by dynasties, needed to embark on its own initiatives, given that the political process was stalling. The disastrous Botha speech and its economic fallout added a renewed desperation by business to involve themselves in the process. The constraints on the economy, which many had believed to be strong and robust, even in the face of sanctions, were beginning to throttle growth and opportunity. This had a severe impact on the country's business leaders, who felt they had to engage in the process more forcefully than they had up until then.

Michael Spicer said that the Anglo-led visit to Mfuwe Game Lodge cut this 'Gordian knot' and played a big role in helping white businessmen gain a better understanding of the ANC. 'It opened the doors to a deluge of missions that went up to Zambia. The Idasa meeting in Senegal, Danielle Mitterrand's Paris summit … there were just vast numbers of people who went up after that and it undoubtedly had a major and profound impact on opening up perspectives all around,' he said.

Mitterrand's South Africa summit near the French capital in 1989 was attended by journalists such as Max du Preez and other newspaper editors, while various business groupings and captains of industry also made the trip to France. Trevor Manuel accompanied other ANC leaders, including Thabo Mbeki, Joel Netshitenzhe (who later became Mbeki's policy chief), Tito Mboweni and Kader Asmal. Significantly, Cosatu general-secretary Jay Naidoo also attended, with Alec Erwin, who'd also played a leading role in the internal resistance movement.

Spicer is convinced that Anglo's initiatives, like the Lusaka safari and Sunter's 'scenarios' process, led the way, because after that groups of 'self-styled progressive businessmen' like Neal Chapman, chief executive of Southern Life, and Mike Sander, managing director of AECI, started to reach out to leaders of the UDF, in which Manuel was playing a leading role.

Manuel acknowledged this and said the mid to late 1980s saw the opening up of perspectives and the creation of opportunities to meet a cross-section of leaders in apartheid society, including in the business world. 'I left Grootvlei Prison outside Bloemfontein in 1989 – it was my last incarceration – and within days obtained a passport to go to Paris to attend the Mitterrand summit. It was almost unheard of that someone who had been banned and imprisoned was allowed to go to Paris. But it shows how things were opening up, and how important the need to talk became. It was a very important signal about the immediacy and the imminence of political change.'[5]

It's calculated that between 1983 and 1990, approximately 167 meetings between the ANC in exile and various South African groupings took place.[6] Nineteen of these were in 1985, and 27 in 1986, and they increased in volume up until the movement's unbanning in February 1990.[7]

South African business leaders, who for so long had ignored the ANC, were now trying their best to 'rapidly build bridges' with black leaders. 'It was fascinating to watch the sudden confusion of businessmen as they hedged their bets and tried to distance themselves from apartheid,' Anthony Sampson wrote. Even Oppenheimer – who seemed 'exasperated … at last' by Botha – asked Sampson if he knew any ANC leaders. 'I would like to meet Oliver Tambo,' he said.[8]

In October 1985 – the month after the Relly meeting in Lusaka – Sampson arranged for Tambo to do the rounds in London, including a speech at Chatham House (where Tambo implored Britain to impose more sanctions on South Africa, and defended the armed struggle),[9] a tea party at the House of Lords, a luncheon at the offices of *The Economist* and a private gathering with some of Britain's biggest investors in South Africa, including mining houses Gold Fields and Rio Tinto Zinc, as well as BP and ICI. Sampson recalls the group was 'clearly apprehensive [about] meeting the leader of a terrorist, part-Marxist movement'. Mbeki – who travelled everywhere with Tambo and was considered the ANC's 'minister of foreign affairs' – did most of the talking, fielding questions about nationalisation, but without convincing the businessmen, who wanted more contact with the ANC. According to Sampson, by the end of that week, even *The Times* proclaimed in its lead story, 'Talk to Tambo', meaning that the time had come for the South African government to also talk to the ANC, like British business was starting to do.[10]

But South African big business – capital – was still reluctant and wary to talk to people whom the state still regarded as communist agitators at best, and murderous terrorists at worst. And there was a retreat from the intended rapprochement when a bomb exploded in a shopping centre in Durban shortly before Christmas 1985, killing five people. Tambo denied that the bomb had been planted by the ANC.[11]

Interestingly, Nafcoc had met the ANC on a regular basis while the organisation was in exile. In May 1986 alone, Nafcoc's president Gabriel Mokgoka and eminent businessman Sam Motsuenyane met the ANC twice, first in Lusaka, then in Paris. In fact, the organisation became known as 'the ANC in business' and its contact was much more regular than that between the ANC and 'official' and 'organised' business from white South Africa.

In June 1986, Chris Ball from FNB and Neal Chapman from Southern Life held talks with Oliver Tambo in London, after which the BBC carried a debate between them.

In November 1986, Cosatu's leaders Chris Dlamini, Sydney Mufamadi, John Gomomo and Alec Erwin travelled to Lusaka.

In July 1987, Frederik van Zyl Slabbert, who'd resigned as leader of the opposition the year before, citing the sterility of the white political environment, led a delegation of mostly dissident Afrikaners to meet the ANC in Dakar, Senegal.[12] Delegate Eloff later reported that it was clear that the sides were on different sets of tracks: 'We believed in a market economy, and they in socialism. I do think, however, they were careful not come across as overtly Marxist. It was obvious that there were differences, and I think both sides realised how deep those differences, especially in relation to the economy, were.' He added, 'We told them, "Gentlemen, you simply cannot import a socialist system to South Africa."'[13]

Eighteen months later, in November 1987, the first of seven meetings between Afrikaner intelligentsia, led by Stellenbosch philosopher Willie Esterhuyse, and the ANC, led by Mbeki, was held,[14] with the connivance of the South African National Intelligence Service (NIS). Most of the meetings took place at Mells Park, a private estate in the English countryside. This initiative is credited with having been an important unofficial channel between the government of the day and the government in waiting. According to Esterhuyse's account of events, discussions were about finding common ground, investigating mechanisms for negotiating, and matters such as the armed struggle and the release of Mandela.

'The reason why the Mells Park discussions are so significant is because the ANC felt it could talk to the Afrikaners. They were, after all, in power,' said Jürgen Kögl, a Johannesburg businessman who worked closely with Mbeki and others when they returned to South Africa in 1990. 'The English business establishment remained very condescending towards the ANC; they always were condescending. They couldn't bring about change.'[15]

And South African NIS negotiators Maritz Spaarwater and Mike Louw held three off-the-grid meetings with Mbeki and Jacob Zuma between September 1989 and February 1990 in Switzerland.[16]

The main thrust of these high-profile engagements was the political situation and discussions on how to bring about fundamental change. But the economy – its current hardship and its future shape – was never far from the top table of discussion.

The ANC was an organisation deeply under communist influence, having established formal links with the SACP very early on during the liberation struggle. The SACP prided itself on being 'the vanguard party' in the liberation movement, often articulating and formulating political theory, strategy and tactics that were adopted by the ANC. (It was the SACP that determined that the South African problem was 'colonialism of a special kind', which has become part of the ANC lexicon and denotes a society where the colonists are born in and live in the colonised country.[17])

ANC leaders were regularly elected to the highest structures of the SACP, and vice versa, and although Mandela has denied this, evidence suggests that he became a member of the party as early as 1960, during the SACP conference in Johannesburg when a decision was taken to establish the ANC's military wing, uMkhonto weSizwe (MK).[18] It's unknown when his membership lapsed, or whether he renewed it after his release from prison.

During the 1980s, the SACP influence on the ANC was at its strongest, with senior leaders such as Joe Slovo and Chris Hani playing leading political and military roles. (Slovo was somewhat of a bogeyman for white South Africa, and Relly's group specifically asked that Slovo not be part of the 1985 Zambia meeting, for example.)

Stephen Ellis said the SACP aim was always 'to control the ANC politically'.[19]

When, in 1985, the ANC, after its consultative conference in Kabwe, Zambia, officially opened its national executive to all races, Slovo and Ronnie Kasrils, a leading light in the SACP, were elected to the ANC leadership, 'reinforcing the party's grip' on the ANC.[20] During this period the SACP played a leading role in all discussions about the economy, and 'remained a fierce adherent of a Soviet, Stalinist orthodoxy until the early 1990s'.[21]

But the SACP didn't have it all its own way. Even socialists like Jeremy Cronin, who later became the long-serving deputy general-secretary of the SACP, and Ben Turok, an academic who later became a respected member of parliament, were uncertain about the future shape of the South African economy, with the former apparently arguing that the SACP would have to take its line from Moscow, and Turok being critical of the seemingly dogmatic imposition of Soviet models on a vastly different South African environment.[22]

According to the SACP at the time, a year after the 1985 Kabwe conference, 'well over two-thirds' of the ANC's governing body, numbering 30 people, were SACP members. 'Tambo was the perfect frontman, since he was not a communist, his manner was disarmingly mild, and he could generally be relied upon to deliver whatever speech was put in front of him by his aides, of whom Mbeki was the most important,' said Ellis.[23]

Mbeki chaired the last SACP congress outside South Africa, in Havana, in April 1989, at which the party adopted a programme for a two-stage revolution in South Africa, with the first stage the overthrow of the apartheid state in a national democratic revolution, and the second the push for a socialist system. The new national democratic state 'was to root out domination by foreign capital and create the industrial and technical base for Socialism through democratic ownership and control of the economy ... [including] ... mining, heavy industry, banks and other monopoly industries.'[24]

But Mbeki had by then started to loosen himself from any socialist or communist pretence; his biography notes that the 1980s were a period where he came deeply under the impression of the inadequacies of the Soviet system.[25] In fact, in 1984, responding to a Canadian scholar's accusation that the ANC 'had betrayed its socialist principles and sold out to the bourgeoisie',[26] Mbeki had stated that 'the ANC is not a socialist party. It has never pretended to be one, has never said it was, and is not trying to be one.'[27]

Mbeki, noted Spicer, was 'the most cosmopolitan guy of every one of them. He was the most thoughtful and had the most exposure on economic issues because he travelled the globe for the ANC. He dealt with businesspeople, diplomats, journalists…everybody. Mbeki was way beyond all the guys sitting in Lusaka or Angola or Tanzania; he was aware of what was going on in the world. And, unlike Cyril Ramaphosa in present-day South Africa, he backed his people. He supported Trevor, he backed Maria [Ramos, an economist who was to become director-general at National Treasury], he backed Tito [Mboweni, also a trained economist and later governor of the SARB as well as labour and finance minister]. His policies were rather clear, actually.'[28]

This is significant, because by the time Mbeki landed in Cape Town on a flight from Lusaka on 28 April 1990, he'd already moved beyond any notion that South Africa was to lurch towards socialism, as many in the movement's leadership with SACP ties wanted. And it was to prove very significant, given capital's fears about the ANC and communism, and also the decisive role Mbeki was to play in directing the post-apartheid economy. His membership of the SACP later lapsed.[29]

The ANC's complete focus after its banning in 1960 was the political struggle against apartheid, which meant that economic policy development was almost completely subjugated if not abandoned.[30]

With Tambo completely engaged in the political struggle, and Mbeki as the movement's chief diplomat, development of economic policy was left in the hands of a few, including Ben Turok and Vella Pillay, an academic who worked for a Chinese bank in London. The ideas prevalent in many left circles in the 1970s, influenced by debates on class and the plight of blue-collar workers in Britain and with the rise of Thatcherism, weighed heavily on those like Turok and Pillay, who were engaged with ANC economic thinking. Margaret Thatcher had advocated a belief in free markets and a small state: rather than planning and regulating business and people's lives, government's job was to get out of the way, she believed.

Add to this Marxist theory taught to cadres of the movement in exile in Moscow and East Berlin and elsewhere, and it was logical that the ANC would be strongly in favour of a command economy where the state was the leading economic actor. Kingston, the banker, said that Turok's thinking was 'symptomatic of current thinking by a lot of people': 'they acknowledged that the private sector had a role to play – but I think it was a subordinate aspect'; it entailed 'the developmental state, heavy hand on the tiller ... the private sector is there to be used, and I would say in certain instances the private sector is there to be abused'. He said this thinking is to this day 'embedded in the DNA' of the ANC.[31]

The ANC's economics unit, established in 1982, functioned more as a study group looking at sections of the South African economy than as a body generating economic policy alternatives. At its peak, about 50 economists were involved, split between Lusaka and Tanzania, with London-based economists linked to the Communist Party of Great Britain carrying great influence. While the exiled movement declared in internal memorandums that 'preparations for economic emancipation cannot be postponed until freedom day', and despite the establishment of a department of economic planning in 1985, there's 'no evidence that this objective was met, and after 1990 the ANC scrambled to develop such a policy-making capacity'.[32] Certainly, the department of economic planning doesn't seem to have been as dynamic and active as was to be expected from an organisation that conceivably could take over the leadership of South Africa.

Despite this seeming lack of active economic work, the department was involved in arranging seminars related to the South African economy. During one in Lusaka, there was an argument in favour of a mixed economy with 'a degree of nationalisation' – which, it was warned, would come with costs. At other seminars, Pillay put forward ideas on anti-monopoly and anti-trust policies to deal with 'powerful conglomerates' that would be able to 'undermine a democratic state', while Rob Davies, a senior SACP leader, spoke of the need to meet people's 'basic needs' and improve 'the conditions of working people'.[33]

According to Clem Sunter, the role of the economy was always going to be a determining factor during the transition – and the Anglo scenarios illustrated that. For the South African political transition to be successful and sustainable, the economic transition had to be just and efficient.

Kingston said that up until 1990, everything related to the economy was on the periphery for the ANC. 'There was no debate about the economy in the context of the role that the private sector or business could or should play. But I think that the levels of mistrust that are still perceived to exist today were already prevalent then.' For decades, there was never serious contact with the ANC by foreign business – like the big British investors – nor local business, said Kingston, who argued that this contributed to the distrust that existed.

But there was no doubt that before the ANC's unbanning, and during the final years of exile, it was committed to something other than a market economy. Said Kingston, 'Marxism, statism, occupying the commanding heights of the economy ... it was at the front and centre of their philosophy. It certainly wasn't investor-friendly policies.'[34]

Trevor Manuel said that before Mandela was released, he'd started receiving delegations of black business figures like Richard Maponya and Sam Motsuenyane, who'd pressed the incarcerated liberation leader about nationalisation – which they did not support – and other ANC policies. Mandela rebuffed their pro-capitalist overtures, sticking to the established ANC line: 'Madiba just said that the policy of the ANC is the nationalisation of the banks, mines and monopoly industries,' said Manuel. 'It was just the reality of what happens when you're stuck in prison.'[35]

Jay Naidoo concurs that big capital's fears were well founded at the time. 'A lot of the intellectual heavyweights of the ANC were aligned to the SACP, and they had a model, and that model was the Soviet Union.'[36]

Band was one of the few businessmen who had semi-regular contact with the ANC in London. 'I had had a couple of informal meetings with the odd ANC people in London, principally because we had a very mixed stable of black artists and we were trying to further their international careers. So I'd actually met a few people through those contacts when I'd been in London, and I had had relatively positive discussions with them, sympathetic discussions, so I didn't personally have a hostile feeling about the ANC. But I was under no illusions that from an economic policy point of view, they were very, very focused on left-wing socialist interventionist economics.'[37]

The realities of the changing geopolitical landscape, which had a serious bearing on the economic environment countries found themselves in, was to prove more of a determining factor than anything the businessmen could have hoped to achieve. 'Whatever the ANC wanted to do and implement, it was going to be subject to the tests of time and reality. There was a belief that as the ANC returned to South Africa and saw the complexities, as they were tested by reality, they would adapt, become less theoretical and more practical,' said Spicer.[38]

5

Big capital starts planning the future

'Influx control is not only an affront to dignity,
which is the political side. There's the other side. You can't run
a country like that. You can't run a business. It's incompatible
with the private enterprise system, isn't it?'

– Mike Rosholt, chairman and chief executive
of Barlow Rand, 1982.[1]

'I don't have time for this bullshit,' said John Hall, a senior executive at
Barlow Rand, the giant diversified industrial and investment company
based in Johannesburg. He slammed his fist down on the table before
storming out of the meeting room.

It was late 1990. Mandela had been freed and various liberation
movements unbanned. For about three years, the Consultative Business Movement (CBM), a hodgepodge of senior business leaders,
had been facilitating meetings between white leaders of big business
and leaders of the internal Mass Democratic Movement (MDM), a
loose alliance of the UDF and Cosatu. They'd been trying to generate
dialogue and understanding, but mostly just introducing people to
each other – because white business simply didn't know who the black
internal leadership was.

46

At that meeting between CBM members and the leaders of the Azanian People's Organisation (Azapo) in the hamlet of Broederstroom, northwest of Johannesburg, the divide was deep and wide. 'The businesspeople were all about the market economy, and the Azapo guys were immovable on a socialist future,' recalls Eloff, then the executive director of the CBM.[2] 'Hall then stood up and left. It was a helluva thing.'

But the Azapo meeting was just one of hundreds that the CBM organised between 1988 and 1995 (when it disbanded) to enable business to engage with internal liberation leaders, returning exiles and ANC negotiators. These meetings, between groups from diametrically opposed ideological positions, had interesting dynamics, Eloff said. 'It was always set down for Friday afternoons to Sundays at lunchtime, and [certain people] were always late, only arriving at 5 pm, 6 pm or even 7 pm. Irritation was then already visible. Then we had dinner and chatted, and on Saturday mornings our discussions started in earnest.'

Although things sometimes grew 'heated', he said, 'the delegates would keep on talking, and it always ended up being good engagements. I think the businessmen started to understand more about injustice, discrimination and poverty, and the other guys started to understand a little more about where money comes from and how the economy works,' he said.[3]

The CBM agitated for a democratic dispensation – but it also believed, as Spicer said of business in general, in 'enlightened self-interest'.[4] 'We had to convince the corporate leadership in South Africa that the role of business was to stay in business. They therefore had to become involved. And there was going to be something of a mixed market economy,' said Eloff.[5]

Business, by and large, was caught betwixt and between: it saw the urgency for negotiated reform, but at the same time it was reluctant to antagonise the security state, not to mention shareholders and customers who were extremely averse to talking with the enemy.

In an interview in 1982, Barlow's chairman and chief executive, Mike Rosholt, who later became deeply involved with the CBM, was described as similar to Oppenheimer: someone who wanted to see progress but needed to balance it with realities. Rosholt didn't 'want to be perceived as a political enemy of a government dominated by Afrikaans-speaking whites who are just starting to overcome an almost hereditary mistrust of the English-speaking business establishment. So, this soft-spoken former accountant insists that his public stance is apolitical.'[6]

Still, capital could have done much more, much earlier. As Rosholt put it, 'Very few liberals want to face a situation where there's an immediate equality, and I don't believe it's necessary. I'm a great believer in evolutionary stages. But there's got to be movement. Black people have got to see it.'[7]

Besides the fact that business did not capitalise on the Relly safari, it also refused to sign up to another significant attempt to get capital to use its ample muscle to lubricate the stalled political process. In 1986 it rebuffed an attempt by former judge Jan Steyn and the Federated Chamber of Industry to get business to subscribe to a business charter of human rights.

It was against this backdrop that Chris Ball, chief executive of First National Bank (which came into being when Britain's Barclays Bank disinvested, with Anglo taking a controlling stake), asked Christo Nel, an executive at timber company PG Bison, to 'set up contact between legitimate black leaders who enjoyed mass-based support and white mainstream business leaders'.[8]

Ball, described as South Africa's 'highest profile business radical',[9] was the subject of a commission of inquiry set up by PW Botha to investigate whether he'd paid for newspaper advertisements celebrating the ANC's 75th anniversary.[10] Testifying before the commission – and accompanied by bodyguards – Ball denied paying for the newspaper ads. He admitted that he'd supported calls to legalise the ANC the year before, but that he'd since changed his mind. 'Given the presence of the Communist Party in the ANC and the issue of violence, it is not possible to talk blandly about unbanning the ANC,' he said.[11]

His outspokenness seemed to rile his biggest shareholder – Anglo, with Relly at the helm – and he was seemingly silenced by his board.[12] But Ball, supported by Neal Chapman, chair and chief executive of Southern Life, Mike Sander, chief executive of AECI, Chris van Wyk, chief executive of Trust Bank, Zach de Beer, director at Anglo, Mervyn King, chairman of Tradegro, and ex-judge advocate Anton Mostert,[13] banded together to get a form of dialogue and contact with MDM leaders off the ground.

Eloff recalls that 'most of the legitimate leaders were either in hiding, in detention, in jail or in exile.'[14] Ball and co's contact 'on the other side' was Albertina Sisulu, wife of jailed ANC leader Walter, and then-president of the UDF, Azhar Cachalia, who was the UDF's treasurer, Murphy Morobe, also from the UDF, and Mewa Ramgobin, from the Natal Indian Congress.[15]

The first engagements were difficult. Business leaders were 'shit scared'[16] of what was coming, and distrust between the groupings was real. They were also afraid of the Botha government, and the legal implications of meeting black leaders.

In June 1987, after the state of emergency was extended, MDM leaders Morobe, Cachalia and Eric Molobi (a former Robben Islander) requested a meeting with business leaders to brief them about the situation in the townships, and also to explain that it was increasingly becoming difficult for the MDM to control escalating violence – a direct result of state repression and the state of emergency.[17] Their request 'was simple': could business leaders issue a joint statement calling for an end to the state of emergency and restrictions placed on black leaders?

It never happened. After days of phone calls and appeals, it wasn't possible to get more than six business leaders to support such a statement.[18]

A couple of months later, in October 1987, Sisulu and Cachalia again told the business grouping that they would commit 20 senior UDF leaders to meet a similarly numbered business delegation in order to kick-start a formal relationship and to engage in dialogue about the country's future. Eloff records that 'rapid support' for the initiative came from a number of business leaders, and that 18 of them arrived ahead of time at the meeting venue to be briefed about what to expect. They were told who was coming, including leaders from the UDF, civic organisations, trade unions and youth formations; some of the MDM delegates were under restriction orders, which, according to law, made meeting them illegal.

'When the preparatory meeting for the business delegation ended, 12 of the 18 potential participants excused themselves. When a delegation of 18 black leaders arrived, only six white business leaders met them.' Although the delegates 'nevertheless discussed how business could contribute to breaking the sociopolitical logjam', 'this meeting indicated that the road to be travelled was still a difficult one'.[19]

In 1988, according to Eloff, 'conditions deteriorated very rapidly'. Business leaders involved with the nascent activities of the still-to-be-established CBM were seemingly being targeted and harassed by apartheid security forces, with activists working for the group being followed, threatened and arrested, and their homes subjected to raids.

By February 1988, most of the black leaders with whom contact had been made by business leaders were banned or under severe restriction orders.[20]

But momentum was picking up, and the CBM was given permanent office space by PG Bison at their head office in Main Street in Jeppe, Johannesburg.[21] By then, more and more business leaders were joining the initiative, and it was decided that they couldn't again approach leaders of the MDM without a firm commitment that they were willing to engage despite whatever consequences could follow.

In April 1988 there was a breakthrough, thanks to the intervention of Sisulu and Cachalia, who arranged a meeting between business and Cosatu's Jay Naidoo and Sydney Mufamadi, and after Christo Nel met the ANC's Tito Mboweni and Steve Tshwete in Lusaka to ask for their assistance.[22]

What followed, according to Eloff, were 'several hundred meetings across South Africa' between local businesses and MDM leaders. 'The meetings had one purpose in mind, namely, to establish a movement of business leaders who would commit themselves to actively creating relationships with recognised black leaders of established mass-based sociopolitical movements.'[23]

'We [big business] simply had to facilitate dialogue with the exiled movements and with the leadership at home, and we … spent virtually every weekend in discussions. We went up to Harare, Tanzania … all over the place. We were meeting all these groups and people,' said Spicer.[24]

Business saw what was coming, and now there was no turning back.

The CBM was formally established in August 1988, after more than 18 months of false starts, and a year before De Klerk replaced Botha as head of state. The movement formally began life at a meeting that came to be known as the 'Broederstroom Encounter', which was attended by 40 white business leaders and 40 black leaders from the MDM. At the time, it was the only business-led initiative established after 'direct consultation with the largely black leadership of mass-based organisations'.[25]

The peculiarity of that period is perhaps best exemplified by Cachalia, one of the co-chairs, who said in his opening remarks that his restriction orders forbade him to speak with or address more than four people. 'By being here, you are breaking the law of the land. So I will not talk to any of you. I will limit my communication to only one of the people right here at the front of the room. Maybe in that way, I will not be breaking any of the strange laws of the land. It's

51

up to you whether you want to break the law by listening to me!'[26]

Eloff explained – and Spicer concurred[27] – that the purpose of the CBM wasn't to formulate policy or to write economic action plans for the South Africa of the future. Its purpose was purely to create a mechanism through which business leaders, large and small, could interact with and contact leaders of the MDM. 'The 40 individuals who established the CBM just knew the country was in trouble, and they weren't driven by fear of the ANC, they were driven by fears of an economic wasteland,' said Eloff. 'The government was refusing to negotiate, economic sanctions were getting worse, and the ANC wanted to immediately implement socialism when they took over.'[28]

But the CBM, which then proceeded to create and maintain a nationwide network of business in contact with liberation leaders – and which was to play such an important role during the actual negotiations – was never intended to be a lobby group for capital, although it became one of the principal conduits of economic orthodoxy later channelled into the transition process. Eloff said the organisation always consisted of individuals, not corporates. 'A company like Anglo, despite Mike's [Spicer] claims, initially didn't want to go in boots and all, despite the involvement of the leadership of many of its subsidiaries. Anglo allowed guys like Mike Sander from AECI and Southern Life's Neal Chapman to take part, but...the chief executives never got involved.'[29]

But the CBM eventually became heavily influenced by Anglo, with a number of Anglo companies, their leaders and Spicer taking a leading role in the movement's activities. In contrast, Afrikaans-speaking companies 'weren't very keen on this', said Eloff, with very few becoming involved. The Ruperts' company, Rembrandt, was never part of the CBM, and Eloff ascribes that to their involvement with the Urban Foundation, established by Harry Oppenheimer and Anton Rupert to help finance and establish housing projects for urbanised blacks. 'I think they did not want to be involved in an activist organisation.'[30]

Jürgen Kögl, however, dismisses the attempts by CBM, Eloff

and Spicer to engage the ANC as 'clumsy'. Spicer, Kögl said, 'over-emphasised' his role during the transition, although he conceded that 'he did a reasonable job for Anglo American'. 'It was very obvious that they were only there to protect their interests, as opposed to con-tributing to a solution. The solutions that they did propose were to protect them and their interests, rather than in the interests of the whole country.'

Kögl established a consultancy with Frederik van Zyl Slabbert, helping big capital position itself ahead of democracy in 1994, and became a sounding board for senior ANC leaders attempting to understand industrialist South Africa. He said that in the consultancy work they did, 'we were very conscious of ensuring that we should find solutions for the whole country'.[31]

Big business – which included Anglo, Old Mutual, Sanlam, the banks and others the Van Zyl Slabbert-Kögl consultancy assisted – were 'confused … and scared' and looking for solutions to enable them to remain in the country.

Despite the formation of the CBM, and the quickening of the politi-cal current around them, business struggled to define its sociopolitical role. Most business leaders were reluctant to play too much of an activist role, although they recognised the damaging and detrimental impact of the political system on their businesses. They also under-stood that their workforce, largely black, had reached the end of their tether, and that if they were to enjoy a sustainable future, visible and systemic change had to come.

Eloff said the CBM leadership – he, Nel and Colin Coleman (who was to become chief executive of investment bank Goldman Sachs) – had to work hard to convince business that they couldn't separate economics from politics, and that they were operating in a political economy. Eloff said for many 'the thought was just scary'. He cited Rosholt, who maintained that politics isn't the job of business, 'and that the business of business is business'.

But this changed with Rosholt and John Hall's increased involvement in the CBM. 'Mike told me he became a convert when he realised that business couldn't just sit back and do nothing. The business of business, he said, was to stay in business. And from there the philosophy of enlightened self-interest was born.'[32]

The CBM leadership held its first official meeting in February 1989 under the chairmanship of Mike Sander, chief executive of chemical manufacturer AECI (part of the Anglo fold), and Murray Hofmeyr, of the Johannesburg Consolidated Investment company (JCI), a South African mining house founded in 1889 by flamboyant mining pioneer Barney Barnato, who made his first fortune in diamonds in Kimberley in the 1870s and his second in gold on the Witwatersrand after 1886. Spicer was Anglo's official representative, and other major companies represented included Southern Life (Neal Chapman), Eskom (Ian McRae) and miner Gencor (Naas Steenkamp).

Shortly after that, companies that had representation included another mining giant, AngloVaal (Clive Menell), Barlow Rand (Hall) and Nedcor (Chris Liebenberg, who later became finance minister under Mandela).

The CBM established regional structures in the western Cape, Natal and eastern Cape, and with local MDM structures arranged a series of meetings and dialogues. Spicer and Eloff recall that they spent thousands of hours in discussions with MDM leaders, including people like Eric Molobi, Mohammed Valli Moosa, who was to become a cabinet minister, Terror Lekota, a grassroots organiser and later also a minister, Sisulu, one of the ANC's big three leaders alongside Mandela and Tambo, and many others, as well as regional leaders at grassroots level.

Eloff said one of the CBM's big successes was the ability to formalise contact and to introduce a process element into dealing with change and overcoming differences. Contact between business and the MDM was run almost according to principles of industrial psychology. 'You know, we often sat there and just drew diagrams on pieces of paper, saying to each other, right, this is where we are, where do we want to go to? I think making it process-driven helped us create a better understanding between people.'[33]

But it wasn't easy, Eloff reiterates, and there were many business-men whose fears and trepidation got the better of them. During one meeting of the CBM, leaders of the MDM and businessmen were caucusing in separate rooms, when one businessman said, pointing at the closed door behind which the MDM group was sitting, 'I don't trust any of those people as far as I can throw them. They are all a bunch of communists who are only interested in taking over or inter-fering with my business!' Eloff said this wasn't representative of the general feeling, but that it shows that many were struggling with what was unfolding.[34]

There were some casualties. Ball, the chief executive of FNB who'd initiated the whole thing in 1987, abruptly resigned from his position in 1989 after enormous pressure was seemingly brought to bear on him.[35] 'Many of these business leaders paid dearly for their involve-ment, professionally and in their private lives. Hall was repeatedly harassed; his house was shot at, and dead animals [were] left in his swimming pool. It was clearly meant to intimidate him,' said Eloff. Hall and his family left the country soon after.

6

Reform accelerates

'In 1989 the Berlin Wall goes down. Socialism is fundamentally discredited and then the Soviet Union breaks up ... From a global economic point of view, it means that capitalism and globalisation and technology and human progress are absolutely dominant.'

– Michael Spicer, then special assistant
to Anglo's chief executive.[1]

In July 1986 secret meetings between Nelson Mandela and apartheid justice minister Kobie Coetsee started taking place,[2] with similar meetings between Mandela and NIS head Niël Barnard commencing in July 1988.[3] Barnard met with Mandela many times, in order to inform him about the political situation outside the prison and advise him on how to negotiate with first Botha and then the new president, De Klerk.

The pace of South Africa's 'reform' programme, previously glacial, suddenly speeded up in the momentous year that was 1989, with fundamental change in the country's domestic political environment mirroring a shift in geopolitics with the fall of the Berlin Wall and the collapse of communism in Eastern Europe.

After the Second World War, the Soviet Union had gradually erected an 'iron curtain' across Europe, splitting the east from the west, and democracies from communist states. Defeated Germany had been similarly divided up by the occupying powers, into east and west, and the city of Berlin had been split into four zones, with British, French and American areas in the west of the city, and a Soviet zone in the east. The notorious wall had been built in 1961 because East Berlin was haemorrhaging people to the west.

Jürgen Kögl visited Leonid Brezhnev's USSR and then West Germany in the late 1970s. 'Those visits cured me of any infatuation with any interpretation of a communist-socialist dispensation,' he said.[4] He saw that socialism, and Soviet-style communism, simply didn't work. 'At the entrance of every restaurant there was somebody watching, and at the end of a hallway at a hotel, there was somebody sitting there watching, usually a woman. And everything was shoddy ... There was no colour. It was black and grey. And when I flew from Moscow to West Berlin and suddenly there was colour ... yellow, light. In the Moscow of Brezhnev, it was grey – grey, grey, grey and black, and dirty ... dirty snow.'[5]

Kögl said he was strongly opposed to the type of system where there was a standing order to shoot anyone who crossed from East to West Berlin. 'There was absolutely no moral basis for that kind of regime. On the other hand, one had to say about all the liberation people, whether it was Swapo [South West Africa People's Organisation], whether it was the East Timor people who had an observer post, whether it was the Palestinians ... all of those with observer status were shunned by free marketeers, by western market economies, [by] the social democrat economy in West Germany. Nobody from that camp of ideological convictions talked to these guys and offered help. In fact, they were banned or sanctioned. So the liberation movements, however humanist they may have been, were trapped in an environment in which the business, and commercial, free enterprise markets were never there to engage them in a friendly way.'[6]

For a young Kögl, disillusioned with South Africa and his native South West Africa, it came as no surprise that Swapo and the ANC were deeply under the influence of the Soviet Union, East Germany and the social-democratic Nordic countries. 'They were left to their own devices … No one offered help, except those countries.'[7]

By the 1980s, the Soviet Union was facing acute economic problems and major food shortages. The cold war had become enormously expensive, and the cost to maintain the USSR's involvement in various proxy battles around the world – including in Angola – simply became too heavy.[8] The ANC's annual budget was reportedly somewhere in the region of $100 million, with half dedicated to the armed struggle.[9] Moscow started losing interest in the ANC's African struggle, and pressured Lusaka to look at alternative ways to solve the conflict with Pretoria.

The installation of Mikhail Gorbachev as general-secretary of the Communist Party in the Soviet Union in 1985 led to a series of reforms driven largely by the economic crisis in which the giant repressive state found itself. Gorbachev introduced a policy of 'glasnost' (openness) and 'perestroika' (restructuring).

On 4 November 1989, about half a million people gathered in Alexanderplatz in the heart of East Berlin. Three days later, the government resigned, and finally, on 9 November, the Berlin Wall dividing communist East Germany from West Germany crumbled.

Certainly, the fall of the Berlin Wall and the subsequent collapse of communism in Eastern Europe was a big setback for the ANC, which had historically received millions of dollars a year from the USSR in cash and in kind, in addition to other forms of support from East Germany.

Sunter said that Anglo's 'scenarios' had anticipated that the Soviet Union was going to collapse under the weight of the system.[10] Confirmed Spicer, 'We saw that the Soviet system was untenable and that the American tactic of just upping the ante and outspending them on defence systems was eventually going to pay off. And if you make them spend too much money, the whole edifice collapses. And it did.'[11]

With the last vestiges of material support for the ANC coming from the Scandinavian countries and the United Nations, African leaders began to put pressure on the ANC to change strategy, which materialised in the form of the Harare Declaration of 21 August 1989.[12] This declaration, adopted by the Organisation of African Unity, called for an end to apartheid, and called on the apartheid regime to create the conditions for negotiations, which included the unbanning of political organisations, the release of political prisoners, ending the state of emergency, and ceasing all political trials and executions. The document also laid out a set of principles to be the basis of a new constitutional order in the country, including that South Africa should become a united, democratic and non-racial state with equal citizenship and a bill of rights.

The statement was vague on the economy, merely stating, 'There shall be created an economic order which shall promote and advance the well-being of all South Africans.'[13] There was no indication of the type of economy the ANC foresaw for the country.

Meanwhile, in Pretoria, PW Botha had increasingly come into conflict with his own cabinet, and a second stroke in January 1989 (according to Giliomee, he'd suffered a first stroke in 1985, which was concealed[14]) forced a period of convalescence during which it became increasingly clear that the status quo could not continue. He gave up his position of leader of the National Party a few months later, and was finally forced out completely in September, on the eve of an all-important election.

He was replaced by FW de Klerk, a prominent member of the party's more conservative wing. De Klerk gave no inkling that he was inclined to make any drastic moves or introduce any structural changes. He was known to be a party man, and always found himself on the reactionary side of national debates or in the governing party's caucus.

De Klerk's ascension was unexpected, and it was unclear what to expect from him. Doug Band recalls that he was with De Klerk's brother, Willem, a respected academic and widely considered miles more progressive than his younger sibling, when it was announced that Botha was stepping down. 'I said to him, "This is a very interesting development. How do you see it? I know you're not politically aligned with your brother, but you obviously would have a view about his capabilities?" And he replied, "You know, my brother's going to surprise everybody, because, despite the way it's projected, we come from a relatively *verligte* [enlightened] family in the way we behaved at home towards black people." He added, "I think we'll be amazed at what might transpire."' And while Willem turned out to be right, said Band, he added, 'I don't think we expected the radical change to unfold as quickly as it did.'[15]

'At the time, it wasn't at all certain that change was coming, and it certainly wasn't unavoidable,' confirmed Eloff, who later worked with De Klerk as executive director of his foundation.[16] 'If he'd succumbed to the pressure being exerted by the military and the securocrats, and listened to them, the apartheid government could have held out for seven, eight or nine more years ... obviously with more bloodletting and violence.'[17]

As it happened, De Klerk didn't know everything his government had been up to before he took the reins. He was never part of Botha's inner circle, nor part of the securocrat establishment constructed by Botha to maintain law and order. So he got a rude shock after becoming president and learning that the South African government was already in direct contact with the ANC in Switzerland, where Spaarwater and Louw, both NIS agents, had met with Mbeki and Jacob Zuma.[18]

Spicer said that the biggest development of the period undoubtedly was the changes in the Soviet Union. 'In 1989 the Berlin Wall goes down; socialism is fundamentally discredited and then the Soviet Union breaks up. And that, by the way, is significant, as we know, for movement on the Namibian and other fronts, because the sort of dreaded communist ogre, according to lots of the old NP stalwarts, disappeared. But from a global economic point of view, it meant that capitalism and globalisation and technology and human progress were absolutely dominant.'

At the same time, the cost of sanctions, apartheid misadventures and the security state had become 'too expensive to bear'. 'Government had been exporting two per cent plus of GDP to settle its international debt and couldn't borrow any more,' he explained, referring to the fact that the state was using this percentage of its gross domestic product – the total value of goods produced and services provided in the country during one year – to pay foreign debt. 'It had gone on huge spending sprees, for all the security operations and the security state ... so what alternative was there [besides negotiations]?'[19]

But journalist Patti Waldmeir said that the economy, although tepid and sluggish, hadn't been brought to heel by sanctions, disinvestment and the ban on foreign lending. She said that many of the economic issues of the time were structural, and had very little to do with the international economic and financial campaign against apartheid South Africa. Exporters still found ways of getting South African goods onto the international market, while divestment created opportunities for local businessmen.

Rather, she said, 'Afrikaners were rapidly outgrowing their ethnic paranoia, and worried as much about their swimming pools as their language; and Africans wanted development more than they wanted democracy ... both sides were coming round to the view that the price of victory was simply too high.'[20]

Businessmen with international links – like Band and the Anglo set – began growing frustrated, with Henri de Villiers from the Standard Bank Investment Corporation saying, 'In this day and age there is no such thing as economic self-sufficiency, and we delude ourselves if we think we're different. South Africa needs the world. It needs markets, it needs skills, it needs technology and above all, it needs capital.'[21] De Villiers, like First National Bank's Ball, knew what he was talking about, because towards the end of 1987 Standard

Bank Investment Corporation's largest shareholder, London's Standard Chartered, had divested because of apartheid, with its almost 40 per cent share gobbled up by, among others, Gold Fields and Rupert's Rembrandt.[22]

Two significant events in 1989 that greased the gears towards negotiations were the end of the Angolan conflict, and elections in Namibia. Shortly after De Klerk became head of state, Namibia held its first elections, the result of years of negotiations between South Africa, Angola, Cuba, the USA, the USSR and the United Nations. The result was that Cuban forces returned home, ANC bases in Angola were packed up, and South African forces withdrew. For De Klerk's government, this removed the communist threat on the border of Namibia and marked the end of its conventional campaign against Russian-supported agitators and formations. It also forced the ANC to largely retreat to Zambia, which meant that the organisation was even farther removed from what was happening in South Africa.

Trevor Manuel, the UDF organiser who'd been released from detention late in 1989, said that inside the country it seemed clear that the environment had been changing rapidly – and intimates that the De Klerk speech on 2 February 1990, in which he announced the unbanning of exiled liberation movements, the end of the state of emergency – which had been in place for five years – and the release of political prisoners, hadn't come completely out of the blue. 'There were a couple of things that sort of indicated to me that the tide was turning. Of course, the apartheid regime had lost its ability to govern unfettered, but also, over the course of a couple of years, groups of people started travelling to and from Lusaka, and then Tony Heard, editor of the *Cape Times*, published an interview with Tambo. And that seemed to suggest that the banning of the ANC wasn't having the desired effect,' he said.[23]

'You also must factor in other forms of protest, including things like the Afrikaners meeting the ANC in Dakar, and [Frederik] van

Zyl Slabbert and Alex Boraine breaking away from the Progressive Federal Party and forming Idasa, and so the scene was set for a different set of arrangements. At the same time there was, among business in South Africa, a more enlightened attitude, with the formation of the CBM that set as its objective an approach of trying to bring these vastly separate bodies of opinion together in some way.'[24]

PART II

CONTESTATION

1990–1996

7

Return from exile

'Well, you know, everybody tried to find their hook,
their leverage, their relationship that they thought they
needed for business reasons and strategic reasons ...'

– Jürgen Kögl, a stockbroker, business consultant
and ANC benefactor during the 1980s and 1990s.[1]

South African business might have been 'shit scared' at was coming at
them, as Martin Kingston explained earlier, but the end of the 1980s
and the early 1990s was still a period of money-making and excess.

Said Jürgen Kögl of South Africa in the early 1990s, 'It was the
roaring Wall Street years – you know, the Reagan years – of conservative economic policies espoused by Thatcher and Kohl. And it was
The Bonfire of the Vanities and also *Wall Street* the movie ... Hedge
funds, all those sorts of things. People made a lot of money.'[2]

Ronald Reagan, the Republican president of the USA between 1981
and 1989, deregulated the American economy; Margaret Thatcher,
Conservative British prime minister between 1979 and 1990, was of
the same ideological bent as her American peer; and Helmut Kohl
was chancellor of West Germany, and then of a unified Germany,
between 1982 and 1998. All three were staunch proponents of the free
market and small government.

And both the movies Kögl mentions depict the excess and debauchery of capitalism and easy money in 1980s New York City, much of which was replicated in Johannesburg in the same period. Everyone beat a path to glitzy and glamorous Sun City – capital of putative independent homeland Bophuthatswana – for dirty weekends of adultery, gambling and seeing international acts defy the cultural boycott, including Queen and Rod Stewart.

Fridays at the JSE in Diagonal Street were, despite political events moving apace, often spent enjoying the spoils of rapacious capitalism. And Kögl, at that stage, partook royally of 'the famous Friday afternoon lunches'. 'You start having lunch at the Bulls & Bears [pub and restaurant] in the JSE building, and by the time you had a steak after a ton of prawns and 15 beers, it was 5 o'clock, and then you hoped the girlfriend or the wife wasn't angry.' He remembered bets being made late in the afternoons, after long lunches, on who would be willing to pay for the first picture of boorish extremist leader Eugène Terre'Blanche and Jani Allan, the svelte blonde columnist for the *Sunday Times*, who were engaging in a quite unexpected and public affair. 'It was a very normal, white South African experience.'[3]

For returning cadres, having been banished for years and decades, Johannesburg was a shock. They had prepared themselves in theory but had no knowledge of the complexity of modern South African apartheid society; they'd had no exposure to business, capital markets, pension funds, medical schemes or the free-market economy's workings. 'They had to learn where to go and how best to navigate daily life. They had real fears about safety and that they could be killed. It was after the assassination of Anton Lubowski, Stratcom with their destabilisation operations, right-wingers were still trying to take revenge after the Hein Grosskopf bomb …'[4] (Lubowski, Namibian anti-apartheid activist and advocate, and a member of Swapo, was shot dead outside his home in 1989. Stratcom, or Strategic Communications, was a counterintelligence operation run by apartheid intelligence operatives. Grosskopf was a young Afrikaner dissident who planted a bomb at an army base in Johannesburg in 1987, an incident that shook Afrikanerdom.)

'So when they came home, they had no intentions to take chances; they were very, very scared. Everyone tried to live in high-rise buildings as opposed to houses. There was very little prospect of the ANC being able to protect them: they had to do their own stuff,' recalled Kögl, who very quickly became a bridge between the ANC and business.[5]

Apart from Mandela, Mbeki, Tambo and a very few others, ANC cadres – ordinary fighters and activists – were largely left to fend for themselves. Kögl said that, although not quite despondent, the air among the returnees wasn't at all chipper. 'The feeling was very much one of, we have no money, or very, very little money, a lot of uncertainty about personal security, they had no network and a dominant leader [Mandela] who had very little capacity or inclination to address them.' This was because Mandela had just been released from prison and the ANC didn't have the means to let him travel all over the country; and also, Kögl said, because Mandela felt removed from the rank-and-file.

Mbeki's biographer, Mark Gevisser, quoted the angst of a returning exile asking, 'Where will I live? Where will my children go to school? Will I be able to get a job?' Exiles, he concurred, were most concerned with safety and anonymity.[6]

He also wrote that many exiles returned with foreign wives and children, many of whom did not speak the local languages. They established themselves in some of Johannesburg's inner-city suburbs like Yeoville, which became the heart of the returning-exile community.

Shortly after returning and setting up a makeshift headquarters in Johannesburg, Thomas Nkobi, then the ANC's treasurer-general, determined that officials and employees would receive a monthly living allowance of R2000. Kögl said this 'caused havoc because in Johannesburg, certainly, you couldn't live on groceries for R2000 a month, you just couldn't. And in that context, it created these dependencies to businessmen and hustlers, to this day, just because they supported somebody with school fees and things like that. There is no doubt about that the origin of patronage, the way that's become so brazen and primitive now, was created by that R2 000-a-month syndrome,' he said. 'But people had to survive.'[7]

After the unbanning of the ANC and the release of Mandela in February 1990, although some exiles started returning to the country, there wasn't a massive influx of people immediately landing at the then Jan Smuts Airport in Johannesburg. The ANC in exile, Stephen Ellis said, had a very poor grasp of South African politics and of the apartheid political leadership in general, and were therefore almost caught by surprise.[8]

And it was clear that there were vast differences between the returning exiles and those who'd fought in the struggle inside the country. Spicer said that, apart from Mbeki, the exiles were all at sea on the economy and the realities of a modern, overtly western, society. 'Somebody like Cyril [Ramaphosa] had worked and lived with big business, so he was much more attuned … not necessarily that he agreed, but he understood business a lot better than the exiles.'

The exiles, he said, 'lived in this paranoid bubble, where all you had to do was to be against something. Only the most sophisticated, like Thabo, who'd travelled widely and was the diplomat, thought about bigger issues.'

While noting that it was 'understandable', Spicer said that a lot of the returning exiles 'didn't have the slightest clue' about what South Africa had become. 'South Africa was the most sophisticated econ-omy on the African continent, completely different to being in Dar es Salaam or Lusaka or any of those places. And it takes a totally different set of skills to run and grow an economy in a complex, sophisticated, industrial democracy. This is not something you can do with mechanistic, top-down control. And it's not amenable to … dirigisme and statism without breaking all sorts of things.'[9]

Manuel admits that because the MDM was 'quite engrossed with the task of trying to destroy the apartheid edifice', they 'didn't pause to think about economic policy nuances going forward'.[10] While it was necessary to engage with a cross section of South Africans, including business leaders, he conceded that 'there weren't very detailed discussions at any point about the future shape of the South African economy.'[11]

Jeremy Cronin, an opponent of Manuel inside the ANC, said that the political struggle – and divisions over how the armed struggle should be waged – were far and away the main debates within the internal resistance movement, not future economic policy.[12]

Despite the fears that the ANC wasn't up to the task of adapting to modern economic thinking and that they could still seek to implement the central tenets of the Freedom Charter – such as nationalisation – Spicer said people at Anglo hoped that 'time and reality' would sway them. 'But the difficulty was how to move from a liberation movement, which is a big tent, to a government.'[13]

In the big tent everybody is in, Spicer explained, and you have an alliance with everyone from Stalinists to free marketeers, and every conceivable view in between. And that works while you're united by opposition to apartheid. 'Now you are the government, you must start making choices, and it's very difficult if you want to continue as a movement.'[14]

For exiles returning from abroad, including the members of the ANC's leadership at all levels, it became clear that they had to find ways of sustaining themselves in a country they didn't know, in a system that was hostile to them, and without resources to speak of. South Africa of 1990 was a vastly different country to the one Tambo, for example, had left 30 years before, when HF Verwoerd was prime minister and before the country was declared a republic.

When Tambo, his family and other exiles returned to Johannesburg at the end of 1990, Kögl 'had to introduce them to dentists, chemists and doctors and things like that ... just the basic stuff so that they could function. They didn't know, and no one helped them.'[15] Mandela stayed with Archbishop Desmond Tutu in Bishopscourt, Cape Town, for a period before returning to his Vilakazi Street home in Soweto, while Mbeki initially was put up in Anglo's Carlton Hotel in central Johannesburg.[16] Later – after Frederik van Zyl Slabbert told Mbeki in the winter of 1990 that he couldn't 'continue to live off Anglo'[17] – Mbeki and his wife, Zanele, moved into Kögl's penthouse apartment in Hillbrow.

Kögl also helped the Mbekis acquire their first property in South Africa, a flat in Rivonia, Johannesburg, and he helped Zuma acquire a flat in Morningside, Durban, when he came back from exile. Tito Mboweni and Penuell Maduna (who later became Mbeki's justice minister) were also given 'a flat in Hillbrow to share', Kögl said.

But apart from living arrangements, other crises had to be dealt with – including Winnie Mandela's huge debts, estimated by Kögl to be in the region of R3 million, a big sum even today, but at the time an immense debt. 'Thabo and I tried to alleviate those debts and looked around for money to pay it. And we spoke to the churches who ran the Free Mandela fund, in the hope that they could help, and all the money was gone.'[18]

Business, big and small, started offering support, mostly in the form of employment so that returnees could pay their way. Whether it was purely benevolent, or business had an ulterior motive, is impossible to say. It certainly presented opportunities for capital to insert itself even more prominently into the process, to seduce and charm and lead even the most hardened freedom fighter away from total socialist revolution to negotiated compromise and a rights-based free market. Many saw it as an opportunity to ingratiate themselves with the presumptive ruling political class – but many others saw it as their duty to support individuals who had been fighting the apartheid system and had no material gains to show for it.

Manuel said business didn't adopt a 'single, monolithic' approach to the ANC or returning leaders. 'The CBM companies were very involved, though, and I'm thinking of the Lubners, Bertie and Ronnie, and Peter Wright who was with them, for example. One of the companies they had that was quite active in Stellenbosch at the sawmills, PG Bison, and what firms like that did was to create employment for people coming out of prison, whether this was [from] long-term detention or coming from Robben Island.'[19]

Eloff, in charge of the CBM, said business never quite believed that the ANC would drop its socialist aspirations, and they had to keep agitating and networking and convincing the incoming elite about what the future should look like.[20] Spicer reiterated that 'everyone' in big business was doing their bit to ensure that socialism and massive, uncosted and unaffordable leftist programmes never saw the light of day. 'We were working all the time to convince (the ANC) … we had workshops every weekend, for years … we published books … Anglo was doing its bit, but so was everyone else … Barlow Rand was doing its own thing … Gold Fields had their thing going,' he said.[21] Every conglomerate or large company did what they had to do to meet, mingle and talk to the ANC.

Kögl said people who previously had contact with the ANC, like Relly and Bloom from Anglo, were inundated with requests for help from returning exiles for support and logistics – and that it was given. 'There is no doubt about it that the Anglo group, with Southern Life … and Sanlam and Johnnic, or JCI as it was called, with Gordon Waddell as the chief executive … all of those guys lent support to the ANC. When legal advice was sought, hotshot lawyer Michael Katz was roped in. And then came Marinus Daling from Sanlam, who was the first guy from Sanlam to really start talking to the ANC …'[22]

Sanlam, the giant life insurer and one of the proudest and most significant Afrikaner-owned businesses,[23] was established in 1918 as the Suid-Afrikaanse Nasionale Lewens Assuransie Maatskappij Beperk. One of the first Afrikaner-owned companies in the country, it marketed itself as a 'genuine Afrikaner people's institution' with a motto 'Born out of the volk to serve the volk'.[24] Daling, known to be an enlightened Afrikaner businessman, had become the youngest member of Sanlam's general management in 1974, and in 1997 was appointed executive chair of the company.

Sanlam's strategic investment vehicle, Sankorp, had sought 'meaningful contact with black business leaders' as early as 1987, well before a 'strategy of negotiation' had been accepted by politicians, according to economist Natalie Phillips. 'Sankorp management realised that with the changing economic environment, unless large numbers of blacks enter higher employment categories, the South African economy would be forced to a standstill as a result of a managerial shortage.'[25]

Manuel and a colleague had gone to see the Sanlam people before the unbanning. 'These guys were actually very scared of association with the ANC,' Manuel recalled. 'It was one of those spy-movie things: we kind of drove to some building, a mall around Tyger Valley Centre [in Cape Town] … and from there we were taken in two different cars to another place, where those cars were left, and then we were taken to a house, where we had supper.'[26]

Soon after, with the ANC unbanned, Sanlam came calling again. 'Sanlam invited Mbeki to meet with its leadership at their head office in Bellville. The invitation came from Marinus Daling. So there we were, at Sanlam's head office, and Marinus was saying, "I am sure that there are some of you saying that our founders are turning in their graves because the ANC has now come to meet with us in Bellville."'[27]

Arriving back in the country, the ANC also had nowhere to set up shop. Its first legal and official meeting inside the borders of South Africa for 30 years took place on 29 April 1990 at Vergelegen, a lush wine estate in leafy Somerset West owned by Anglo American. Spicer explained that the company had decided to expend 'enormous resources' to influence the political and economic reform and transition process, and offering the use of one of their premier vanity assets seemed like a good way to curry favour with the incoming political elite.

The movement – before it was registered as a political party – was initially housed on a couple of floors in Munich Re House in Sauer Street, Johannesburg, while Southern Life's Neal Chapman also offered some space in their office in the centre of town. Reinsurer Munich Re's chief executive Ernst Kahle was in fact severely reprimanded by his board in Germany for being too accommodating of the newly legalised liberation movement, for fear of antagonising the National Party government.[28] Munich Re House was eventually sold to the ANC, who renamed it Chief Albert Luthuli House, and it is the ANC's headquarters to this day.

With the ANC unbanned, back in the country and busy setting up structures and systems, the conversation about the future of South Africa – including its economy – started becoming increasingly urgent. But the ANC were on the back foot. They didn't have an economic framework at the ready, returning exiles were unsure of their new environment, and they were up against corporates who were very clear in what they wanted to achieve: a free market system, with minimum state intervention.

In June 1990, Kögl accompanied Van Zyl Slabbert to a meeting between the ANC and Nafcoc, at the exceedingly luxurious Johannesburg Sun and Towers (hotel rooms had their own computer terminals to help guests check in and out, as well as a sushi bar – a first for South Africa). On the agenda were the consolidation of black business in the country, as well as possible black empowerment schemes and policies. 'Mbeki was there, Aziz Pahad [an executive committee member who would go on to be appointed deputy head of the ANC's department of international affairs] ... But none of the economics unit of the ANC was there.'[29]

The uncertainty was felt on both sides. 'Well, you know, everybody tried to find their hook, their leverage, their relationship that they thought they needed for business reasons and strategic reasons. [Sun International founder] Sol Kerzner, for instance, was very nervous, because of his casino licences and his bribery scheme in the Ciskei and the Transkei ... R5 million to [then Transkei premier] Kaizer Matanzima ... so these guys were very, very nervous about what democracy would mean.'[30] Kerzner admitted to bribing Matanzima in order to 'preserve' his gambling empire Sun International's licences in the apartheid homeland of Transkei.[31] The charges against him were later dropped when the person who supposedly received the bribe died.

Cosatu, one of the constituent parts of the MDM, had by then already commissioned studies and working papers about the country's economic future,[32] while the CBM, with Eloff and Colin Coleman, were working hard to bring business into contact with the liberation movement's leaders.[33] With the heavy involvement and support of Spicer and Anglo, they were arranging meetings across the country, bringing together local business leaders and representatives of the MDM. It was almost like a grand coming-out, with both groupings now seeing the inevitability of change and the imperative to talk.

'There were a lot more interactions at local and provincial level thanks to the CBM, because of the need to try and break down the sense of fear that the ANC represented,' said Manuel.[34]

At the same time, black business, as small and fragmented as it may have been, used its proximity to the ANC and the liberation movement to press its case for fundamental change. And although it was big capital – white business – that eventually introduced the idea of empowerment, black business during the period also launched initiatives of its own to influence the process.

Manuel, as head of the ANC's department of economic planning, often engaged Nafcoc, headed by Sam Motsuenyane, and the Foundation of African Business and Consumer Services (Fabcos), led by Jabu Mabuza. Fabcos, an umbrella body of black business organisations, was established in 1988 to bring together the formal and informal sectors of the economy. Manuel said that even though there were disagreements over various issues, there was consensus on the need for greater black representation in the economy.

'In 1993 black business, led by Nafcoc, invited a group of us to the Mopani Rest Camp in the Kruger National Park for a weekend of engagement. One of the issues that was starting to gain momentum was a policy proposal by Nafcoc which they called 3-4-5-6. The proposal went something like 30 per cent of the board seats, director's seats, of a JSE-listed company must be black, 40 per cent of the equity of listed companies must be black-owned, 50 per cent of their inputs must be black-owned and 60 per cent of the managers must be black.'[35]

The Black Management Forum, established in 1989, worked with Nafcoc especially on the issue of managers, said Manuel, who cited businessmen Lot Ndlovu, Don Mkhwanazi and Reuel Khoza as 'campaigning vigorously' to improve representation.

8

Capitalists and comrades

'These may sound like harsh words, but the reality that is unseen inside the boardrooms, by those who exercise power, across the length and breadth of this country, is harsher still. The anger in the heart of Shylock is abroad in our society.'

– Nelson Mandela, referencing Shakespeare's
The Merchant of Venice, in a speech to businessmen at
the Carlton Hotel, Johannesburg, 23 May 1990.[1]

If there was one advantage that organised business had during the early part of the transition years, it was the fact that relationships between corporate captains and liberation figures had progressed much farther down the road to understanding than between the ANC and the NP government.

In early 1990, President FW de Klerk and his senior cabinet colleagues had yet to personally size up their opponents, while Tambo, Mbeki and others had already had extensive contact with Anglo, the CBM, the NIS and progressive Afrikaners. They understood each other in broad strokes, and they'd met eye to eye a couple of times.

And, added Spicer, 'Business had the advantage because it was concentrated. You could get the entire business community round a 10- or 12-seater table. Once you have the big mining houses, Liberty, and the banks, it was 10 or a dozen people.' So, he said, if 'Relly, Rosholt and the Barlow Rand leaders and people of that stature' were brought together, 'you could get a coherent view relatively quickly. And they, among themselves, agreed that things needed to change, and they could play a role.'[2] And if Harry Oppenheimer was on board, more often than not, the rest followed.

Naidoo said he doesn't blame big capital for trying to do what they could to direct events. After the fall of the Wall, in a unipolar world and without the threat of communism 'at the gates', capital sought to 'swing' Mandela and the ANC to a more reasonable economic policy. 'If I was big business, then I would have done the same thing. You know, it's not unusual, it's not secretive. They wanted to influence the agenda. They had a legitimate right to want to protect their interests,' he said.[3]

And Anglo, considered by Kingston to be in a different league as far as engaging the ANC was concerned,[4] was completely under-estimated by the liberation movement, said Cronin. He had by the early 1990s become more closely involved in economic debates within the ANC-SACP-Cosatu alliance, and later came to believe that they should have been more sceptical about capital's motives. 'I think we seriously misread people like Michael Spicer and what their agenda was. Obviously, they were genuinely committed to democracy of a kind; I would say low-intensity democracy,' Cronin said.[5] But capital, he felt, was much more focused on self-preservation than anything else after the reality of doing business under apartheid started to bite from about 1985 onwards.[6] Big business, Cronin believed, came to see the enormous possibilities that a Mandela-like president could hold for it. 'Big capital in South Africa didn't trust a future ANC government, and they were desperate to get their bottled-up investments out of the country as quickly as possible; because they were uncertain about the future,' he said.[7]

During the first flurry of activity – Mandela's release, exiles returning, the government preparing for talks, the international community in a frenzy about imminent change – business set about 'staying in business', as Rosholt had put it.[8]

Anglo's approach was based on the company's scenario planning process, which was premised on a negotiated outcome and a new constitution. Anglo even commissioned a book – a guide, Spicer said – on how to craft a new constitution, as well as one on empowerment, based on the Malaysian policy of affirmative action, or Bumiputera. 'This range of activities was possible because business was taking this hands-on, coordinated approach, and because there was a coherent view,' he said.[9] But it was clear that business would have to put in the hard yards to influence the ANC.

Two weeks after Mandela's release, he invited Relly to visit him in Soweto – the first business leader to do so. Spicer accompanied Relly, and Ramaphosa sat beside Mandela. The Anglo pair spent 45 minutes with Mandela and Ramaphosa while almost a hundred journalists waited outside to hear what capital's most prominent emissaries had discussed with the ANC's headline leaders.

Spicer recalled that despite nationalisation being the most talked-about economic issue at the time, it was never discussed at that meeting, because Ramaphosa, the former National Union of Mineworkers (NUM) general-secretary, directed conversation to labour relations.

When Relly and Spicer emerged 'from this little house in Soweto', the press stuck their microphones 'up Relly's nostril and said, "Mr Relly, Mr Relly, what about nationalisation?"' Relly, knowing full well what was at stake, said Spicer – and that persuasion, influencing and treading softly was the only way forward – uttered one sentence: 'Well, we didn't discuss it, but you know, nationalisation is one of those things that will be subject to the test of time and reality.' 'Full stop,' said Spicer.[10]

Band, who at the time was in charge of the Argus newspaper group, one of Anglo's more strategic investments, said 'the nationalisation and redistribution of wealth' debate was concerning for capital, and he had serious fears about what could happen, warning idealistic colleagues about 'the rocky road' that lay ahead. One of his first 'official' engagements as Argus head with the ANC was when a delegation led by Gill Marcus (who was later to become governor of the SARB) visited Newspaper House in Cape Town. 'Everybody was calling each other "comrade" – "comrade this", "comrade that" – and by the time you'd finished the meeting you weren't sure if you weren't in Stalingrad.'[11]

Band was also visited by a Pan Africanist Congress (PAC) delegation led by one of its firebrands, Benny Alexander, who later changed his name to Khoisan X. Alexander and his colleagues marched into Newspaper House and demanded of Band when Anglo was going to offer ownership of its assets to black South Africans, Band recalled. 'There were all sorts of threats. It was quite an ugly meeting. Afterwards, I went to lunch at a restaurant … near the Company's Gardens, and I saw Alexander around the corner in the restaurant enjoying a bottle of very expensive wine. And I thought to myself, oh well, maybe things weren't going to be that bad after all.'[12]

On 23 May 1990 more than 300 mainly white businessmen packed into the ballroom at the Carlton Hotel in central Johannesburg to listen to Mandela's first major and public engagement with South African capital, at an 'options for building an economic future' conference arranged by Theuns Eloff's CBM. 'Businesspeople then did not include black businesspeople, because there weren't many. They were businesspeople but they didn't fit into the corporate category. Black businesspeople were mostly running corner shops and the like,' Manuel explained.[13]

'It was a very strange speech,' he continued, because Mandela quoted the children's rhyme 'Baa-Baa Black Sheep', as well as paraphrasing John F Kennedy (ask 'what are you prepared to do for your country, rather than what your country can do for you') to impress on the assembled business leaders the imperative for fundamental economic change. Manuel, though, added that it was a significant marker on the road to demystifying the ANC and its recently released talisman.[14]

Mandela, although acknowledging that South Africa at the time had its own unique challenges and that the country should design solutions to address its own particular problems, was clearly still committed to the organisation's basic economic tenets, including nationalisation and a programme of growth through redistribution, meaning higher public expenditure, which would then lead to economic growth. He took a hard line with the overwhelmingly white audience, telling them that it was unsustainable that less than a thousand white directors oversaw 10 conglomerates on the JSE 'that control almost 90 per cent of listed shares'. He explained that there was latent anger and frustration among the majority of the country's population about the structure of the economy and the resultant power dynamics. This – everything – had to change, he told them.

After reciting the children's nursery rhyme to the gathering, he asked, 'Could it be that when the children composed this simple verse, they understood that it was only the figurative black sheep that would, because it was itself excluded, have sufficient sense of justice and compassion to remember the little boy down the lane? Was it because they had seen in practice that the white sheep apportioned only a tenth of its wool, or none at all, to the little boy down the lane?'

He quoted Shakespeare's Shylock and said that 'bitterness' and 'hurt ... lurks in the breasts of many whom this society has considered and treated as disposable cyphers'. White people, he said, had had total power over the lives of blacks. 'Questions such as these, whether about black sheep or the universal nature of human pain and suffering, can only be posed by people who are discriminated against, in a society that condemns them to persistent deprivation of the material artefacts and the dignity that are due to them as human beings. We pose them for the same reasons,' Mandela said.

'These may sound like harsh words, but the reality that is unseen inside the boardrooms, by those who exercise power, across the length and breadth of this country, is harsher still. The anger in the heart of Shylock is abroad in our society. This is a fact to which we should be very sensitive, without any attempt at self-deception.'[15]

Mandela's speech (and Thabo Mbeki, who wrote it) took aim at the business leaders, and the oratory revealed the depth and extent of distrust and animus towards capital. South Africa was a country of two worlds: one white and rich, the other poor and black. And the capitalist system was at the centre of perpetuating the inequalities codified into law by the apartheid state.

Mandela swept through some basic economic ideological and policy positions, and reading the speech 30 years later revealed that the ANC at the time was still antagonistic towards private capital, and that it wasn't about to easily conform to the tenets of apartheid capitalism. The economic power structure of private ownership and private property might be considered 'a fact of life', Mandela said, but the ANC was in the process of looking at other models and that the end of white domination in the exercise of economic power was the goal. He emphasised the need to break up the conglomerates (such as Anglo, and over which Spicer and Manuel were to clash) and floated the idea of government-appointed directors to the boards of companies 'to balance the pursuit of private gain with the need to promote common good'. And despite saying that he didn't want to go into the debate about nationalisation, the ANC hadn't ruled it out.[16]

'There should be no debate among us about the centrality of the issue of ensuring a rapidly growing economy,' he said, adding that the state was going to have to intervene because, left to its own devices, market forces wouldn't be able to bring about meaningful socio-economic change to those who had systematically been shut out of the economy.[17]

The *Workers Hammer*, a radical left periodical in Britain, accused Mandela of 'backing off' at the Carlton conference, accusing Anglo of 'co-opting' trade unions, 'orchestrating' Mandela's speech and trying to 'mould the shape' of the country's post-apartheid economy.

'Imperialists are courting Mandela' and using 'treacherous schemes' to keep on subjugating blacks, it said.[18]

For Spicer, too, the speech was a disappointment, if not for the same reasons. 'The ANC was still clearly wedded to nationalisation. After that we did say to them, "Guys, get real. The Wall has fallen, socialism has essentially been consigned to the rubbish bin, and you're still talking the language of the old world. There are all these new ideas ..." Look, we weren't playing politics. We were telling them that whatever role they, the ANC, were going to play, they had to get up to speed with economic thinking and with the way the world was changing."[19]

Thirty years after that day at the Carlton, Spicer conceded that the ANC – and blacks in general – had reason to be distrustful and vengeful of capital, because, for many, apartheid and business were two sides of the same coin. And mining – and Anglo – had played a central role in the economy and socially destructive systems such as migrant labour.

'It was a source of great pain and anger for many,' he conceded – many of whom didn't distinguish between business and the National Party.[20] But he was nonetheless sharply critical of the ANC's approach to the economy at the time, and of their poor grasp of reality in a changing environment.

And the socialist dogma that characterised the movement then continues to haunt it and South Africa today.

Jay Naidoo was scathing about the ANC's lack of commitment to negotiate and prepare for a post-apartheid economic dispensation – and said that Cosatu had had serious difficulty in engaging the organisation even before it was unbanned. 'In our attempts to try and negotiate with the ANC about what would be the post-apartheid economic framework, we were often told that we should leave that to a democratic government,' he said. And that meant 'the ANC-in-government'.[21]

During the pre-1990 period, Naidoo said that Cosatu, which had been launched in December 1985, 'had the responsibility' to be the platform on which the MDM could be constructed, and that it engaged in economic policy development from the beginning. In 1986, it launched the Economic Trends Research Group, a body of researchers to look at a post-apartheid economic model with the purpose of ensuring that workers' rights would be protected during a political transition.[22] It was involved in various other research efforts, and it supported the later Macro-Economic Research Group (MERG) to investigate and develop alternative economic policies for the ANC (see chapter 11).[23]

But, said Naidoo, it was 'anathema' for an African liberation movement to negotiate economic policy proposals with a trade union movement; and the ANC did not want to engage the internal MDM, believing that fundamental discussions about the country's future – economic and otherwise – was its province alone. 'We had to assert our independence and that's when we started to approach the ANC and the SACP, saying we want to discuss economic restructuring with you all,' Naidoo said.[24]

'We had one conference in Harare [in 1988] and then one in Lusaka [in 1986]. [These] didn't really produce much, because, again, the ANC view was that they had this all tied up, they had it sewn up.'[25]

Naidoo said that the ANC-in-exile believed its political pedigree to be above that of the trade union federation and its leaders, and that despite the policy development efforts Cosatu had launched, the ANC wasn't interested. And their lack of insight and preparation showed. 'They were completely unprepared when they returned from exile,' said Naidoo. 'And they were tied to their old Soviet economic model.'[26]

Naidoo and Cosatu were fiercely protective of their independence and wanted to engage the ANC on its (the federation's) own economic positions, which it believed were not wholly aligned with that of the exiled liberation movement. Cosatu wanted a pact between itself and the ANC, and in exchange for that support, wanted an agreement on a programme of action to fundamentally transform the South African economy. 'You know, for us, transformation wasn't just about political transformation and deracialisation; it was about deracialisation of the broader economy, including the land question.'[27] (The 1955 Freedom Charter called for restrictions of land ownership on a racial basis to be ended, and all the land redivided 'among those who work it', and noted that 'all shall have the right to occupy land wherever they choose'.)[28]

The tension between Cosatu and the ANC – and between Naidoo and the ANC leaders – really started showing when Mac Maharaj and Siphiwe Nyanda were infiltrated into the country to establish an underground network.

The run-up to this began with the Nkomati Accord, a non-aggression pact signed in 1984 between Mozambique and South Africa (the signatories were Samora Machel and PW Botha, respective leaders) focused on preventing Mozambique from supporting the ANC to undertake violent actions in South Africa, and South Africa from supplying the Renamo anti-communist movement in Mozambique. Although, even before the Nkomati Accord, the ANC leadership in exile had been asked to address the issues of leadership and control within South Africa, following the Accord, the prospects for a negotiated settlement seemed ever more remote, and it appeared that a protracted struggle was on the cards, so problems of leadership on the ground had to be dealt with. The ANC's national executive committee (NEC)[29] decided that senior leadership had to be sent into the country for the day-to-day running of the underground, and Operation Vula was the result, with senior ANC cadres Nyanda and Maharaj asked to take up internal leadership positions. In June 1988, the two infiltrated South Africa and began working underground.

To Naidoo it felt as if they simply wanted to co-opt Cosatu into the ANC, disregarding its views on the economy and liberation – and he had to assert the federation's independence early on. 'The ANC saw Cosatu as a labour wing, and therefore wished it to just follow the instructions of the ANC. I felt it was an attempt to try and hijack the union movement and turn it into a conveyor belt of the underground,' said Naidoo.

He resisted attempts where the ANC sought to 'undermine institutions that we had built through mass struggle and mandates and reportbacks'.[30]

Finally, Oliver Tambo conceded to Naidoo that Cosatu 'was an independent organisation with an independent programme and therefore we had a legitimate right to put on the table, as part of building the tripartite alliance, a programme of action.'[31] 'When the debate came about formalising the alliance, we had then consolidated our views on a reconstruction pact, and that's what we took into the discussions around the new alliance, the tripartite alliance with the ANC, the SACP and Cosatu. And we made that the basis, a programme of action that would then determine the programme of the tripartite alliance's three independent organisations.'[32]

Like Spicer, Naidoo saw a big difference between those who'd been exiled, and those who'd fought for liberation inside the country. 'The ANC in exile believed they were a government in exile. They had the hope, and there was the expectation, that when they marched in, it would be on top of a tank, carrying an ANC flag. And when they returned, they were like, "Oh, thank you, guys, you've done your job, now let us take over."

'And then you had the group that came out of prison, like Mandela who, of course, had missed the critical period of mass action in 1987, 1988, but who still supported us.' That was important, said Naidoo: 'Mandela respected the union movement, and so did Oliver Tambo and Chris Hani.' But, he added, 'You know, I don't think it went further than that.'[33]

Naidoo leveraged those relationships to start talking to the ANC about the economy, about how to restructure it in order to close the massive inequality gap that existed (and still does).

He attended the CBM's Broederstroom Encounter in August 1988 on behalf of trade unions – and he did so despite 'getting roasted' by his own people when he suggested they should engage with big capital, or 'the employers', as he called them. 'This process starts, where big capital is starting to peel off its National Party sticker. They initiate a process of conversation with the MDM, so I go to the Cosatu congress and to the central executive committee and say, there is this process, and my view is that we should make sure that we are part of it. I get roasted at the central executive committee meeting, but I still maintain that it is important that we don't exclude ourselves.'[34]

Naidoo said the Broederstroom Encounter made him realise that the apartheid government's edifice was showing strain. 'While we were participating in this meeting, it became clear to me that without the support of big business, the National Party couldn't last too long. They would be forced into negotiations. I became convinced of that. And this prepared the ground for the later meetings between the ANC, us and the business community. And it was an important step, because it's an onion; we were peeling off layers of support.'[35]

9

Brenthurst and meeting Oppenheimer

'It was very important that he did that because we didn't
know where the country was headed, and we had to create some
stability. And we had to leverage our relationships with business.'

– Jay Naidoo, on Nelson Mandela's meeting with
Harry Oppenheimer in the early 1990s.[1]

The ANC in general, never mind its department of economic planning, had a tough time of it in 1991 and 1992. Vusi Khanyile, an
activist who was in charge of ANC fundraising after its unbanning and
was later the chief executive of Thebe Investments, said the party had
to start from scratch when it returned to Johannesburg. 'The apartheid
government, when it banned the ANC, took everything from it. It
took all its assets, so there was nothing when we returned. And it was
no use to start trying to retrieve it,' he said.[2]

So it had little to go on; it was reliant on donations from mainly Scandinavian countries to remain afloat. And its nascent national
structure was scattered about the centre of the city, housed in various
buildings where companies like Southern Life and Munich Re offered
up working space.

Trevor Manuel became head of the department of economic

planning in August 1991, taking over from Max Sisulu.[3] The department wasn't a dynamic and creative policy-development unit and didn't set the world alight with analyses, proposals or even internal lobbying. At that time, in fact, it was the London-based group of Marxist economists, under the leadership of Vella Pillay, who believed their technical economic views would hold sway.

Manuel – whose leadership grouping included people like Maria Ramos and Tito Mboweni doing the work on the ground in South Africa – said he found it 'curious' that the London-based group thought they would run the organisation's policy development from the UK's capital city, and that there was even a measure of disgust from the London group when the ANC's NEC took policy decisions that didn't accord with what the leftist researchers were proposing.

By contrast, organised business in South Africa – through the companies affiliated with the CBM and other initiatives – were doing scenario planning and drafting policy proposals, with university academics investigating other economic transition experiences elsewhere in the world. In the early 1990s a couple of economic policy papers were drafted, most notably ahead of the ANC's first national conference back in the country in June 1991.[4]

The fact that the MDM internally had more capacity – and certainly more exposure and experience in actual economic matters – made business and the apartheid government's persistent approaches to the exiles rather than to the 'inciles' that much more galling, said Kögl. 'There were no attempts by business to speak to the MDM leaders inside South Africa; none,' he said.[5]

Spicer said Anglo held fast to the Relly aphorism that 'everything will be subject to the test of time and reality'.[6] But Manuel faced a problem, in Spicer's estimation: how to craft a modern economic policy that embraced the realities of the global environment and the South African economic situation, and the dire need for complete social transformation as Mandela had articulated at the Carlton Hotel.

Nelson Mandela's visit to the World Economic Forum's annual gathering at Davos in Switzerland in January 1992 was a major turning point in both locating ANC economic policy development in South Africa, and in sobering up the debate on nationalisation, which Mandela had clung to up until then.

The World Economic Forum, founded in 1971, is funded largely by its thousand member companies. It views its mission as 'improving the state of the world by engaging business, political, academic, and other leaders of society to shape global, regional and industry agendas'. 'Davos' has become shorthand for 'international capital'.

Mandela had left for Switzerland planning to sell a future government's policies to an international community querying what an ANC government's priorities would look like. And nationalisation was still part of its suite of policies to be implemented once it took power.

'The guys in London had prepared Mandela's speech which he was to deliver at Davos, but when the ANC delegation that accompanied Madiba saw the prepared remarks, they rejected it,' Manuel said. 'They said, "Nelson Mandela cannot be expected to give a speech that resembles something at a high school debating contest!"[7] He had to look presidential. So they shredded the speech that they believed was inadequate, and there was a stand-off because the London group didn't quite understand that there was a shift, that the ANC was now in charge of its own economic affairs.'[8]

But that's only part of the story. The other half is that 'at that stage Madiba was going around talking about how we're going to nationalise the mines because that's what the Freedom Charter said,' Manuel recalled.[9] But at Davos, Mandela was told that times had changed, and that nationalisation was no longer the central plank of modern socialist countries, or countries following a developmental model. And these admonishments didn't come from the west, but from countries that were close to the ANC, such as Vietnam and China.

'He came back, and in a quite undefiant way, said, "No, I've been

91

convinced that you can't just go ahead and nationalise, that we mustn't just nationalise."[10]

Spicer, who developed a good working relationship with Mandela, said that despite all the talk about nationalisation and the Freedom Charter – and the fact that left economic positions carried great store in large quarters of the organisation – key people in the ANC started moving away from it very early. 'I'm not making a hard-right judgement here, but very quickly Mrs Thatcher's immortal phrase "there is no alternative" became clear to people like Trevor and Thabo, the people who were actually going to run the economy.' Thatcher often used the phrase to describe her belief that despite capitalism's problems, there was no alternative to it as an economic system, and that a political approach that favoured free markets, free trade and deregulation must push back against socialism as the only way that modern societies could advance themselves.

Mandela's visit to Davos, Spicer believed, was a big setback to the statists in the ANC, precisely because the warnings about nationalisation came from countries whose leaders Mandela trusted. 'He did obviously get an earful from the businesspeople at Davos but surprisingly, shockingly, he also got the view from the Vietnamese and the Chinese. They told him, "What are you doing? We are determinedly paddling downstream, away from absolute state ownership of the economy. In the modern era, this doesn't work, and you'd be well advised to stay away from it."

'And he comes back to South Africa and tells his comrades, "Guys, regretfully, that dream is over."'[11]

Mandela was seemingly starting to see the world differently. It had been three years since the Berlin Wall had fallen, and a year since the collapse of the Soviet Union; and it was his own second year of freedom. In addition, China's modernisation programme, unleashed by Deng Xiaoping, was starting to harness the forces of globalisation and technology, and the Chinese shared all that with Mandela.

'South Africa was the flavour of the month, internationally. There was huge goodwill, there was vast investment, everybody was willing to help, and that would have come to a crashing end if they had set off on [the socialist] road,' said Michael Spicer.[12]

But capital's fight wasn't over just because of Mandela's experience in Davos or the ideological contestation inside the ANC. 'And this was one of the reasons why we were so intensely engaged and deployed so many resources over an extended period of time. And it wasn't just Anglo who were doing it, either. There were many other corporate players, and all, to some extent, working together, but also working on their own account,' said Spicer.[13]

Mandela might have come back from Davos chastened, and Manuel might have been starting to exert his influence over the department of economic planning, but capital wasn't taking any chances. The fight over the future of the economy was only just beginning.

In and among all of this intense contestation and lobbying, the ANC and many of its leaders seemed open and amenable to the approaches of capital and South African big business. Both capital and the ANC now moved into the twilight zone of patronage and influence. An informal network started taking shape, with employment being offered to ANC returnees without corporates really expecting their new employees to come into the office or, quite frankly, to work at all.

Among all the conglomerates' efforts to assuage and cajole, to convince and persuade, Anglo was considered to be 'in a class of its own'.[14] The biggest player, the company provided cars and drivers for people like Archbishop Desmond Tutu and made company planes available so that ANC leaders could move around more easily.[15]

Mandela and Oppenheimer met regularly as part of the 'Brenthurst Group'. Named for the Oppenheimers' expansive Johannesburg estate, the Brenthurst meetings, which were held from 1990, have always been shrouded in mystery, with many believing that it was here that big business managed to beguile the ANC and seal the deal for capitalism. The gatherings of business leaders and ANC representatives were a regular feature of the evolving relationship between capital and the liberation movement, and became the source of much speculation about the actual influence that business was able to exert on the ANC.

Jeremy Cronin believed 'a deal was struck between the Mbekiites and big business' at Brenthurst and that black economic empowerment (BEE) was first initiated there.[16] And Spicer concurred that 'Thabo was a key, key, key player': 'We should not underestimate that he, despite all of his quirks, essentially was convinced that a relatively orthodox economic policy was required for South Africa at that time.'[17]

Bobby Godsell, later chief executive of AngloGold, kept minutes of the meetings and said the regular gatherings between business and the ANC at Brenthurst weren't all that lore made them out to be – in fact, he called them 'thoroughly insignificant', a 'magnificent non-event'. Although, he said, 'Mandela generally came with quite an impressive group of ANC leaders', 'we had no meaningful economic discussions. We did speak about BEE, about how to make people capitalists if they had no capital. That's what I would say was most meaningful.'[18]

Godsell recalled one significant exchange, however. 'It's quite interesting that the person who caused it to happen was [deputy chair of Anglo American] Leslie Boyd. It was during the third, fourth or fifth meeting of the Brenthurst Group, and Leslie was getting a bit impatient with the fact that we just were nice to each other.' (Godsell noted here that this was 'very true of the relationships between the white elite and the ANC, that they were always nice to each other, and they never actually – either side – said what they were really thinking'.) 'And therefore, you never really got to any kind of resolution. Anyway, Leslie lost his cool and gave a long speech about Zimbabwe, and the fact that even at that relatively early stage, the perception was that the ANC wasn't prepared to be in any way critical of black leaders anywhere else on the continent, and particularly not in Zimbabwe.'[19]

The ANC group left that meeting, said Godsell, 'knowing that business thought what was going on in Zimbabwe was a hell of a bad thing.'[20]

In Spicer's opinion, the Brenthurst meetings were important post 1994 because they kept 'the lines open' when economic policy was 'contested and unclear'.[21]

Manuel recalled one such get-together of the venerated freedom fighter and the doyen of South African capitalism at the Oppenheimers' Brenthurst Estate. 'He was larger than life,' Manuel said of Oppenheimer, who reportedly regaled them with details about the size of the Soviet Union's diamond stockpile.[22]

'Dealing with Harry wasn't a complete shock, as my seniors had dealt with people like that all the time,' Manuel said,[23] offering the example of Tiny Rowland, the British magnate and head of Lonrho, the multinational with roots in mining in southern Africa. Rowland maintained a sprawling network of contacts throughout Africa, and regularly briefed apartheid intelligence services on his contact with African leaders and American spies.[24] 'Tiny was a big mover and shaker at the time, and looked out for Oliver and Adelaide Tambo during tough times. He wanted to support them.'[25] In fact, Kögl said, Rowland bought the Tambos a house in Sandhurst, the same Johannesburg suburb where insurance billionaire Douw Steyn built his grand house.[26]

The eccentric and slightly odd Steyn also saw opportunity in the returning exiles and grabbed it with both hands. At the beginning of 1992 Steyn invited Frederik van Zyl Slabbert to his home, where the former leader of the Progressive Federal Party found Steyn 'alone in this enormous mansion'. Steyn told Van Zyl Slabbert that he could use the Sandhurst estate for anything – meetings, workshops, accommodation – as long as he introduced him 'to the new lot'.[27]

After his separation from Winnie in 1992, Mandela moved into Steyn's mansion and lived there for six months before he moved to a house in Houghton. And in the late 1990s, after Mandela left office, Steyn built a private villa for Mandela on his Shambala

Private Game Reserve in the Waterberg in Limpopo.

Steyn's efforts clearly paid off. When his home was converted into the Saxon Hotel in 2000, Mandela made a speech at the opening of the hotel – which boasts a Nelson Mandela Platinum Suite, the very room in which Madiba had temporarily lived. Van Zyl Slabbert 'quietly left' the event after Mandela declared that apartheid would not have been defeated 'if it weren't for businessmen like Steyn'.[28]

Kögl was clearly not a Steyn fan, describing him as having 'a tacky record': 'He never had anything to do with the ANC and certainly only ended up with Mandela and gave money to Mandela, but nobody else.'[29]

Doug Band recalled a lavish party one year at the Steyn mansion in honour of American actor Whoopi Goldberg, who was in the country in 1992 for the filming of *Sarafina!*, a musical drama based on Mbongeni Ngema's 1987 musical of the same name. 'Anant Singh, the movie director, called me and said that he's having, at short notice, a party for Goldberg, because she's been a great supporter of the struggle and it's going to be held at Douw Steyn's residence, and that Madiba's going to be there. So off I went, and we had a fascinating evening, including Whoopi sitting there completely bemused by the fact that there were all these struggle heroes, dining out on crayfish and smoked salmon at Douw Steyn's place, with old Douw wandering around and everybody asking him how the hell he got to where he was!'[30]

Spicer said he – and others at Anglo – realised what problems unchecked patronage and loose money could cause. 'We had people who had nothing, and they've got large families, and then they see how others are living who have been here and they've built up capital, and then they say we should be on that level, and why aren't we?'[31]

The dilemma was how to ensure that the incoming political elite, who didn't have anything like accumulated capital or economic opportunity, never mind pension funds, had the security to govern responsibly, without seeming like they were being bribed or pressured.

'It was a conundrum, starting with Mandela. People did give him a lot of financial help, and it's not an issue only with South Africa. You know, if you don't pay politicians and bureaucrats reasonably well, they will look for extra sources of income.'[32]

There was a belief that someone of Mandela's stature, and given the role everyone was expecting him to play, couldn't live like a pauper. Spicer said deciding how to help Mandela without being seen to bribe or unduly influence him was difficult. 'Those were tricky conversations. But support was given. It was seen as necessary to make the wheels go round and to get through this transitional period.'[33]

Apart from Mandela, there were also whispers about Mbeki's proximity to the capitalist establishment, made worse by his friendship with people like Tony Bloom, the Anglo businessman who'd accompanied Relly on the safari to Zambia. And Mbeki's 50th birthday party was allegedly paid for by hotel magnate Sol Kerzner.[34]

Many in the ANC, including senior figures, very quickly moved very close to the moneyed establishment. ANC treasurer-general Thomas Nkobi, Tokyo Sexwale, a former Robben Islander, and Mzi Khumalo, also a former Robben Islander, who later became a flamboyant and empowered businessman, quickly saw opportunities that business brought.[35] One of Nkobi's protégés was Schabir Shaik, who worked as an advisor to the treasurer; Shaik, whose company's name was Nkobi Holdings, was later convicted of corruption and fraud related to bribes allegedly paid to Jacob Zuma.

Band said companies in the Anglo stable 'tried to push things along' by introducing blacks into middle and senior management positions 'to offer advancement to qualified black people, and to try, wherever possible, to find ways of encouraging a new way of thinking'.[36]

The principal obstacle to that was that there weren't very many qualified black people, he said. 'There were obviously a number of black lawyers, and one saw them starting to emerge in some of the bigger practices after being given opportunities, but there were very few black qualified chartered accountants, for example.'[37]

As slow and hesitant as it was, the introduction of a small number of black professionals into white management and boardrooms was a big step that showed big capital's intent. Said Manuel, 'There was a small group of professionals coming through, who were also brought into these engagements at various points. For example, Don Ncube was in human resources at Anglo American. It's not an insignificant point. Don frequently was brought into these kinds of engagements, and later became the key to the establishment of Real Africa Holdings. There was a company with headquarters in Cape Town called Norwich Life that eventually was taken up by Fedsure, which eventually was taken over by Investec. And one of the guys working in the bond market at Norwich Life was Khaya Ngqula, who later became chief executive of the Industrial Development Corporation, and thereafter chief executive of SAA.

'So there was a cadre of black professionals starting to come through, and to some extent it also was a function of the general orientation of the boards and management of these companies. The guy who headed Norwich Life had by 1990 appointed Mamphela Ramphele onto the board of Norwich Life – not because it was a legal requirement, [and] this clearly demonstrated a lot of foresight in the way in which he went about things.'[38]

10

Living in the real world

'You go and borrow money to finance a car, and
when you stop paying your instalments on the car, the
bank repossesses the car, and you are still liable for the
value of it ... Well, we can't repossess your country,
but by God, we'll teach you how to budget!'

– Edward Jaycox, a senior World Bank official, to an ANC
delegation in 1992, according to Trevor Manuel.[1]

By early 1991, violence was wracking the country, with the East
and West Rand, as well as the Natal midlands, having been turned
into killing fields as ANC and IFP self-defence units and impis, the
latter aided by government-sponsored training and arms (the so-called
third force), engaged in a bloody battle. 'War had broken out,' recalled
Jay Naidoo. 'There were hundreds of people getting killed every week
and our job was to protect the transition and human lives.'[2]

On 18 April 1991, FW de Klerk suddenly announced that the
government was to hold a multiparty conference to discuss the
escalating violence in the country – without consulting with the ANC.

Mandela immediately announced that the ANC would not be
taking part, arguing that such a conference should be held under

the guidance of an independent third party, given the ANC's belief that the government was fomenting the violence through the state-sponsored third force.[3]

Both leaders were now in a pickle: De Klerk couldn't call it off, and Mandela was coming across as intransigent.

Eventually a delegation from the CBM, headed by Barlow Rand's John Hall, went to see both De Klerk and Mandela to try to negotiate a compromise. 'John Hall first went to the president, who said he wouldn't postpone the conference. And Mandela stuck to his guns, saying he wouldn't attend. Eventually the parties agreed that the conference would go ahead, but would not take any decisions, and that the ANC wouldn't condemn it,' recalls Eloff.[4]

The CBM's role in helping to broker a form of compromise – alongside the churches, which played a crucial role in this 'shuttle diplomacy', as mediators travelling between the two parties – led directly to its involvement in the very first multiparty negotiating meeting, held at Barlow Rand's corporate headquarters in Sandton, Johannesburg, on 22 June 1991. The purpose of the meeting was to prepare for a national peace conference, which all parties to the political conflict needed to attend, to prepare for fully fledged constitutional negotiations. It was the first time in South Africa's history that the apartheid government, the ANC, the IFP and other political parties such as Azapo, trade unions (with Cosatu as the representative federation), churches and business came together to discuss issues like violence and the future. The meeting was co-chaired by Desmond Tutu and Barlow's Hall, with Theuns Eloff and Anglo's Bobby Godsell attending as rapporteurs.

'It very quickly became clear it was going to be tough to reach some form of consensus,' Eloff recalled. 'It was such an historic event, but it was almost unmanageable. At around 5 pm in the afternoon, Tutu suspended the meeting, because we were going nowhere. I was sitting at the back, and I was a nobody, and thought to myself, *Surely it shouldn't be so difficult?* And I started scribbling on a flipchart, drawing some lines from this point to that point, and took it to Tutu.

"Archbishop, why don't we try it like this?" And he looked at it and asked me to present to the plenary. And eventually we agreed on the process that made the National Peace Accord possible.'[5]

According to Naidoo, Cosatu pushed strongly for a peace process based on already-established relationships with capital and existing protocols on how to manage conflict. 'I met André Lamprecht, who was an executive at Barlow, and said to him that this fucking shit is going to crash if we don't do something – South Africa is going to be the *Titanic*. We spoke about the system of collective bargaining, and how we should negotiate a recognition agreement to create a system to adjudicate and arbitrate in the conflict.'[6]

Eloff said that the negotiating parties started to see the value of process and procedure, a discipline of industrial psychology embedded in how businesses operate. 'They started understanding the value of determining, for example, how to get to a goal from your point of departure. And after the preparatory meeting for the National Peace Convention, we broke into committees and sought compromises.'[7]

The ANC understood it couldn't lead the process because it was a party to the conflict – and both the ANC and Cosatu were content for the process to be led by John Hall and representatives of the churches, including Tutu and Rev Frank Chikane.[8]

The committees, consisting of three members of the ANC-SACP-Cosatu alliance, three from the government, three from the IFP, one religious leader and one business representative, met over a period of months at Barlow's head office, thrashing out issues like codes of conduct for security forces and political parties (which, said Spicer, were based on the agreements reached by Godsell and Cyril Ramaphosa during the great mineworkers' strike of 1987[9]), socioeconomic issues and procedural matters.[10] Thabo Mbeki was the chair of the ANC's delegation, while Roelf Meyer led the government's team.

It was during these negotiating sessions that people started to see each other as fellow human beings, Eloff said. 'Personal relationships started playing a role during those meetings. Suddenly the ANC started seeing their opponents not as these caricatured, die-hard capitalists. I reckon there's a PhD to be had on the role that alcohol played in our peaceful transition to democracy, because we often, after arguing and fighting, retreated to John Hall's office to drink whisky and talk. And we started finding each other, with some in the ANC starting to see that even though the person in front of them might work for Harry Oppenheimer, he is also just a human being.'[11]

The CBM was appointed to provide secretariat and organisational services to the National Peace Convention, which took place on 14 September 1991, and which paved the way for the Convention for a Democratic South Africa (Codesa) I and II, and eventually the Multiparty Negotiating Forum (MPNF), which produced the interim constitution. The National Peace Accord, which established provincial and regional peace committees to enable constitutional negotiations going forward, was the product of months of talks, and created an independent entity with its own set of norms, standards and goals.

Manuel said it helped 'reframe' the objectives for everyone involved in the negotiating process.[12]

As Naidoo put it, 'It didn't matter whether you came from Inkatha, or you came from the ANC, when you were sitting in the peace group, you were talking about maintaining the peace, despite the deep connections you had.' He believed if it wasn't for the peace accord process, 'there would have been no negotiations. We wouldn't be talking today. We would probably be a completely failed state and war would still be continuing.'[13]

The peace process created the architecture within which parties could not only engage each other, but also start taking part in normal political processes, like marches and demonstrations. 'It set down protocols so that if the ANC is going to organise a march, or Inkatha is going to organise a march, they first have to meet at the police station, the station commander has to be there, the peace monitors have to be there, all the parties have to be there, and we agree where do we march, how we march, and that process is guarded, and then linked to statutory powers.'[14]

But where Eloff said the peace process was a victory for business and process, Naidoo claims it as a trophy for the union movement. 'The peace process establishes the foundation for negotiations. It's an initiative that comes out of the union movement in conversation with business. We were used to negotiating with and engaging big capital. It wasn't like we had a view that no, this was collaboration. No, I'm a fucking negotiator, you know ... pragmatic. I don't give a fuck about your ideology, the only question for me is, how do I secure the present?'[15]

After the peace accord was signed on 14 September 1991, Eloff told Roelf Meyer that the negotiation process had momentum and that all parties should move ahead quickly. 'And he told me no, the government and the ANC still had to sort out some differences, the time wasn't ready for constitutional wrangling.'[16]

In early December, Meyer called Eloff and said that both the government and the ANC had agreed that he should head the independent, but fully representative, secretariat to support the imminent inaugural meeting of Codesa. 'It was a vote of confidence in the CBM, I believe, and the role business played in the run-up to the constitution-making process. Afterwards I was told the government had wanted the department of constitutional development to be given the role, while the ANC had preferred a highly regarded consulting firm. Neither of them wanted to relent, and they settled for second best. De Klerk personally was very sceptical of me,' Eloff said.[17]

So although the CBM wasn't officially involved, because the secretariat was designed to be nominally independent, it was the CBM's staff and skills that were appointed to ensure that the negotiating process succeeded. In this way, the CBM used its ample resources and abilities to ensure that it became the support structure on which the actual constitutional negotiation process was constructed.

'Our first goal was to ensure that business remained in business.

Our second was to transform our own interests into enlightened self-interest. And thirdly, we had to ensure that we had a mixed market economy.'[18]

By around mid-1992, the debate about the future shape of the economy had started to intensify in the ANC and the broader liberation movement, with initial economic-policy documents being drawn up and papers like 'Ready to Govern',[19] which set out the ANC's guidelines for a democratic South Africa, including a framework for a future government, being published. But internal contestation was fierce, with leftist arguments in favour of social-democratic policies of growth through redistribution being punted hard, while rejecting economic orthodoxy – a neoliberal system believed to be forced on the developing world by the Bretton Woods institutions of the World Bank and the International Monetary Fund (IMF), both international institutions funded by member states that provide assistance to countries in the form of development finance. (Bretton Woods refers to the system of international finance rules that were agreed on by Allied nations in 1944, out of which the IMF and the World Bank were born.)

But things were changing: Mandela had had his chastening experience in Davos, and big business was lobbying hard in support of a free market economy. And the gravity of what the ANC was about to undertake hit Trevor Manuel, the head of the ANC's department of economic planning and part of Mbeki's inner circle, square between the eyes in the northern-hemisphere spring of 1992 – and it was an American drawl that hammered the message home: if South Africa borrowed money from the World Bank and couldn't pay it back, it would be the World Bank that would call the shots, not any ANC government.

Manuel was part of a group of around 15 representatives of the MDM attending a session at the World Bank in Washington, DC, which included Tito Mboweni and Jay Naidoo, and Cheryl Carolus, who was in charge of the department of economic planning's social-welfare arm.[20] This was the result of Mandela's request to the president of the World Bank during the latter's visit to South Africa in February 1992, 'to help train these people so that we can govern the country'.[21]

At that meeting, Edward Jaycox, the World Bank's vice-president for Africa, proceeded to spell out the realpolitik of international high finance in no uncertain terms. 'We're a bank. We lend money. We borrow money from the capital markets, we lend it to countries, we add some interest on it, and that's how we exist within the global system,' he said, according to Manuel.[22] So the World Bank and the IMF would assist countries in dire straits, Jaycox spelled out, but those countries would then have to conform to policy frameworks and policies set down by the institutions.

'Now, one thing that I want to make clear to you is that all banks are the same, whether it's the World Bank or your local bank,' Jaycox continued, according to Manuel's version. 'You go and borrow money to finance a car, and when you stop paying your instalments on the car, the bank repossesses the car, and you are still liable for the value of it. Similarly, if you take out a mortgage on a home. Well, we can't repossess your country, but by God, we'll teach you how to budget!'[23]

By the end of the trip, Thabo Mbeki had joined the delegation and held a number of 'roundup meetings' with various institutions, including the IMF. 'And they were all very cordial and helpful and so on,' said Manuel, 'but we took stock of the situation and asked each other how we were going to conduct ourselves to prevent getting into a situation where we had to subject ourselves to the World Bank.'[24]

The ANC had no standing among international financiers and development-finance institutions or on the bond market. It had never run anything. And the ample talk among members of the tripartite alliance about grand spending plans and higher taxation to redistribute wealth had replaced talk about nationalisation – and made many people nervous. Manuel – and Mbeki and Mboweni – understood that if South Africa was to succeed under the ANC's leadership, it would have to follow a path of conservative fiscal consolidation.

Returning from the US, Manuel said he was under no misapprehension about what lay ahead, and the concept of 'golden handcuffs'. 'It was clear there was to be some form of disciplining needed ... There was this fear across Africa about what happens if you borrow from the World Bank and can't repay, and Zimbabwe presented us with wonderful examples from their first decade.'[25]

Zimbabwe fell into debt during the 1980s after it took loans from international development-finance institutions, including the World Bank, which it struggled to repay.

Manuel said, '[*New York Times* columnist] Thomas Friedman talks about these golden handcuffs that you put on. And it's not the same as structural adjustment programmes [interventionist economic policies aimed at addressing structural problems in the economy], but if you borrow from capital markets, they will impose a certain discipline on you. That, for me, was actually a helluva lot more important in understanding how disciplining works than some secret deal struck with business.'[26]

Mandela, meanwhile, was enthusiastic about training his people in the relevant and necessary financial skills, and used his influence to ensure that his officials and policy teams got as much exposure as possible.[27] He persuaded the president of the German central bank to take on economists for training, used his relationship with New York mayor David Dinkins to place another group at some of that city's foremost banks, and, thanks to Mboweni's intervention, a group that spent two weeks with Goldman Sachs in New York included Lesetja Kganyago, who later became director-general of the National Treasury and president of the SARB, and Maria Ramos, also to become director-general at the National Treasury and Absa chief executive.[28]

'When Tito and Maria and a bunch of people were taken to New York and were shown globalisation in play, and as they were exposed to these big New York firms, they saw this was the world in which you're going to operate, so you'd better get used to it ... And they saw

South Africa was not some sleepy African backwater detached from the global economy. We were part of it,' said Spicer.[29]

Jay Naidoo described his frustration – and that of colleagues like Sydney Mufamadi and others – at the ANC's approach to the economy from the very beginning. He said that Cosatu had agitated for whole-sale changes to the structure of the economy, and that he believed he could 'bring along' big business because employees and employers had a recent history of negotiation and compromise. But the ANC, he said, was reluctant to engineer the same economic transformation it was pushing for politically.

Big capital was watching from the outside, and Spicer said they were able to identify who the main actors were during this period of internal contestation. It was natural, he said, that in a broad movement like the ANC there would be evolution, and they kept a very close eye on developments. 'It was in flux all the time. There was contestation with Jeremy [Cronin, from the SACP], with Jay [Naidoo, from Cosatu], all of them contesting what policy should be.'[30]

Perhaps, Naidoo intimated, the ANC's approach was to a degree informed by that first meeting between Oppenheimer and Mandela in 1990, at Brenthurst in Johannesburg. 'If you go back to the Brent-hurst meeting, the first one, with the captains of industry ... I went to the meeting with Mandela, but basically, I knew what they would be saying at the meeting as big capital: don't rock the boat. And I felt that, well, we should rock the boat! But we didn't want the boat to capsize, you know; we walked that tightrope a thousand times.'[31]

Big capital wanted to sway the ANC – as executives from Anglo and others repeatedly said – to adhere to a more 'reasonable policy',[32] and during the negotiation years, 'don't rock the boat' seemed to become the organisation's mantra in relation to the economy, said Naidoo. 'And so, consistently, post the release of Nelson Mandela, when Cosatu challenged the apartheid state, for example, on the issue of mobile licences in the early 1990s [when the government issued licences for new cellphone networks], we built a campaign on the slogan of "no unilateral restructuring of the economy". Even at meetings of the transitional executive council [the multiparty body that oversaw the functioning of the apartheid government during the last year before democracy], the thesis was "don't rock the boat". And for us, we had to rock the boat! And we had allies in that, whether that was people like Joe Slovo, Chris Hani or even the broader ANC, including Nelson Mandela, that we actually had to rock the boat. And so we took up that issue.'[33]

One of Cosatu's biggest campaigns at the time was against the imposition of value-added tax (VAT), and, despite failing to prevent its introduction, it did give the federation a burning issue around which to mobilise support and strengthen the coalition against the apartheid government. 'The VAT issue was really important and became a watershed event, because we built a campaign that included black business. It included the broadest coalition of organisations in this country and our slogan was again "no unilateral restructuring of the economy, no taxation without proper representation".'[34]

In November 1991, Cosatu led a massive, nationwide strike against the process driven by finance minister Barend du Plessis, and apart from the bread-and-butter economic issues related to the new tax, Naidoo believed the clash to be an opportunity to weaken the government 'and the interests of local and global capital' that the National Party represented. 'Du Plessis gave us the ammunition on a silver platter, because eventually we ended up in negotiations, and at the Carlton Centre during a meeting between delegations from Cosatu and the government, he said he is prepared to make some concessions and is prepared to exempt basic foodstuffs. And he said he also will exempt offal. He then looks at me and he grins, "And we are also prepared to zero-rate lentils …"'[35]

Naidoo remembered the day with a great deal of black humour, and laughed when he recalled how he turned the offer by Du Plessis into a rallying point. 'So, of course, I go out there to the membership and the country and I say, "Look at this fucking finance minister! He wants to give us offal and lentils and he thinks that we are going to give him the mandate to go and implement VAT!" We built a campaign that caused the biggest strike in the country, because this was something that not just black South Africans or the MDM were concerned about. Every single person, including white people, felt that this is just a new tax. The coalition we built was probably the broadest coalition of any national action we've undertaken in the country. And it basically shook the government to its core, because De Klerk was forced to fire Du Plessis and, in his place, he puts in Derek Keys, seen as an independent, but somewhat trusted by big capital.'[36]

Naidoo said – and Manuel concurred – that Keys was a good negotiating partner. A former managing director of mining giant Gencor, he wasn't a politician. 'We had a great relationship, and he recognised that you could not only talk about this deracialising the politics and the political architecture of the country. You had to deal with making sure that the economy itself would be somewhat acceptable, broadly, to both the MDM and the apartheid state,' said Naidoo.[37]

Some years later, in November 1997, the Truth and Reconciliation Commission convened a special hearing in Johannesburg to listen to testimony by the country's business establishment about its role during apartheid. This included Anglo, Rembrandt, Barlow Rand, Tongaat-Hulett and the Chamber of Mines, among others. Naspers, or Nasionale Pers, refused to take part.

One of the central questions during the hearings – and in the broader national debate at the time – was how much organised business could (and should) have done to resist and protest apartheid. Big capital's detractors argued that apartheid 'was part of a system of racial-capitalism' constructed on cheap, black labour, while business contended that apartheid had in fact been bad for business, had raised the cost of enterprise, had eroded the country's skills base and had undermined long-term growth.[38]

Economist Ann Bernstein's argument was that 'corporations are not institutions established for moral purposes. They are functional institutions created to perform an economic task – the production of goods and services and so on. This is their primary purpose. They are not institutions designed to promote some or other form of morality in the world. Other institutions exist for this purpose.'[39]

And Sanlam, the Afrikaner-owned conglomerate from Bellville, protested that the power and influence of business over government should not be exaggerated. 'Any notion that business could have acted as a watchdog of the government as far as human rights violations are concerned is totally unrealistic and should be dispelled. Business was unable to act in that way in the past and will not be able to do so in the future ... government is so powerful and dominant that a business organisation will seriously jeopardise its prospects of success by crossing swords with politicians.'[40]

The commission found that 'business was central to the economy that sustained the South African state during the apartheid years' and that mining was 'involved in helping design and implement apart-heid policies'.[41] Indeed, the commission was particularly scathing of mining in its findings, declaring that the industry influenced and often directed apartheid legislation to its own benefit, and to ensure a steady supply of black workers. 'Thus, the mining industry bears a great deal of moral responsibility for the migrant labour system and its associated hardships,' it found.[42]

11

Ready to govern

'The RDP was the biggest and most comprehensive economic policy document to serve as an election manifesto in the world.'

– Jeremy Cronin, co-convenor of the RDP writing process, on the launch of the RDP in 1994.[1]

In May 1992 the ANC adopted 'Ready to Govern',[2] an ambitious policy framework document that it presented as the basis on which it was to administer a future South Africa.

Trevor Manuel described the convoluted, complicated and quite chaotic process before the framework was finalised. 'You've got all of these streams and you need to kind of convene them. You need to convene a stream that understands the state of the economy and what policy will matter. You need to have a stream that is doing the listening from groups like Nafcoc and Fabcos. You need to factor in the views of the trade union movements. You need to factor in the views of civil society, the views presented by the churches and so on. And you need to build this base that can demonstrate the capability to govern, which in the cold light of day and after a gap of 30 years, you look back on and ask, "How the hell did we take chances on these things?" But we did.'[3]

After the adoption of Ready to Govern, at an alliance summit held outside Johannesburg, it was decided that the policy framework needed to be transformed into a programme that people could refer to and identify with.[4] Manuel, Jeremy Cronin and Alec Erwin were assigned to initiate discussions and planning around this programme, 'and that was the genesis of what was to become the RDP'[5] – the Reconstruction and Development Programme.

But, according to Manuel, it was extremely difficult to devote the time and energy necessary to the project, given what was happening in the country. Negotiations with the apartheid government were floundering and violence had caused hundreds of bloody deaths. 'It wasn't like we could stop everything, go to university and do some research. We had to do a million different things. We had grassroots work to do in trying to establish ANC branches. We had to campaign among our people. There were wars being fought, Boipatong happened, which we had to deal with.'[6] In the June 1992 attack on the residents of the township of Boipatong by supporters of the IFP, 45 people died.

'When you run a project like that, and you're up against the clock, and you're trying to do things that none of us had ever been involved with ... You're trying to develop policy perspective, you're trying to inform an election campaign, and you're trying to develop a programme that may be more durable than just for the elections.'[7]

The original plan for the RDP came from the National Union of Metalworkers of South Africa (Numsa), the then largest affiliate of Cosatu, whose leadership was 'very suspicious of the ANC', and who developed the idea for a reconstruction and development pact with the organisation, recalls Jeremy Cronin. 'Numsa's leadership argued that these national liberation movements always sell out the workers after using them to obtain power. And so, it was the [SACP] that agreed, and said it was a good idea, let's develop a comprehensive perspective on what we are trying to achieve with what was obviously within a matter of years going to be an ANC-led government of one kind or another.'[8]

Jay Naidoo said the creation of the RDP was a creative, positive and dynamic experience – and he had high hopes that it would serve as the foundation of a reimagined and fundamentally different South Africa. 'I went from people's forum to people's forum – you know, there is a plethora of forums which were so vibrant. There was a health charter process, there was a workers' charter process, there was an education charter process, a women's charter process, labour market restructuring taking place, there was a plethora of input coming from everywhere. It was a process that created a social consensus, even with employers. Even they knew change was coming and that they had a role to play. It was a social consensus we achieved,' said Naidoo.[9]

Cronin concurred that the RDP was a policy that came from the grassroots, informed by community organisations, the civics, the broad liberation movement and the ANC's historical positions such as those in the Freedom Charter.[10]

Spicer's view was somewhat different; he said that 'typically ANC, there were numerous processes going on all over the place, simultaneously, without them speaking to each other'.[11]

Manuel, meanwhile, repeatedly acknowledged the frantic nature of the process – which, it should not be forgotten, was very much secondary to the fraught constitutional and political process of the time.

While all this was going on, a major fight was brewing in the ANC and broader liberation movement about what Manuel – under the aegis of Mbeki – was doing. Some thought that Manuel's department of economic planning was dysfunctional and alienating itself from the broader liberation movement.[12] And, indeed, the department battled to establish functional regional offices (only the western Cape functioned as it should, with the Witwatersrand region – where the ANC was headquartered – considered one of the weaker regions), didn't have enough basic resources, such as a typist or secretary, and had no heads of subsections like mining or energy.

Moss Ngoasheng, an official in the department and later a businessman, said that the department 'and indeed the whole movement had no experience in formulating concrete economic (technical) policy, not to say anything about implementation'.

The ANC didn't have the resources or the skills to compete with whatever alternative policy proposals were being crafted by the apartheid state, which had a massive budget and various departments and institutions to call on, or big capital, which had infrastructure, economic research departments, money and the skills to influence the process. The ANC, Ngoasheng said, sought to address its problems by 'farming out work to outside researchers, to associate members and sympathetic economists located in other institutions'.[13]

Manuel and the department of economic planning thus 'became alienated from its original aims. Its members simply ignored all that was going on around them within the movement itself and turned elsewhere for their economic ideas. [It] was understaffed, poorly organised, and its leadership appeared to make little to no effort to mobilise the relevant experience available at some of the universities.'[14]

The source of the conflict in the ANC, with the left particularly wounded, was the process of the Macro-Economic Research Group (MERG), led by economist Vella Pillay, an ANC stalwart and lifelong employee of the Bank of China in London. MERG was intended to investigate and develop alternative economic policies for the ANC.[15] It was staffed by local and international economists who worked alongside research teams, and was guided by a steering committee, chaired by Manuel as the head of the department of economic planning. But it was run by Pillay, who returned to his birth city of Johannesburg in 1992 to coordinate the work and oversee research done by MERG associate academics at historically black universities such as the Western Cape and Durban-Westville. And a range of left economists from across the world, including Britain and Canada, became involved with Pillay's efforts to keep the ANC to its historic, statist latter-day socialist convictions.

But relations between the MERG economists and researchers, and the department of economic planning, were never good. Significant ideological differences soon emerged, with the department of economic planning believing that MERG ignored ANC policy positions as decided on at the organisation's 1991 conference, and policy documents like Ready to Govern.

The ANC at executive level, and even the department of economic planning, appeared 'to have been only perfunctorily engaged in the debates about drafting MERG policy proposals, choosing [instead] to spend time with World Bank officials and local business leaders'.[16] This is in apparent reference to the visit by the World Bank's president to an ANC lekgotla in Johannesburg, and to the meetings between Mandela and Oppenheimer.

The SACP's Ronnie Kasrils said the ANC succumbed 'to a neo-liberal, free market economic embrace because some of us were fast asleep'.[17]

Economist Bill Freund argued that before Manuel was appointed head of the department of economic planning, its pronouncements were 'fairly progressive': against low wages, and for raising capital locally, higher corporate taxes and unbundling of conglomerates. 'Later, under Manuel, the [department] may have been guided to believe that there was no alternative to a market-friendly approach to post-apartheid reconstruction and development.'[18]

But Manuel stridently – even furiously – rejected this censure, saying that the co-author of these criticisms, Vishnu Padayachee, a researcher at MERG working directly under Vella Pillay, didn't understand that it was the ANC, not the London socialist academic set nor anyone else, that was in charge of developing and designing economic policy. 'Vishnu's concerns relate to the fact that he didn't understand that these shifts happen … The problem that Vishnu didn't see is that this network operating out of London believed that it would decide what the ANC does. But that, in fact, was not the case.'[19]

And, indeed, a shift had occurred in the ANC: the closer it

moved to obtaining political power, the closer attention it paid to the economy. And it didn't feel beholden to the leftist academics who seemingly for years had arrogated the movement's economic policy to themselves.

'There was a stand-off, because the London group didn't quite understand that the shift meant that the ANC would be taking more of its own decisions … in fact, all its own the decisions. The ANC didn't come across from Lusaka with truckloads of filing cabinets filled with policy documents. There were core issues, and these needed to be developed in South Africa,' said Manuel.[20]

After more than a year's research and fieldwork, the MERG report of more than 300 pages was finalised and officially presented to the ANC at an event in Johannesburg on 3 December 1993. It proposed massive spending increases in basic and adult education, health and nutrition, and housing, and a statutory minimum wage. It was, however, the position of the SARB that was the centrepiece of MERG's macroeconomic plan, which argued for the effective nationalisation of the country's central bank.

Three weeks earlier, Vella Pillay had given a speech in the presence of Nelson Mandela and other leaders during which he'd lifted the veil on what the final policy proposals would entail, saying that the SARB 'should be subordinate to the government such as to allow monetary, interest and exchange-rate policies, and the flow and direction of credit in the economy, to be consistent with the democratic state's policies in the areas of public sector expenditure and taxation, in trade, industrial diversification and development, employment generation, and social and economic infrastructure investments.'[21]

But Manuel said that proposals like that on the SARB were 'never part of ANC macroeconomic policy'.[22] And he said that despite the protestations of individuals like Pillay and Padayachee, even the MERG report itself 'was leaning towards independence for the SARB'.

Other MERG proposals differed from the Normative Economic

Model, the National Party government's economic policy position, and those proposed by the Nedcor-Old Mutual planning scenarios (similar to Anglo and Sunter's modelling), because they were 'carefully costed and situated in what appears to be a sound macroeconomic model'.[23] The plan steered clear of massively increased government spending, and instead focused on the demand side. It was, said one economist, 'a bold attempt to reconstruct the South African economy, boost growth to 5 per cent per annum by 2004 and create 300 000 jobs per year'.[24]

But MERG, the product of the left-leaning development economists from London and locally, with big dreams of massive social spending and strong government intervention, was never going to cut it – not with Manuel in charge of the department of economic planning, and Mbeki setting the course for a future economy.

After receiving the report, Manuel denounced it, as did his department officials in charge of health, housing and social welfare.[25] He rejected criticism more than thirty years later that the department of economic planning had been 'out of touch' or that it had 'succumbed' to the overtures of 'neo-liberalism' in its repudiation of MERG – the left's first big policy assault on the ANC after its unbanning. Rather, he said, they simply hadn't been consulted. 'I was the chairperson of both the department of economic planning and MERG, and nowhere was I or any other member of the [department] leadership invited to be part of this thing.'[26]

Manuel did not, of course, act in isolation in rejecting MERG. Being part of Thabo Mbeki's inner circle meant that he was intimately aware of what the country's future president was thinking and planning. Spicer has no doubt that Manuel was able to do what needed to be done – reject MERG, link with the World Bank and the IMF, and so on – because he had the support of Mbeki.

British economist Ben Fine, one of the authors of the document, said he was 'bewildered' by 'these people, rubbishing my work'. Manuel, Fine said, not only said the issue of the independence of the SARB shouldn't be put forward as a policy proposal, but that it 'shouldn't even be discussed'. Fine was shattered, apparently refusing South African citizenship offered to him later because of the MERG rejection.[27]

Jeremy Cronin said that 'the expulsion of outstanding British economists dealt a serious blow to economic policy debate', and created the momentum for agents in the ANC, politics, business, civil society and academia to 'abandon independent and critical thought and fall behind a default market-friendly economic policy position that could be summarised as "there is no alternative".'[28] There being no alternative was, of course, exactly what Spicer and Anglo wanted to convey to the liberation movement. And the MERG people finally had to concede that economic policy would have to be measured against 'time and reality', as Relly had put it.[29]

Where capital was concerned, a problem with MERG was that it failed to address business confidence, and that some of its more aggressive state interventions would 'deter, rather than encourage' investment.[30] And Spicer said that big business was concerned that 'all this MERG stuff was going to win the day. We didn't see it by any means as a done deal, where we could sort of sit back and say, "Oh, these guys [the liberation movement], they'll come around eventually." Not at all, because there was this crescendo of activism from the left as well.'[31]

After the RDP's adoption by the ANC as its election manifesto in January 1994, Jay Naidoo had no doubt that it would inform the government of national unity's policy framework. Naidoo explained, 'The fundamental focus of the RDP was around meeting the needs of people, around ensuring that the deep legacy of apartheid when it came to jobs or quality education and training was addressed and built into the system, [and] the right to quality education and quality healthcare. It was an organic process, an extrapolation from the Freedom Charter.'[32]

Naidoo argued that during the formulation of the RDP he could sense a shift in ANC economic policy thinking, and cited the fact that ANC leaders such as Manuel had by then gone on 'Goldman Sachs-sponsored' junkets to New York and elsewhere. 'Of course, some of our policies and proposals were watered down *because* they came from Cosatu, but all of this was negotiated and there was give and take ... but the fundamental thrust of the RDP was about how the people, who played the most critical role in our freedom, continue to exercise that role in a post-apartheid South Africa.'[33]

The RDP process, and its subsequent adoption as policy, enabled the ANC to gain a foothold among the poor, said Trevor Manuel. But he admitted it was the product of many different streams, with many different perspectives with interest groups involved that wanted various outcomes. 'Eventually, once the framework was there, we were trying to do too many things at the same time, I suppose. We were trying to build capacity; we were trying to ensure that we would know what to do when we stepped into government,' he said.[34]

He said that even though the document and policy fulfilled a specific role at that stage, the new government's macroeconomic policy couldn't be premised on it. He said the RDP was a tool to build the ANC and the broader movement, to ensure that it had direction. 'Out of that, we could distil a set of views ... so you needed to formulate documents such as the RDP. But you also needed to formulate something a little bit more detailed.'[35]

And he conceded that the RDP did contain flights of fancy and misjudgements. 'There was a view, [and] it may have been exceedingly naive at that time, that cutting military expenditure would free up so many resources that you could fund this,' he said, referring to the chapter in the RDP document titled 'Financing the RDP'. 'There were ... numbers in the body of the document that were very ambitious, and they became slogans in the electoral campaign, so it was "A million houses in five years!" "Jobs, jobs, jobs!" All of those came from the RDP.'[36]

After the adoption of the RDP as the ANC's policy framework, Cronin said there was great optimism for what lay ahead. 'Madiba would often say that through the negotiated settlement we were part of the third wave of democracy ... The same things were happening in Eastern Europe, in Nicaragua, El Salvador, the Philippines, and South Africa was a bit of a poster child in 1994 and 1995. We thought that we were a bit like Western Europe in 1945 and 1946, that there would be a wave of Marshall Plan-type inflow.' The Marshall Plan was a US programme providing aid to Western Europe following the devastation of the Second World War, and provided more than $15 billion to help finance rebuilding efforts on the continent. 'We thought there would be this post-apartheid dividend, and that if that was coupled with this effort of getting water to the poor, getting electricity and energy, housing, and having a major redistributive effort through the RDP, we could really change the country.'[37]

But big capital didn't believe the RDP was either appropriate or feasible, said Anglo's Michael Spicer, who regarded the plan as an attempt to put together some sort of 'socialist cum social democratic vision'. 'And I use the word "vision" because the RDP was not a plan. The RDP was a wish list, but it was, as always with the left, uncosted. It assumed resources that simply weren't there, it assumed an implementation ability that wasn't there, it wished away the severe state of the South African economy, which people like Trevor [had] got to grips with very quickly. A new government had to stabilise the economy, rebalance the books and accrue some capital. It could not do that by going on a fantastical spending spree, spraying social welfare payments around and indulging the fantasies of the left.'[38]

As far as Spicer was concerned, it was all fantastical. 'Remember the Relly story, where he said that nationalisation was one of those things that would be subject to the test of time and reality? Same here. The ANC was untested, hyper-theoretical, paranoid, dealing with a changed world, and was confronted by reality faster than they ever thought they would be. And it's also the reality of a South Africa they hardly recognised, because it's a modern industrial economy, it's a world that is just vastly different from their imagined world of the 1950s and 1960s when they were put into exile. And they lived in a sort of time capsule, in the camps in Tanzania and Zambia and Angola and so on. There are very few who were outside the time capsule, and so, you know, shock therapy was needed.

'But many of their supporters – the academics on the left – who didn't accept any alternative, who hated globalisation and hated all these developments, encouraged them to perpetuate the idea that you could turn back the clock to the 1950s and 1960s and govern the country as if nothing had happened.'[39]

'I assumed that, even if there are other processes, we have now agreed on the RDP,' said Naidoo of those times. 'Of course, everybody has an agenda, but formally I present to the SACP, I present to the ANC, and we agree in the tripartite alliance on the RDP. No one stands up and said this RDP is not relevant, or this RDP is unrealistic. No one.'[40]

He rejected big capital and Spicer's criticism that the RDP wasn't costed and was unaffordable, and said that at no point did the left argue that the new government should 'print money' – a reckless policy that would inevitably have led to hyperinflation and economic strife.

'[The RDP] had a macro-economic view on the society that we could not just spend our way through the crisis, because essentially the government we inherited was bankrupt. In fact, we knew the statistics: 93 cents in every rand were already going towards paying off debt and carrying the expenditure of the civil service. The RDP wasn't a spending programme.'[41]

Naidoo said the whole point of the RDP wasn't to throw money around, but to implement a new set of developmental policies, laws and expenditure that 'cut across' government. 'For me, the RDP was never about money. It was about restructuring the policy, legal and institutional framework of the country so that we could re-allocate programmes, both in terms of budgets and in terms of the civil service, to now go beyond meeting the needs of a white minority, to the needs of all South African citizens. That was my view.'[42]

The RDP wanted to change a socioeconomic environment that excluded most people based on colour, Naidoo said. And he was certainly ready to implement the RDP. 'And, having sat several times with Madiba and gotten his assurance, and then sitting with people like Joe Slovo and particularly Chris Hani, why would I doubt that this would be a reality? Ja, I was confident. I was confident that, with Mandela's backing, it would happen.'[43]

12

The left loses its lustre

'There was a pretty broadly held naivety that, somehow, we were going to switch on the lights, and it was all going to be … sunny and the future was going to be rosy.'

– Banker Martin Kingston, about South Africa post 1994.[1]

When Trevor Manuel stepped into his Pretoria office as the new minister of trade and industry in May 1994, shortly after the ANC's victory in the country's first democratic election and Nelson Mandela's inauguration as president, he found it close to empty, aside from a giant ministerial desk and – curiously – a chaise longue reclining couch in the corner. 'I wondered why the minister would need a chaise longue,' Manuel said.[2]

He could never figure out why the piece of furniture was there. He was also reluctant to say how often he used it. Given the gargantuan task faced by the newly elected ANC government, it was probably not very regularly.

Besides the couch, the giant desk and an old computer, Manuel only had two documents to guide him in his newly created ministry, one called 'Trade and Industry Policy in a Democracy' and the other 'The First 100 Days in the Ministry of Trade and Industry'. 'That was it,' he said. 'We had to formulate the RDP in more detail than we had going into the election, and we had to do it for the whole of government, even though we didn't completely understand how it all worked yet.'[3]

There was 'great unevenness' across government in those first days of democracy, and not every department or ministry had clarity about what they should do or tackle first. One other ministry Manuel could recall that did have a policy document in place was the department of minerals and energy, 'except that the first minister of minerals and energy was Pik Botha, and Pik wanted nothing to do with the stuff, as you might imagine.'[4] (Botha, a former National Party minister, desperately wanted to remain minister of foreign affairs.)

For Jay Naidoo, appointed minister in the presidency in charge of the RDP, there wasn't even the mystery of a reclining couch. 'I walk into the office Mandela has set aside for me, above his office at the Union Buildings, and there's not even a kettle in it. That's where I start. First day at work, I walk into an empty office. And I think, what the fuck have I done here? No secretary … Nothing, nothing.'[5]

The reality of what he'd taken on hit Naidoo. In his bare office on the top floor of the west wing of the Union Buildings, straight out of leading Cosatu from mass action to national strike, and into government as minister in charge of the RDP, he looked around and saw trouble. 'I've done many crazy things in my life, but this is fucking ridiculous,' he remembered thinking.[6]

The economy that the first democratic government inherited from its apartheid predecessors was in a tepid state. Ever since the foreign debt crisis of 1985, the apartheid economy, which essentially functioned as a siege economy, with high state intervention, under-pinned by a skewed labour architecture (with black labour excluded from high wages and decision-making structures) and industries protected from competition in an artificial environment, had ground to a halt.

The high rates of GDP growth that had marked the 1960s and

early 1970s had plateaued in the late 1970s and come to a shuddering halt in the early 1980s, when GDP started to decline, with the economy contracting by 0.4 per cent in 1982 and 1.8 per cent in 1983. Apartheid president PW Botha's disastrous Rubicon speech and subsequent events saw the economy decline by 1.2 per cent in 1985, although there was some recovery in the late 1980s.[7]

The 1980s and the early 1990s were some of the worst-performing years in the country's recorded economic history, and when the Mandela government took the wheel in mid-1994, South Africa had just emerged from the longest downward economic phase since the SARB had started keeping such statistics after the Second World War: 51 consecutive months of negative economic activity. And while GDP recovered in 1993 (1.2 per cent) and 1994 (3.2 per cent) from the negative growth of 1990–1992, it was still way too low to start making a significant impact on unemployment and socioeconomic inequality.[8]

Investment in the economy was also at its lowest point ever. Big capital had started to hold back on new investments from around 1976 (after the Soweto Uprising, when the number stood at 32 per cent of GDP), and gross fixed capital formation declined sharply from around 1985. (Gross fixed capital formation indicates how much investment is being done with profit, as opposed to how much of those profits are consumed; it's essentially an indicator of business confidence.) And whereas 24.6 per cent of GDP was ploughed back into the economy in 1985, by 1993 only 15.8 per cent was invested, increasing slightly to 16.1 per cent in 1994.[9]

Foreign investment was also at a low: foreign direct investment stood at 25.5 per cent of all foreign investment (which included indirect investment, such as buying into a property investment without actually buying the property itself directly). In 1990 foreign direct investment represented a mere 8 per cent of GDP. The rand, which historically – and thanks to South Africa's gold exports – had held its own against the dollar, depreciated rapidly in the 1980s, and in 1993 lost more than 11 per cent of its value from the previous year. When Mandela became president, a rand was worth less than a third of a greenback.[10]

Government finances were in trouble. The budget deficit (when expenses exceed revenue) had reached an eye-watering 7.1 per cent of GDP in 1992–1993, during the height of the violence and crunch-time for negotiations. When the ANC took power in 1994, the deficit stood at 5.4 per cent.[11] (In February 2022, the budget deficit stood at 5.7 per cent, considered very high by economists.)

In 1994, the debt-to-GDP ratio (basically, comparing what a country owes to what it produces) was the worst since the early 1980s. While foreign debt was low (1.2 per cent of GDP, and 2.7 per cent of total debt), total debt stood at 43 per cent, and would worsen to 49.7 per cent two years later.[12]

The socioeconomic environment, shaped by apartheid and years of institutional discrimination and racism, was completely skewed. Unemployment was high, with a fifth (20 per cent) of all South Africans of working age unemployed; that number rose to 31.5 per cent on the expanded definition, which included those who'd given up looking for jobs.[13] This disproportionately affected blacks: officially, 24.7 per cent of blacks were unemployed, compared to 3 per cent of whites, 17.6 per cent of coloureds and 10.2 per cent of Asians.[14] And that number rose dramatically on the expanded definition, with 39.2 per cent of blacks jobless.[15]

The skewed pattern was replicated elsewhere, with more than 45 per cent of blacks living in informal or traditional housing in 1996, just more than 49 per cent of households not having electricity (and the vast majority of these being black) and only seven million households having access to piped water.[16]

These challenges were the product of deep-rooted patterns of economic activity, constructed not only on cheap black labour but also on expensive skilled labour. The latter became expensive because white labour was protected from black competition so that whites' standard of living could be maintained and raised. Employers could absorb these high costs 'as long as they were protected from foreign competition, enjoyed rising demand from white consumers or the state, and could secure an abundant supply of cheaper, unskilled African labour when necessary'.[17]

The normalisation of labour relations after apartheid, with the accompanying pressure on employers' balance sheets, as well as the opening up of the economy, and a lack of skills and training, would have profound effects on the new democratic government's ability to redesign society.

The new government, although it seemed to enjoy the warm and fuzzy goodwill of freedom-loving democrats across the globe, remained an unknown quantity. Big capital, consistently engaged with the transition process since the 1980s, tentatively went about 'staying in business', with foreign investors and their governments taking a cautious approach. Mandela sought to reassure international high finance and local business that it would follow a responsible and conservative fiscal and monetary path by reappointing Derek Keys as finance minister; when Keys resigned a few months into his presidency, Mandela replaced him with Nedcor's chief executive Chris Liebenberg.

And there were other 'smart people' in the then department of finance, said Martin Kingston, naming Maria Ramos and Ketso Gordhan. They were, he said, 'open-minded individuals who had a view of how the world worked, who acknowledged that the private sector and business community had a role to play and that this was a mixed economy. They did not ignore the role of the state but had a pretty well-informed assessment of the fact that it wasn't necessary for the state to be involved in a whole load of things that it didn't have the capacity, skills or capital for.'[18]

Still, the government's reserves were low and demands on its resources high. The RDP's lofty promises of a developmental state where a million houses would be delivered within five years, while hundreds of thousands of jobs would be created, seemed an impossible ask, given the state of the national accounts.

The so-called post-apartheid dividend, which Jeremy Cronin had described as a type of Marshall Plan for South Africa, also never materialised. And despite adopting the RDP as its overarching policy for a democratic South Africa, the country did not have a clear, sellable macroeconomic framework.

Jürgen Kögl, who was close to Thabo Mbeki and Tito Mboweni, said there was no 'proclaimed economic policy'; that this was 'implied'. 'There was just, "We have to batten down the hatches to make sure that we can get out of the debt trap and, because of that, then become creditworthy again."'[19]

Trevor Manuel concurred, saying, 'A lot of the policy initiatives hadn't quite been bedded down. Whether it's competitions policy or early BEE stuff, that was pretty nascent ...'[20]

Allister Sparks, the former editor of the *Rand Daily Mail* who in a series of books covered the transition in detail, said the RDP was the nearest the ANC had to an economic policy, but that in fact there was none to implement on day one. And he described the RDP as 'inadequate and problematic' – 'really an election manifesto rather than a systematic set of policy programmes'. It made enormous promises, with the dominant view of 'growth through redistribution' being the guiding ideology.[21]

The RDP's economic section 'was riddled with ambiguities', Sparks wrote. 'While making a raft of promises, the RDP also pledged the government to "avoid undue inflation and balance of payments difficulties". It would redirect government spending rather than increasing it as a proportion of GDP. And while pledging to "pay attention to macro-economic balance", the RDP also promised to "meet the basic needs of the people – jobs, land, housing, water, electricity, communications, healthcare and social welfare".'[22]

Said Spicer, 'The RDP was the last-gasp idealistic attempt at socialism on the part of people like Jay Naidoo. It was quickly seen to be unrealistic. All the idealistic goals of lots of goodies to distribute to everybody, à la the RDP, was not possible. We had to rebalance the economy. We had to pull in our horns and that was politically all very difficult.'[23]

Big capital had hoped the party would adapt to realities (as it saw them) and would be guided by pragmatism instead of hard ideology. This proved a challenge, Spicer said – something the ANC up to 2022 has not been able to move beyond. 'You can't govern without making choices, and the whole point about political economies is that you have limited resources, and politics is about the allocation of those limited resources. This requires you to divert resources into some areas and away from others. And inside this process, you have all these vested interests, including big business.'[24]

Kingston said there were four significant concerns about the new government from the perspective of big capital and foreign investors during 1994 and 1995. The first was whether the new national executive was able to govern. The ANC had never run anything and had no record at any level of governance; its leaders were largely unknown to the public and remained difficult to gauge among business and investors. No one knew what would happen. 'There was no reason why anyone would assume that Trevor Manuel was capable of being the minister of trade and industry. This concern, as it turns out, was misplaced, and I believe they had better capacity in 1994, 1995 and 1996 than they have today.'[25]

The second big issue remained the dominant influence the SACP continued to have on the strategic thinking of the ANC and, by extension, the new government. 'They provided much greater thought leadership than they do now, and disproportionate thought leadership relative to the ANC, in my view.' A concern was that the SACP would significantly influence ideology, 'because they went hand-in-glove with the statist view that they could run everything, which they manifestly couldn't,' said Kingston.[26]

The third big concern was the rise of crime and corruption. 'At the time there wasn't an acknowledgement that the private sector was anything other than an enabler of resources to flow to the state. I'd spent a lot of time in some very insalubrious countries, like the former Soviet Union and other parts of Africa or parts of Latin America or parts of Asia, and in my head, South Africa was never going to go down that route.' What happened in reality, said Kingston, is that 'not only did we go down that route, but we've outdone them all. There's a level of crime and corruption that I consider to be completely systemic.'[27]

Kingston's fourth and biggest concern about the future of the young democracy that was South Africa in 1994 was the legacy of apartheid. In hindsight, Kingston said, there was a naivety about how the country would change, and would have to change. The naive belief that 'the future was going to be rosy' was, for a period, 'exacerbated and magnified by the post-1994 halo effect. The halo effect wasn't just Mandela, although he was a personification of the halo effect. But we were accorded significance way beyond our status, we punched above our weight, we were admitted to the G20 [Group of Twenty intergovernmental forum that works to address major issues related to the global economy], accorded special privileges … There was a disproportionate level of focus and attention on us. South Africa was connected in ways that almost no other countries were connected. I was concerned that the fissures in the country would be masked for too long by this halo effect, because many of the fissures [that remain prevalent today] were already there.'[28]

Trevor Manuel, having helped to write the RDP and been in conversation with big capital since 1990, was clear about the most urgent and pressing courses of action the new government had to take. Chief among them was establishing domestic and international credibility. 'When I think back to my first few years at the department of trade and industry, part of what we had to do was to take the country onto the global map, and to use the Mandela presence to do that.

We had to persuade investment in South Africa, and to try and get past the apartheid isolation,' he said.[29]

This required conversations with 'several constituencies simultaneously' and building trust. The new South African government had to convince the world market that it could be a predictable and dependable investment destination, and that it would manage the country's finances prudently and responsibly.

Manuel explains the SARB's efforts at 'defending the rand' in the 1990s as a major test for the country's new leaders, both internally and externally. (Defending a currency refers to monetary or policy interventions made by a government to artificially prop up a currency, like buying or selling foreign reserves.) Internally, the government had to draw a line in the sand and ensure that the central bank understood its role, and externally it had to transmit that it could make difficult decisions – and stick to them.

Manuel explained the difficulty the new government faced, including having to deal with the SARB's purchasing of foreign currency to fund payments for imports (the net open forward position). 'We started out with negative reserves because of the net open forward position, and before you could build up reserves, you had to get rid of that $25 billion [in foreign currency the SARB had bought]. And no sooner had you done it, by 1997, and the SARB tried to defend the rand and borrowed ... and it built up a new net open forward position of $27 billion.

'Now, that stuff is not insignificant. You see, the SARB had used reserves to try and defend the currency. And the background is that George Soros was known to have bankrupted the Bank of England because he drew them into the market to defend the pound, and he was just taking money as fast as they were throwing money at it.' Manuel was referring to Britain's 'Black Wednesday' on 16 September 1992, now known as the day when speculators – hedge-fund manager Soros among them – 'broke the pound' by 'shorting' it (selling it, with the intention of repurchasing it later at a lower price), after the government had tried to artificially buoy the pound by raising interest rates.

'And so, the idea that you could use reserves, especially reserves you didn't have, to defend the currency, wasn't the smartest approach. It was one thing that we needed to deal with, and at that time all those international negotiations were done by the SARB rather than by the ministry of finance. The SARB needed to understand that the Constitution gave it instrument independence, not goal independence.'[30] 'Instrument independence' refers to the ability of the SARB to decide what instruments (e.g. inflation rates) it could use to achieve whatever goal government set for it; but it could not pursue goals independently from the government.

Manuel says the ANC government was deeply focused on signalling to the world that it would be a responsible government. He recalls the first global roadshow to sell government bonds in 1994, when new government officials travelled from Japan to the United States. 'The truth of the matter is, it was an incredibly expensive bond which we had to mop up later, and it was expensive because the South African government was new and it didn't have any credibility. It didn't even have a credit line [with international finance institutions]. What we had to do was build trust.'[31]

In building that trust, said Manuel – who was nothing short of livid that much of the trust and credibility that was built up in the early years of democracy was squandered later – these issues of managing the economy responsibly and establishing policy certainty became quite important. 'You must understand that trust is important because we know what happens when you put into the ministry of finance people like Des van Rooyen [a little-known ANC backbencher who was appointed minister of finance by Jacob Zuma in 2015, and who lasted only four days in the position, but cost the country dearly when the rand lost value and an estimated R500 billion was lost on the markets] and Malusi Gigaba [minister of finance from February 2018 to November 2019, during which time he was a pivotal character in the spider's web of state-owned enterprises caught up in state capture during Zuma's administration]. Trust must then be built *ab initio* [from the beginning] ... and the people who you're trying to rebuild trust with are saying, "We've given it to you before, and you screwed it up."'[32]

Jay Naidoo and Jeremy Cronin were up against it. Cosatu and the SACP had held a firm line that they wanted to see a social-democratic/socialist macroeconomic policy implemented when the ANC took power, but had seen these hopes dealt a fatal blow in the period between Mandela's release from prison in 1990 and his election as president in 1994. Mandela went from saying in 1990 that 'nationalisation ... is the fundamental policy of the ANC and it is inconceivable that it will ever change this policy'[33] to declaring, on the eve of the election in 1994, that the RDP contained 'not a single reference to nationalisation ... not a single slogan that will connect us with Marxist ideology'.[34]

The ANC, having championed massive state intervention for decades based on the Freedom Charter it adopted in 1955, was effectively abandoning its central economic policy tenets. A fundamental and seismic shift had occurred.

'Big capital won the day in the transition,' said Cronin. 'What we needed to do was to discipline it. But capital had huge power during the negotiations, so we couldn't just take it over and nationalise ... and then the economy was liberalised [deregulated], whether it was agricultural boards, exchange controls, and so on. A whole range of things that the apartheid regime in crisis had used to discipline capital for the system to survive, like prescribed assets [the apartheid government prescribed to pension funds where they were allowed to invest, including in government bonds], all of those were kind of progressively – and often quite aggressively – abandoned. And this led to huge capital outflows, some of it legal and huge amounts of it not so legal, lots of tax evasion, or, if not evasion, then creative tax arrangements that enabled it.

'That's why during the lead-up to 1994 there was a big debate around what the essence was of the RDP. Was it growth through redistribution, or growth first and then redistribution?'[35]

Cronin said there was consensus on how much work would need to be done: 'Between Trevor Manuel and myself, there was no disagreement that there was a huge need to address the housing crisis, the employment crisis, the water crisis, and so on. But what we needed to determine was: is it growth as the overriding priority, or is it growth as a priority, but with a genuine attempt at redistribution, a different kind of growth which was of a more redistributive kind?'[36]

Jay Naidoo, rejecting that there was any form of 'selling out the revolution', said there were many agendas at play. With what he said was 'clear alignment' between global capital, the British banks, the financial sector and the mining conglomerates like Anglo American, he contended that the union movement had to help ensure that an agreement could be reached between 'a powerful section of the ANC' and capital. 'One must accept that we were at a very fragile moment. I don't think any of the [macroeconomic] proposals from Cosatu threatened to cause chaos: we had to have a fiscal policy, we had to have a monetary policy, we had to have discussed the position and the independence of the SARB. Clearly, to all of us, the apartheid state was bankrupt ... And that's why Cosatu supported the negotiations process. People said, "Well, you supported the sell-out." But I keep saying to people, "What's the sense of a union movement that doesn't engage in negotiations?" That purist form of unionism would have meant that there were no negotiations.'[37]

Still, both Cronin and Naidoo lamented the subjugation of the left before, during and after 1994 by Thabo Mbeki and Trevor Manuel. Cronin said there was no 'heterodox [conservative] macroeconomic policy that had been able to stand the test of time', and that the language of development economics came 'too late' to the ANC. The new governing party paid insufficient attention to transforming the productive side of the economy and failed to link education and training to it, for example. 'What were our priorities? Those were all difficult discussions. And, of course, you had Spicer and Anglo American loudly saying that you can't do this, you can't do that, and that you shouldn't interfere with the economy and must leave it to the market. So, essentially and at an institutional level, the loosely called Mbeki-Manuel perspective won out in government. But not without ongoing resistance and battles.'[38]

Naidoo described the frustration he'd felt with the ANC since before its unbanning, with the organisation's reluctance to properly engage with macroeconomics, and its refusal to initiate an economic negotiations process to run parallel with the constitutional negotiation process. 'Even Keys, while he was the [apartheid] government's finance minister, agreed to it. It was blocked by a section of the ANC, which felt that negotiations on the future of the economy had to be left in the hands of a democratic government, which in many ways meant left in the hands of the ANC,' he said.[39]

Almost 30 years on, Manuel confirmed much of what Cronin and Naidoo said: the new government was never going to implement any leftist or radically interventionist economic policy. 'We weren't going to nationalise, and the RDP indeed took a very different approach. We needed to stabilise the country and the economy,' he said.[40]

One of the very first interventions the ANC government had to make was in laying down competition policy – and breaking up the conglomerates. This, Manuel said, was needed to address the 'distortions' in the market resulting from capital accumulation and the structure of the JSE.

Referring to Robin McGregor's *Who Owns Whom* economic handbook of South Africa from that period, Manuel quotes some figures as examples. 'In 1990, Anglo American controlled 44.2 per cent of the JSE, Sanlam 13.2 per cent, SA Mutual 10.2 per cent, Rembrandt 13.6 per cent, and so on .... If you took the profile of SA Breweries then, you would find [that it owned] two shoe factories, you would find furniture factories, you would find OK Bazaars as a chain store, and a whole myriad of things. If you looked at Anglo American, they owned the Ford plant, they owned the Mazda plant, they owned large tracts of land for agriculture … you could just run on and on and on with what they were doing.'[41]

Part of what they were hoping to do, said Manuel, 'was to speak to these companies, persuade them that competition meant giving up on some stuff'. 'Early in the process we tried to convince them to give up some of these things, and to try and focus. It was a complex issue, and there were amazing stand-offs.'[42]

He recalled one specific confrontation between himself and Spicer. On the day of a conference about competition laws, Manuel first attended a meeting at the omnipresent Carlton Hotel – the site of many crucial engagements before and after the arrival of democracy. 'And at the hotel I stumbled onto a caucus of business leaders, including Anglo's Spicer and Barlow's chief economist Pieter Haasbroek. These guys were holding court and basically sitting there and strategising how they were going to put us in our place, that they didn't want competition law to feature … They wouldn't let up on it.'[43]

At the subsequent conference, a proposal was put forward detailing how the conglomerates could be broken up. Spicer, Manuel said, 'was very, very angry' and rejected the new trade minister's ideas. According to Manuel, Spicer said, 'This minister said he wants to break up, dismember and tear Anglo American apart, limb by limb. We won't let him. And I need to say to him that ministers have a very short shelf life in South Africa!'[44]

'Mike couldn't have been more wrong,'[45] Manuel recalled, although it was unclear whether he was referring to the unbundling of Anglo or his own longevity as a cabinet minister.

Spicer laughed about the incident and said Manuel was 'quite hot on the subject' in 1994. But, he added, fighting about competition policy was by and large about the only 'sparring' they had. Spicer credited the then-minister of trade and industry with quickly getting his head around the country's economic problems. 'He used that type of language, that we'll be torn "limb from limb", in the beginning, but he soon became much more circumspect.'[46]

The new government was determined to transform the economy and ensure larger black participation, and competition law became one of its most powerful instruments to diversify ownership in the economy. Ultimately, this created business opportunities. So, despite Spicer's initial resistance, big capital saw the opportunities that spinning off non-core assets presented.

Describing the conglomerates as 'just all over the place, and highly inefficient', Manuel pointed out that 'part of the move in competition was to compel [the big conglomerates] to focus, and as they focused, there were then business opportunities'.[47]

This created the first empowerment opportunities – it would be good for business to sell assets to black investors, because it would insulate capital from state intervention. It would also be good for a company like Anglo's balance sheet, because it would enable it to invest in core operations, and it would give black businessmen a chance.

The chance for a few politically connected members of the new elite had arrived. And billions of rands were to be made.

The pact between big capital and the ANC was about to pay off.

13

Betrayal and the end of the RDP

'The RDP was about fundamentally recalibrating the economic and social framework of the country. It created tension, because already finance was becoming the powerhouse of cabinet. So from Keys to Liebenberg to Manuel, and it was clear to me what agenda started dominating the ANC government.'

– Jay Naidoo, then minister in the presidency
in charge of the RDP.[1]

On Thursday 28 March 1996, President Nelson Mandela stood up in the National Assembly chamber and told the house that he needed to make some announcements. It had been just over a year since Chris Liebenberg had accepted the job of finance minister, and democratic South Africa seemed to be on a more even keel.

Mandela, not unaccustomed to theatrics, toyed with the parliamentarians who waited with bated breath. 'Oh, I'm so thirsty, I need some water,' he said at the podium before launching into his speech.[2]

'He announced that I would become the minister of finance, with Gill [Marcus] as my deputy,' Manuel recalled. 'Alec [Erwin] would become minister of trade and industry; Pallo Jordan got dropped from

138

cabinet and Jay Naidoo walked across to the ministry of post and telecommunications.'[3]

Mandela's announcement was huge. With Liebenberg's retirement, Manuel's appointment to the country's exchequer signalled that the ANC not only had confidence in him, but enough confidence in itself to set its own course – and that it believed that society (and the markets) would be able to accept an economic and fiscal path charted by the former liberation movement.

Liebenberg and his deputy, Erwin, a member of the SACP's central committee, had formed a good working relationship with each other, to the point that Liebenberg had told his wife they were so close as far as policy was concerned that he believed himself to be a communist too.[4] The former Nedcor chief executive had taken the job with the proviso that he would be free to pursue market-friendly policies with tight fiscal controls, and Mandela had left him to it.[5]

Liebenberg had been an acceptable face to the investment community, said Kingston, noting that both Mandela and Mbeki were awake to the sort of people needed to drive economic policy. 'The ANC took a fully pragmatic view to endear itself to, rather than alienate, capital providers. It doesn't matter whether Chris was a good or bad finance minister, he was an acceptable face and he tried hard.'[6]

Doug Band, in the Anglo fold as chairman of the Premier Group at the time, agreed that the ANC's approach across the transition years was sensible – but, he added, 'the irony, from a historical perspective, is that [Keys and Liebenberg] weren't particularly successful as ministers of finance, principally because they had no political constituency.'[7]

Mandela also announced that the RDP office would closed. This came as a massive shock to the left, and especially to Naidoo as the minister in the presidency in charge of the RDP.

The RDP office was never foreseen to be a 'command office' or 'command centre', like in the USSR, said Naidoo. It was envisaged to be a planning office that would help to shape the new government's policy priorities. So Naidoo's office used the RDP fund, set by

Derek Keys at R3 billion, to help various government departments redesign their budgets and departmental programmes to align with the RDP's goals and outcomes, whether it was in housing, sanitation, education or health. Ministers could apply for support from the RDP fund if they could build a business case for a project and if they recalibrated their budget accordingly.

But, said Naidoo, 'The fund really was not the main thing for me. I put in a set of procedures where, if you wanted money from the RDP, you had to demonstrate that you were restructuring the budget, based on a new policy framework that you would have to develop, arising out of the RDP. As minister, you had to change your policy framework, introduce a new law that you would put into place for delivering housing, social grants, whatever. And then you could access the RDP fund to bring in new programmes that would take us closer to the implementation of the RDP.'[8]

The RDP office could therefore not allocate funds to departments. However, the RDP fund could be used for specific projects.

But Manuel said the RDP office was problematic because 'it existed as a kind of super-ministry to tell other ministries, "You do this, and you do that," and there was no supporting budget.'[9] There were too many contradictions for the RDP programme to work as originally envisaged, he said. All the slogans that were printed on posters ahead of the election – most notably those that promised 'jobs, jobs, jobs!' – had to be turned into action. 'How we were going to deliver it was a big, big issue.'[10]

Naidoo had an enormous task as a minister without portfolio to convince and cajole ministers to commit to the RDP and to amend policies in line with the ANC's pre-election objectives. 'I was simultaneously turning the RDP from an election manifesto into a policy of the government of national unity, establishing the office with new people, and bringing together various parties so that they could agree how to make the RDP, which gave the ANC its majority at the election, a programme of government,' he said.[11]

But the RDP's grand promises – houses and jobs – were proving difficult to fulfil. And a fundamental shift, which had been underway for some years, was now gaining traction.

Despite the assurances from Mandela that the RDP would be the ANC-in-government's lodestar, and that it would be implemented across the state, Naidoo had very quickly started to feel isolated, and had struggled to enlist the support of his colleagues on the national executive. In fact, he said, he got more support from political opponents like the NP's Roelf Meyer and IFP leader Mangosuthu Buthelezi than he did from ANC ministers.[12]

Naidoo said that he believes, in retrospect, that his inclusion in cabinet in charge of the RDP, which was the only overarching policy programme that the new government had, 'must have caused enormous reaction' behind the scenes.[13] Thabo Mbeki had taken complete charge of economic policy, with Mandela 'not very keen nor able in that department',[14] and Naidoo said that despite his position as Cosatu's most senior representative in the tripartite alliance and RDP minister, he was never part of events in the background that shaped outcomes. He points, as examples, to an $850-million loan agreement with the IMF (agreed to in 1993 by the De Klerk government and the ANC, after much wrangling and hand-wringing), 'the discussions about people from our ranks being taken for training at places like the World Bank, the role of Goldman Sachs and so forth ... Maria Ramos is studying in London, and then gets a position as deputy director-general at the department of finance. And then [after 1994] you have the emergence of the RDP office that was looking at cross-cutting policy functions across government ...'[15]

Naidoo believed the mandate of the RDP office was a threat to others, including deputy president Thabo Mbeki. A section of the ANC, chief among which was the then-deputy president, thought he and the RDP office's role was 'unacceptable', he said, and that there was 'a deep suspicion' of his role as a unionist – especially given Cosatu's stated independence from the ANC.

Within a year of taking office, it became clear to Naidoo that the RDP wasn't being taken seriously by his government. The ANC was no longer adhering to the economic and redistributive beliefs it had held four short years before. 'It doesn't take a rocket scientist to know that you have no political backing for it, [that you are] swimming against the tide,' he said. The left's point of departure, that society and the economy must be reformed by prioritising redistribution, had been discarded. And that conflict was at the centre of why the RDP office was closed down, and why Naidoo eventually left government. 'While in charge of the RDP, I still argued that our approach was growth through redistribution, because that's the model we agreed on and that was at the core of the RDP. And that was the clash, because in fact the new government believed in redistribution through growth. That was the difference, and that's where the schism is within the ANC.'[16]

When the RDP office was shuttered, the 'key policy challenge', according to Manuel, was for the line function departments, like housing or water affairs, to take over the RDP's responsibilities as soon as possible. He was honest in his assessment that the task was enormous, and that the government of the day struggled to keep a hand on all the tillers. 'When you're dealing with a transition as massive as the arrival of democracy in South Africa, it didn't always work very well, and we often didn't have the administrative capability to deal with these things. Bear in mind that at the same time, we were trying to set up nine new provinces, and the way in which the Constitution was constructed … a lot of these responsibilities were concurrent. Consequently, how you resourced them, how you got the policy concurrence, how you got all those things right, became a very particular challenge.'[17]

In mid-1995, travelling abroad to hawk a new issue of South African government bonds, Alec Erwin, Jay Naidoo and Maria Ramos (then deputy director-general in the department of finance) had been caught flat-footed by international investors who asked about the country's macroeconomic direction. 'They weren't interested in hearing you waffle on about all sorts of things. The RDP talks about macro-economic balance, but we had such imprecise answers we couldn't deal with the questions properly because they'd know we were talking crap,' said Erwin.[18]

So a group of economists, under the political protection of Erwin and from inside and outside government, started working on a new macroeconomic policy. This policy, the Growth, Employment and Redistribution strategy, or GEAR, was to become the flashpoint of the biggest political conflict in post-apartheid South Africa – a conflict whose repercussions continue to be felt to this day.

Meanwhile, the South Africa Foundation drew up a proposal in which it implored government to adopt a formal and strict macro-economic framework. The Foundation had been established in 1959 by business and the government working together, to counter the ANC's message advocating for sanctions, and had evolved into a business formation representing big capital.

Spicer said that when the Foundation's Growth for All plan was presented to Thabo Mbeki in March 1996, it didn't go down well, and was taken as patronising. The ANC firmly rejected it, saying that the plan ran the risk 'of pushing our country backwards in a number of respects and the policy proposals contained therein could be a recipe for disaster if they were ever to be adopted by any South African government'. It called proposals around privatisation 'ideologically driven and unlikely to be implemented', labelled labour proposals 'ridiculous', and accused the overall document of being an attempt at 'shifting economic policy to the right wing'.[19]

But Spicer said that business just wanted to see action, and that the new government was reluctant to take it. 'The conundrum was that the whole culture of the movement in exile was to talk. There was no imperative to *do*, and so coming back, part of the culture shock was, "Well, now you're expected to do,' and the propensity of this movement was always to fall back on talking.'[20]

And the role of business was changing. It had taken a strong position since the mid-1980s in trying to influence change in the country and to facilitate contact with the ANC, but with the arrival of democracy and the installation of a legitimate, democratic government, big capital had to start getting back in the game. The open, global market demanded greater efficiency, and changing labour and social relations had to be addressed. 'We became much less absorbed by political issues,' said Spicer.[21]

In March 1995, the CBM and the Urban Foundation were merged into a new body called the National Business Initiative (NBI). Theuns Eloff, who had run the CBM and helped manage the secretariat at Codesa and the MPNF, explained that although business went 'back to business', there was a strong feeling that capital couldn't merely walk away. 'Even after the CBM did its job in helping with bringing people together before 1994, facilitating the peace process and the subsequent negotiations, many in business felt we couldn't simply leave these guys.' Eloff believed the measure of trust that had been established before 1994 enabled business to maintain its relationship with the ANC government.[22]

The NBI, like the CBM, was an expression of the desire by business to work with the government, Eloff said; its purpose was to 'enhance business's contribution to growth, development and democracy … by promoting increased economic growth, reducing poverty and socioeconomic inequality, and supporting effective and efficient governance'.[23] Its constituent members, including individuals and companies, were able to mobilise money, resources, skills and support for the new government.

The most important things the NBI did, said Eloff, was to establish the Business Trust and Business Against Crime.

For the Business Trust, big business came together and pledged a percentage of their market value. 'You can imagine how much it was, given, for example, what Anglo was worth,' Eloff said.[24]

A turnaround for the tourism sector was devised, and 'we also focused on a thousand schools and tried to implement a mathematics and English programme. So great was the dysfunctionality in schools, however, that five years in, the R500-million programme folded.'[25]

The relationships between business leaders and the ANC had been established over many, many hours of negotiations, discussions and often deep arguments, said Spicer, and business consciously cultivated them so that there could always be open channels of communication. 'Something that is under-reported and under-appreciated is the hundreds of hours that senior chief executives gave … It was hours and hours of dealing with things like tourism. They dealt with things that normal businesspeople would never deal with, like how to develop reading programmes that would lift the literacy rate. Pat Davies, the chief executive of Sasol, personally spent hours and hours and hours working on that; he contributed a substantial amount of money and got to grips with the problem. I remember travelling around the country with him to all these damn meetings. He put the time in, he did the long miles …'[26]

Eloff cited Business Against Crime's biggest success as the campaign to force the government to ensure that the vehicle identification numbers (VINs) of cars were engraved into the engines, to clamp down on rampant vehicle theft.[27]

Doug Band, who led a process to help modernise the police, recalled that the initial relationship between Business Against Crime and the government was good. 'I found the attitude of the ANC people and their delegates extremely positive and extremely engaging. And we could agree and disagree on a number of issues, but it was always cordial, and it was always respectful.'[28]

Band said the South African Police Service had become 'completely dysfunctional'. 'It didn't know that its fleet of cars had dwindled to around 20 per cent that were serviceable and on the road. Systems were nonexistent.'[29]

One of the early decisions they took, he said, was to recommend bringing in someone from the private sector to try and restore some financial and administrative control. 'We proposed a couple of names to Mbeki, who was deputy president at the time, but he smiled and said he and Mandela had someone else in mind: Meyer Kahn of SA Breweries. I told him I couldn't see Meyer under any circumstances agreeing to that, and he said we'd be surprised to see what Mandela's power of persuasion is like.'

Kahn was indeed convinced to take the job, although he was unfairly pilloried for failing to reform the police, said Band. 'He was never intended to be the top cop; that was [George] Fivaz's job. He was, however, equipped to sort out a lot of the mess, and he achieved a hell of a lot in a short space of time.'[30]

Mandela's new finance minister Manuel, who took office on 6 April 1996, was already aware of the team 'working day and night' to finalise the new macroeconomic programme – GEAR. Coordinated by Andre Roux from the Development Bank of Southern Africa and Iraj Abedian, economist at the University of Cape Town, the small task team included academics, economists from the World Bank and representatives from the SARB.[31]

'The South African economy had a big problem because of our balance of payments constraints,' Manuel recalls.[32] Balance of payments constraints refers to, among other things, the difference between exports and imports. In the South African scenario, this seemed to suggest that the economy couldn't grow at more than three and a quarter of a percentage point. 'Now you've got to sit down and work through this thing, because the macroeconomic problem is not going to disappear. We don't have adequate savings. We can't borrow. We need to communicate and we're grappling with this because there's no road map here. You must work through all of it, and you must apply the knowledge you have, and you must be clear about who's in the tent and who's not in the tent,' Manuel said.

'It was an unhealthy set of circumstances, which had built up over many years, and what you needed to do was to clean up all of this. So, I knew of the [GEAR] task team's work, and now I had to drill it in, and try and understand what the hell they were talking about.'[33]

That wasn't his only challenge: according to his biographer, journalists actively sought to embarrass the new finance minister, second-guessing him and asking him to explain economic terms and concepts.[34] 'I'm addressing the media after this conference about donor funding, and I get asked a question by the late Greta Steyn [then a journalist on *Business Day*]. "Now that you're the minister of finance, when are you going to lift exchange controls?" she asks. And I'm very smart and I say, "Greta, who wants to know?" And she said the market. I said, "Greta, you're telling me the market sent you?" She said yes, I'm telling you that. So, I said to Greta, "The market is amorphous, how did it send you?"'[35]

But Manuel's remark backfired when it was used to show how little he apparently knew about economics and finance.

It was a rough start for the ANC's first post-apartheid finance minister. He was taking over a department that was putting together a new macroeconomic framework that was sure to rile the left and the ANC's alliance partners. And the 'amorphous markets' reacted poorly to his appointment, with the rand immediately shedding two per cent of its value, and losing more than nine per cent in the following month.[36]

The finalisation of GEAR and its announcement as the macro-economic policy of the government of South Africa was one of the most significant moments in this country's history. Although imperfect, it was emblematic of the Mandela government's best intentions to have the country establish itself as a modern, well-run industrial democracy, given the constraints and realities of South Africa's history.

But it set in motion events that would lead to fundamental and irreconcilable divisions in the governing party, with the conflict between proponents and opponents of GEAR eventually leading to the rise of Jacob Zuma and the era of state capture.

The final shift away from the ANC-in-exile's dreams of a Freedom Charter implemented in a liberated South Africa, to a market-friendly and liberal economic system, also enabled the rise of a new class of ANC cadres, connected to the governing party and desirous of the opportunities that big capital presented.

There was money to be made. Lots of it.

14

The new South Africa accepts new rules

'What we weren't going to do, what we were not
going to do, was to treat this like wage-bargaining
negotiations. We weren't going to propose a three per cent
budget deficit, and then Cosatu says it wants a six per cent
deficit, and then we settle on a deficit of 4.5 per cent.'

– Trevor Manuel, minister of finance 1996–2009.[1]

On 14 June 1996, Trevor Manuel tabled GEAR in parliament as
South Africa's macroeconomic policy.

'What options are open to government?' asked the 25-page document containing the fundamentals of the ANC government's chosen
policy direction. 'An expansionary fiscal strategy could be considered.
However, even under the most favourable circumstances, this would
only give a short-term boost to growth since it would reproduce the
historical pattern of cyclical growth and decline ... Without attention to more deep-rooted reforms, there is no possibility of sustainable
accelerated growth.'[2]

The limited choices were set out in stark detail. Massive spending
was clearly not realistic, and GEAR prioritised economic growth as
the point of departure. Without economic growth, premised on stable
fiscal and monetary policies, the expansion of state and private-sector

investment, accelerated non-gold exports and increased infrastructure development, none of the country's developmental goals 'set [out] in the Reconstruction and Development Programme' could be attained.

South Africa, GEAR said, needed to focus on budget reform, seek to reduce the fiscal deficit faster, relax exchange controls, reduce tariffs, introduce tax incentives to stimulate new investment and speed up the restructuring of state assets, among other measures. The country would also follow a 'consistent monetary policy to prevent a resurgence of inflation' and show 'a commitment to the implementation of stable and coordinated policies'.[3]

It was a bold statement of intent by Manuel, Mandela, Mbeki and the ANC leadership. It signalled that the government was taking a long-term view and that it was prepared to play by the rules that governed the globalised economy – a far cry from the statist and isolationist approach that had characterised the ANC's policies before and shortly after 1990. And it opened the economy to competition, linked it to the vagaries and uncertainties of global financial markets and money flows, and firmly moved away from populist economic policies.

The ANC was now leading a country that had to survive in the modern, ruthless and interconnected world that Relly had feared that Tambo and his colleagues did not understand back in 1985, and the environment of modern technology and rapid advancement that Spicer had tried to explain to ANC leaders returning from exile.

Economist Michael Sachs, a former senior official in Manuel's National Treasury, said GEAR showed the then-government's 'commitment to fiscal prudence'.[4] The policy 'implied a new approach to engagement with the party militants, trade unions and civil society groups that constituted the ANC's broader activist base', he argued.[5] 'GEAR's fiscal objectives were to cut the budget deficit, avoid permanent increases in the overall tax burden, reduce public consumption spending on goods and services, and raise government's contribution to fixed investment in infrastructure. A rebalancing in the composition of government expenditure would reduce the sum of wages, transfers, and the procurement of goods and services by three percentage points of GDP by the year 2000, to enable an increase in RDP-related capital spending.'[6]

The IMF's managing director at the time, Michel Camdessus, later wrote that the IMF did not harbour much faith that the government would embrace fiscal prudence and conservatism. 'History did not provide much basis for hope that a democratically elected government in Africa would take a long-term view and give precedence to financial stability and policy sustainability.'[7]

GEAR was a decisive blow to the left, which had had so much influence on the ANC during its years in exile. There was going to be no profligate expenditure programmes, no nationalisation and no massive programme of redistribution.

Spicer, who as a senior representative of capital had been lobbying for a liberal and market-friendly macroeconomic policy for years, said the unions and SACP weren't fans of GEAR: 'They really, really hated it.' The ANC's alliance partners had always wanted a democratic government to steer away from the Bretton Woods institutions' economic systems and policies – the so-called Washington Consensus, which denotes a set of international economic guidelines. Rather, they had clamoured for a strong and interventionist state and agitated for redistribution through spending – 'Much more tax and more spend, the classic sort of left stuff,' Spicer said.[8]

GEAR finally put paid to that, and this 'led to a crescendo of criticism'.[9]

The outcry from the left was rooted in the belief that it had been formulated without proper consultation with alliance and social partners, that it had happened in secret and away from prying eyes, and that representatives of big capital had had much more say in it than the grassroots – the people who had suffered under apartheid and exclusion.

Critics of GEAR contended that 'secret' meetings at the Development Bank of Southern Africa were evidence of the cloak-and-dagger nature of the process, and that the leadership of the country was unaware of this.[10]

Shortly before GEAR was finalised, Mandela convened a meeting at his house to discuss the matter with the angry alliance partners, followed by a meeting at Shell House, the ANC's headquarters at the time. And cabinet was only informed on the morning of GEAR's tabling in parliament.[11] According to SACP luminary Ben Turok, ANC parliamentarians were ushered into a committee room, where Manuel told them about the country's new macroeconomic policy, and that 'some questions' were allowed but that they weren't allowed a copy of the policy document for fear of leaks.[12]

Jay Naidoo felt blindsided – he hadn't been aware a new macroeconomic policy was being prepared and was only informed shortly before it was announced; the policy-making process, he said, was 'parallel and conducted somewhere else'. 'GEAR emerged out of nowhere,' he said. 'No one understood it. And it looked like it was a secret negotiation beyond the constitutional structures of either cabinet, or the ANC itself, or the tripartite alliance. Where did it come from?'[13]

Jeremy Cronin said the announcement of GEAR made him feel as if the left had lost the battle – but, he said, initially the SACP cautiously welcomed the new policy. 'I was responsible for the SACP's immediate response, as I'm still reminded of it by the left and ultra-left, and we sort of half-welcomed it. And that lasted for a couple of weeks. A front page of *Umsebenzi* [the SACP news journal] at the time, for which I was also responsible, basically said, "Let's give it a chance."'[14]

Like Naidoo, however, for Cronin there was a feeling of a fait accompli to the whole thing: 'The thing is, before GEAR there was room for discussion when there were problems and differences. But when GEAR was announced, it was written in stone.'[15]

Rob Davies said GEAR was developed 'very much in line with the recommendations of proponents of the Washington Consensus' at the time. 'Reform' was held to be a process that was susceptible to being blown off course by 'populist' pressures, he said, so 'the recommended role of "reformist leadership" was thus not to consult with constituencies in advance, but rather [to] develop policy in narrow technocratic circles and then "sell" it to the broader public. GEAR's development had all the hallmarks of this approach.'[16]

But Manuel says the government was determined not to go cap in hand to international finance institutions and wanted to be master of its own fate. And that demanded a homegrown policy solution, not one forced on it from abroad.[17] Democratic South Africa was extremely averse to the overtures of the IMF to consider a borrowing arrangement. The IMF had tried hard to cultivate a relationship with the ANC before 1994, believing that it would play a leading role in a future democratic government, and that, given the inequality and service delivery backlogs, the country would soon apply for IMF financing. An IMF mission to South Africa in late 1993 calculated that 'to equalise government spending on social services for all race groups at the level enjoyed by whites would require a budget increase of 11 per cent of GDP. Clearly, this would be impossible to finance.'[18]

Camdessus wrote that when the ANC took power, he was convinced 'more than ever' that South Africa would seek the IMF's help. But it didn't happen. Towards the end of 1996, as the country's finances continued to deteriorate, Camdessus went to see Mandela in Johannesburg and offered a loan facility to the government – which he said Mandela accepted but the ANC vetoed. 'Although the country's social and financial needs would continue for years, South Africa would forgo all further borrowing from the IMF.'[19] South Africa did not want any help from Bretton Woods institutions.

In preparing the policy document, amid a worsening economic climate and pressure building up, Manuel said they had had to determine who would support the policy change – and who would not. The conceptualisation of GEAR, the way in which it was formulated, the decision-making process behind it and how it was communicated to stakeholders within the governing alliance (the ANC, Cosatu and the SACP) remain a source of conflict to this day.

The policy design team was first introduced to Manuel at the Development Bank of Southern Africa shortly after he became finance minister, and they spent May 1996 working 'late into the night' on most days; in the final days, the policy team worked around the clock to finalise the package, including Manuel's speech.[20] 'It was very, very hard work trying to get everything ready, trying to ensure that the numbers could be tested by people who wanted to test them, and trying to ensure that we got the messaging about growth and redistribution right,' said Manuel. And even though 'the numbers weren't very clear', he said 'there was a lot of trust in the way in which we got there', referring to the work of the technical team.[21]

This positive assessment wasn't universally held. Some critics say that the ANC economics team – including Mbeki, Manuel, Erwin and technical support staff like Ramos – were 'caught off-guard by events, unevenly trained in modern economic theory and policy, somewhat poorly prepared, inexperienced, possibly daunted by the mathematics, the budgeting process, the accounting' and that 'this led to them being intellectually seduced in comfortable surroundings and eventually outmanoeuvred by the well-resourced apartheid state and by local pro-market friendly actors.'[22]

According to his biography, Mbeki and his economic policy ministers agreed to limit consultation with the ANC's allies, fearing leaks and public dissent, which could lead to compromise and further loss of confidence among potential investors.[23] But many opponents of GEAR believed that it was conceived by a small group who were members of the ANC elite, in conjunction with representatives of international financial institutions like the World Bank and the IMF, and that it was a betrayal of the liberation movement's commitment to social spending and alternative economic models. This was especially so because GEAR sought to limit state expenditure and was, in fact, a homegrown 'structural adjustment programme'.

Structural adjustment programmes, which prescribed a set of economic reforms that countries had to follow if they wanted to borrow from the IMF or World Bank, had a very bad reputation in Africa, and were interpreted by many in the continental liberation movements as attempts by the west to subjugate emerging African countries and democracies. They inevitably led to austerity measures, which meant less money to spend on socioeconomic upliftment. And many in the ANC, and the whole of Cosatu and the SACP, were vehemently opposed to a macroeconomic programme aligned to a structural adjustment programme.

But, as amply illustrated, the realities of both South Africa's financial and economic position, and those of the globalised world, did not allow for the new government to pursue the policies for which many lobbied. The post-apartheid 'freedom dividend' in the form of an influx of massive investment hadn't materialised, and the realisation that the RDP was unattainable, and that the ANC government would now have to do what apartheid governments never had to – rein in spending, privatise and reduce the budget deficit – was 'agonising' and 'disillusioned' Mandela.[24] He, along with Mbeki, understood that constructing a democracy on the foundation of apartheid was going to be exceedingly difficult, and that the ANC was going to have to do so within the constraints of the world as it was, not as it should have been.

Manuel, ever since his appointment as head of the ANC's department of economic planning in 1991, had been realistic about where the country found itself. His exposure to big capital, to international finance institutions and, finally, to the state of the national accounts, shaped his views and approach. But while he might have implemented and executed GEAR, it was Thabo Mbeki who was the driving force behind it.

Every single actor in the drama that unfolded in the country after 1990 interviewed for this book identify Mbeki as arguably the most important and consequential figure of the transition years. And considering his position as heir apparent to a septuagenarian president who'd made clear his intention of playing a unifying, non-partisan role, Mbeki took on the responsibility of redesigning the state and crafting policy. And this he did, by all accounts, with a ruthlessness and bloody-mindedness which, 30 years on, looks decidedly quaint in a country where statecraft has become corrupt, unimaginative and staid.

Jürgen Kögl said Mbeki was determined to prove westerners wrong about African democracy and the abilities of an African government to efficiently run a modern – and modernising – economy and society. Everyone in the broad liberation movement negotiated – 'the communists did, the trade unionists did,' said Kögl – but Mbeki never compromised on three issues: BEE, the economy and governance.

He accepted the free-enterprise model to enable economic growth and wealth creation, despite vigorous agitation by the left. 'At a technocratic level, he wanted to show the world that the ANC could run a modern economy according to the textbook. And they did, to the surprise of everybody, while the whole of Western Europe bent the rules with deficits, inflation targeting, sovereign debt ratio to GDP ... On all those things they just didn't give a shit, but Mbeki wanted to do it right.'[25]

If it hadn't been for Mbeki, Manuel would never have had the political space to push through GEAR, said Spicer. 'Mbeki was a tough guy. He ran a proper cabinet, which had cabinet discipline. And when GEAR was announced, Mbeki kept a tight grip on things, even though Jeremy [Cronin] and the unions hated it.'[26]

Manuel confirms the central political role of Mbeki in planning, formulating and implementing GEAR: 'Mbeki was the go-to person in this whole thing, obviously.'[27]

Spicer said there was a definite change in Mbeki's tone and presence from before April 1994, and the first democratic elections, to after May 1994, when the ANC officially formed a government. 'We entered a different era then, with Mbeki and obviously the tripartite alliance, too. Mbeki had his difficulties with the alliance, but he managed relations with an iron fist, and by and large he ran a semi-orthodox economic policy, while he had Cosatu and the SACP constantly chirping. They were not happy at all.'[28]

Naidoo – who noted that at the time 'power effectively sat in the hands of the deputy president; that was the political reality of it'[29] – recalled Mbeki freezing him and the RDP out from the start, while the left, Cronin confirmed, 'were getting hammered by Mbeki'. 'The government was under pressure from big capital, internally as well as externally, saying, "You guys are trying all sorts of things, but what is your macroeconomic fabric?" They weren't convinced South Africa was really biting the bullet.'[30] Mbeki was sure to show them.

In analysing the period over a quarter of a century later, Manuel began by acknowledging, and agreeing with, critics that political consultation with alliance partners fell short of what up until then had been convention. 'I think there wasn't adequate discussion, there wasn't open discussion … but there was discussion,' he said. 'Jeremy [Cronin] has vacillated on this himself, about whether consultation was good enough.'[31]

But then he hammered home that the ANC leadership weren't about to brook dissent in the face of severe economic constraints – that economic policy couldn't be formulated on consensus and committee. 'What we weren't going to do, what we were not going to do, was to treat this like wage-bargaining negotiations! We weren't going to propose a three per cent budget deficit, and then Cosatu says it wants a six per cent deficit, and then we settle on a deficit of 4.5 per cent. You can't deal with a macroeconomic package in that kind of way.'[32]

For his part, Thabo Mbeki was unperturbed by the unhappiness among the alliance partners, and in the face of criticism even declared that people could call him a Thatcherite.[33] He was convinced of the soundness of the new policy direction and displayed 'a belligerence never previously seen in this unconfrontational man'. In fact, two years later, he and Mandela threatened to eject Cosatu and the SACP from the alliance if they continued to resist and reject GEAR.

Naidoo – who by that time had already resolved to leave government after Mandela's term came to an end in 1999 – said GEAR was a continuation of the way in which the ANC engaged in the economy and engaged with its alliance partners. 'In the 1980s there was a reluctance, and sometimes an unwillingness, to engage on future economic policy. And it continued when they didn't want to engage in debating the national economic forum, a process we wanted as a counterpart to Codesa. Their reluctance certainly came up during talks about the RDP,' he said. The ANC, according to Naidoo, wanted to formulate policy alone, and only once in government.

Manuel remained resolute that the policy direction chosen under Mandela and Mbeki was the correct one, despite how it turned out. He said GEAR was but one part of an effort to reconfigure and reconstruct the state, redesign the country and implement a new institutional culture in the public service – 'to induce a system of trying to build government efficiency'. And it demanded policy clarity and fortitude. 'I have done a few different things in my life, but never have I worked as hard as I worked as minister of finance. Just hard, hard, hard, every single day … it's incredibly thankless.'[34]

Because GEAR demanded fiscal constraint – basically, keeping a check on government expenditure – it provided the opportunity for government to introduce new policies. One of the biggest changes that the new government made – and Manuel said it is one of Mandela's most lasting legacies – was the introduction of the Public Finance Management Act of 1999.

The purpose of the Act was, Manuel said, to establish governance systems that 'controlled and contained' public expenditure. 'Now, you need to consider the fact that we allowed health expenditure to increase, [and we also] equalised social grants, and we introduced the child support grant while we were tightening fiscal constraints. So, it wasn't as though we imposed a kind of hardship on everybody, our focus was going to be on efficiency.

'We also understood that among the biggest risks we faced was the fact that the biggest employers were the provinces, and we needed to keep a tight leash on the provinces. We had to improve our systems so that the ministers and the MECs [provincial ministers] could see what was happening in every province, on a monthly basis, so we could contain expenditure.'[35]

And then the rest of the macroeconomic alignment 'started coming right', Manuel said: 'We started feeling the change by about 1998 and 1999. We didn't see all of the positives until 2000, give or take. It's not a light switch you throw, it's a process of managing change and building trust.'[36]

By 2007, Manuel's eleventh year as finance minister, South Africa had a budget surplus – the country had more money in the bank than it had spent.

But not everything that the new government tried to do worked in the long run, and Manuel cited the fact that government departments were given control over human resources and supply-chain management as two interventions that had 'terrible' consequences. 'Part of the modernisation of the state entailed giving departments control over those areas which they deemed important. Of course, now, human resources with cadre deployment and supply chain management, which unleashed a generation of tenderpreneurs, is the terrible underbelly of those modernisation plans.

'There was a measure of organisation and control, but it was very, very difficult running the ship that way [by giving departments more control]. And when things started going bad, they went bad quite quickly.'[37]

PART III

HARVEST

1996 to present day

15

The origin story of the ANC billionaires

'That was the quid pro quo but it didn't always work out neatly.'

– Michael Spicer, then special assistant to the Anglo American chief executive, explaining that spinning off assets and selling them to black investors was intended to create value for the big corporates and provide a foothold in the economy for blacks.[1]

During the 1970s Harry Oppenheimer had come to realise that South Africa would not be able to continue down the path it was on under John Vorster's National Party. The country's economy was starting to slow down, state repression was on the increase and violence had become part of everyday South African life.

'I would argue that two events in the 1970s made it abundantly clear that the system was not workable,' Bobby Godsell said. 'The first was the rebirth of the black union movement in 1973 in Durban, followed by the 1976 Soweto Uprising. Those two things said the blacks are here and they're not going to go away, and they must be accommodated. The pressure meant that a conceptual understanding was developing that South Africa was not a white country, and that a concept of South Africa had to be developed in which black people could play a responsible and meaningful role.'[2]

Describing the Oppenheimers' 'unusual' credentials ('the unique nature of this particular family, which had made a very deliberate decision to remain in this country from the beginning of the twentieth century and who committed to it, serving in the Second World War, serving in the military, serving on the opposition benches for 20 years'), Godsell noted that difficult dialogue 'was possible' with Oppenheimer. 'We went to Oppenheimer and said, "Look, on the issue of trade unions, they've either got to be good for whites and also good for blacks, or, if they're not good for blacks, they can't be good for whites. You've got to be for unions, or against unions. You can't distinguish between them in terms of race."' And Oppenheimer gave a speech in 1974 saying that black unions 'weren't illegal and that if they were representative, business should deal with them', Godsell recalled.[3]

Godsell called Oppenheimer 'a renaissance man'. The son of Sir Ernest was someone deeply concerned about and interested in the human condition and its evolution. 'I mean, he had one of the largest collections of [nineteenth-century British Romantic poet] Lord Byron original manuscripts in the world. He was interested in civilisation, whatever you think it means. But he was a man of ideas ... he was as much interested in politics as he was interested in business.' Despite being South Africa's foremost industrialist and the richest man in the country, Oppenheimer was not merely and exclusively concerned with business and wealth, said Godsell, and he surrounded himself with progressive 'true-blue liberals', even though many in his organisation did not share his political views and were considered conservative and racist. 'He appointed people who had ideas, so he employed [fierce Anglo critic] Alex Boraine as business practice consultant, and Boraine employed me, and they were "odd" appointments.'[4]

It was under Oppenheimer's leadership in the 1970s and the early 1980s that Anglo American accepted that the political arrangement up until then wasn't workable – group areas, job reservation and influx control, the last-named being a range of legal measures that strictly limited how many black labourers could live and work in South Africa's cities, and was one of the strongest underpinnings of the apartheid system which sought to keep cities white and force black South Africans to live in their so-called 'homelands'.

Trevor Manuel identified the Urban Foundation, established in the wake of the Soweto Uprising by Oppenheimer and Anton Rupert, and headed by former judge Jan Steyn, as a significant actor in normalising the presence of black people in cities and society. The Urban Foundation was a non-governmental organisation that helped finance and establish housing projects for urbanised blacks. 'Part of its job was about creating a black middle class as a buffer between black South Africa and white South Africa. In today's terms, that would be quite offensive, but for capital it seemed like a positive move at the time,' he said.[5]

The Foundation tried to improve the lives of black people who were better off, and certainly the black professionals, including black teachers, Manuel said. 'They didn't have to live in the Bantu Admin-istration's houses but could acquire houses in townships.' But, added Manuel, other initiatives were at work at the same time. 'Several com-panies, like SA Breweries, that employed black graduates, helped create this class of black professionals, and add to that the doctors and teachers and lawyers and so on. I remember coming from Cape Town, and the African community was very small there, and didn't have many professionals, and going to Bloemfontein, where I encountered these massive houses in the black areas, but the electricity wasn't connected. So, there was this contradiction between comfortable houses for some black members of this middle class, but without electricity.'[6]

Godsell gave the Urban Foundation more credit than Manuel, and, from an obvious Anglo position, said it didn't only improve the lives of the tiny black middle class, but also helped prepare white South Africa for inevitable political changes. 'The Urban Foundation is an important part of this story, because what the Urban Founda-tion said was, "You've got to at least do something about urban blacks,

165

incorporating them in political structures." I think we were able to help popularise the inevitability and the desirability and the need for political change.'[7]

It was in this context that Gavin Relly, who succeeded Oppenheimer, arranged the visit to Lusaka in 1985 and commissioned the 'scenarios' project – and appointed Michael Spicer to head up public affairs and develop contacts within the liberation movement.

It was during the negotiations period, from about the mid-1980s to the first democratic election in 1994, Spicer said, that big capital came to understand that the structure of the economy had to change.

If the democratic transition was to be successful, the economy needed to remain intact. But if the transition was to be sustainable, then blacks needed to have a stake in economic fortunes and progress. So, during the late 1980s and early 1990s, some conglomerates started employing and deploying young black professionals into the middle- and senior-management echelons. For example, many of today's senior black finance professionals are products of a programme started by Old Mutual during apartheid, in which they were taken in by the company and put through training to qualify.[8]

But that was clearly not enough – and business understood that in order to survive, and to enable a significant black stake in the economy, they had to start giving up parts of their empires.

In the first week of August 1990, Thabo Mbeki met with Jürgen Kögl and businessmen Don Mkhwanazi and Andy Schwarz at the Carlton Hotel in Johannesburg. Kögl had by then positioned himself as a serious power broker between the returning ANC and big business, having set up the consultancy with Frederik van Zyl Slabbert to enable both sides to feel each other out. 'At the meeting, we started discussing the fundamental tenets of what was to become black economic empowerment, its fundamental design and the economic equations before us,' Kögl said. 'If we did not design an evolutionary process – which became BEE – then it would be very difficult to prevent radical interventions in the economic life of the country, such as nationalisation or expropriation without compensation. The fundamental idea of BEE was that property is the cornerstone of economic development, along with private initiative.'[9]

They accepted, said Kögl, that the outcome of a peaceful transition would be that 90 per cent of the political power would reside in black hands, while the economic power would still be in the hands of whites, with only one to two per cent in black hands. 'The economy would still be dominated by white interests, white business, white shareholders, white savers, white pensioners, and white provident owners.'[10]

In 1992, a conference was convened in Johannesburg at which corporate South Africa and representatives of black business met to discuss empowerment structures. Kögl, one of the prime movers behind the conference, said that in addition to representatives from bodies such as Nafcoc and Fabcos, 'We had the black business leaders … like Mkhwanazi, Jabu Mabuza, [medical doctor] Nthato Motlana, Sam Motsuenyane, Richard Maponya … Spicer represented Anglo, Southern Life was there, as well as JCI, Hilton Appelbaum was there representing Donny Gordon from Liberty. But certainly, the most influential in those early engagements about suitable empowerment structures was Marinus Daling, chairman of Sanlam, who was there as the Afrikaner voice.'[11]

At the conference, the Viva Project was launched. Its aim was the creation of a central fund to help finance BEE transactions. Daling's view, Kögl said, 'was that we should raise R5 billion, which was a lot back then'.[12]

He gave some of the background to what was happening in business at the time. 'Corporate South Africa was trying to get out of the sanction-busting and siege economy and back to core business, and therefore disinvesting themselves from non-core interests.'[13] So, for example, he said, 'Anglo would disinvest themselves from Breweries and hotels and newspapers, but stuck to Haggie Steel and AECI and Shaft Sinkers, which were core businesses that were developed for very deep-level mining. And the same would have happened in Old Mutual, looking at what it really needs to invest in for its policy holders, and the same for Sanlam and the same for Liberty and the same for Southern Life.'[14]

The Viva fund would facilitate the purchase of the shares in these businesses' non-core interests, which it would then put into custodianship for black people who wanted to be investors and owners. The Viva Project would also give black people insight and access to the management of those companies; it would enable them to run those organisations after a transfer of skills had taken place.

But the Viva Project failed, even though the corporates initially supported the idea that such a fund would be the best vehicle to help black entrepreneurs obtain valuable assets, and even though black business formations supported the initiative. 'They suddenly discovered that having a black shareholder because of BEE was a competitive advantage to them, as opposed to participating in a national project of upliftment. [For example], Anglo saw they could offer non-core assets, like those in JCI, and do a transaction privately. They realised that if they did those transactions in their own interests and by their own design [rather than doing so as part of a collective scheme like Viva], they would have a competitive advantage related to new business opportunities, like new mining licences and casino licences.'[15]

Anglo's commitment to BEE, from Spicer's perspective, came from a different place: it was driven by the twin needs to ensure that the company would be able to continue operating in a democratic South Africa, and the urgency to help create a black middle class with a significant stake in the country's economy. He said that he – and many of his colleagues on Anglo's executive – believed that capital had the duty to intervene in the creation of black wealth.

He explained that the left thought that big capital cynically supported BEE, and in many instances initiated the first BEE deals, in order 'to capture and seduce the naive and innocent ANC'. But, he said, it was actually 'part of trying to – and this sounds patronising – just to get people to be able to have experience of the market and decision-making and implementation ...'[16]

Manuel said that companies like Anglo acted as quickly as they could to move capital out of the country – and Kögl, by dint of his association with Mbeki and as a consultant, believed that empowerment provided a way out of the country for companies who didn't want to be 'caught by a black government'.[17]

Manuel said the origins of BEE lie in the Constitution. 'Basically, we said, "Okay, so we've got the Constitution and it provides political freedom. But if you only have political freedom where people vote, and there isn't participation in the economy, you're not going to make it." And then, of course, in the crafting of the Constitution, in ... the equality clause, there needed to be a provision that allowed for people who were previously excluded to come into the economy. And that then laid the basis for legislation that tried to solve the problem.'[18]

And Manuel did credit Oppenheimer and Anglo for attempting to bring black people into the mainstream of economic activity, as well as into broader South African society, before and after apartheid. 'There were many strands to the transition and many people who contributed to help create a mass of people capable to take responsibility at the point of democracy. And within this there were people like Oppenheimer,' he said.[19]

Others were the Ruperts in Stellenbosch, who were the prime movers behind the Small Business Development Corporation, an entity that provided loans to small businesses. Manuel recalled, 'We went to see them to enquire whether the state could become the holder of the assets that they had in the [Small Business Development Corporation], because we wanted to use it to advance black business. Old man Anton [Rupert] was very accommodating. He could see the importance of having the government on-side to advance small business initiatives.' (Manuel noted, however, that 'his son Johann wasn't having this' and mentioned that there was some 'screaming' at the meeting.)[20]

And Manuel concurred with Kögl that Sanlam's Daling was pivotal at the time. 'A big, big mover was certainly someone like Marinus Daling – he was a manager rather than an owner but he was a big player in trying to assist in the transition.'[21]

So, as the political transition was happening, the realisation took root that an economic (or financial) transition had to also be initiated. Nothing like it had, however, ever been attempted before.

Spicer spelled it out: 'We had a group that was going to assume political power but had little economic power. They were going to run the country, but, as the majority, they had been rigidly excluded from the economy during apartheid.'[22]

Spicer said that from a purely theoretical economic perspective, black business should have started modestly, by running small concerns. 'Those that were successful would grow to medium-sized businesses and ultimately a few would grow to become large enterprises. And you do this over two or three decades, and then you get a sort of classic development.'[23] But, he pointed out, it was completely impossible to have the relatively fast political transition, and then say that 'economic change would only occur over the following 30, 40 or 50 years'.[24]

'There was no script. We had to create a middle class and some form of business community rapidly, so Keys and others came with the idea that if you unbundle big conglomerates, you short-circuit the process. Initially, the thinking was [first] individuals, and then the second phase was broad-based groupings, so that you spread it a bit more. There were various combinations and permutations, in several phases. Because there was no playbook, it was made up as we went along. And we made mistakes.'[25]

Back in 1994, black people simply had not had exposure to business, economy and commerce that they have almost 30 years on, Manuel agreed. 'We took young black entrepreneurs and professionals to countries like the United States, to expose them to black-owned business and how they were run. I remember on one of those trips, we'd gone to a few cities, and we were in Atlanta, which had a very strong cast of black professionals and businesspeople. And there was this young chap, I think he may have been a candidate attorney or perhaps just qualified as an attorney then, a chap called Patrice Motsepe, who was on this roadshow with us ...'[26]

In 1994, the economy was still dominated by a few conglomerates, including Anglo, which had interests in everything from gold and diamonds, to paper, banks and cars. After the 1994 election, the new government – with Manuel, who was running competition policy, at the helm of the trade and industry ministry – tried to force the conglomerates to focus on their core business, and both big capital and the state saw opportunities to broaden the country's economic base by selling off assets.

'The economy at the time was structurally just not fit for purpose. One of the big issues that we in the ANC had raised was the need for a more aggressive competitions policy. By dealing with competitions policy, you could, for instance, compel these conglomerates that sat over everything to get rid of parts of [themselves],' said Manuel.[27]

Manuel was deeply involved in trying to stimulate the creation of a new black business class, with competition regulations as his primary tool. But many of the new policy drivers implemented by the ANC government had unintended consequences, he said, using the example of Anglo 'sitting on a pile of cash and unable to invest further in mining in South Africa [because many mines were reaching the end of their lifespan]' and then going offshore. 'But there was a rationality to how we approached empowerment. Besides competition and breaking up the conglomerates, we had to get black people into business, and we convened presidential small business conferences in Durban in 1995 and 1996. The idea was to attract small black entrepreneurs through organisations like Nafcoc and Fabcos. We wanted to bring people into business, to try and stimulate something, not in exchange for anything but because we weren't getting to BEE issues immediately.'[28]

171

While 20 empowerment transactions took place during the first year of democracy, by 1998, 20 transactions were taking place each month. And where in September 1995, 11 companies on the JSE were considered black-controlled (and with a market capitalisation of R46 billion), by the end of 1998 there were 26 black-controlled companies on the JSE, with a total market capitalisation of R52 billion, around four per cent of the JSE's total market capitalisation.

Bobby Godsell said that when he was running AngloGold, foreign white executives regularly asked him to identify BEE partners. 'They would visit me in my office on the nineteenth floor of Diagonal Street and they say, "Oh, we want to come and do business in South Africa, we are looking for a black partner." I would take them to the window and say, "Look at Diagonal Street. You know we're a country of about 60 million people, there's about 40 million blacks, black Africans. Go out and find somebody who knows something about your business, somebody you can trust, somebody who will add value to your business. Please don't ask me to anoint someone."'

The first phase of black incorporation, he added, was 'anointing for political connection and without real risk'. 'And, unfortunately, we haven't moved beyond that yet.'[29]

While Manuel and his department were looking at ways to bring black people into the economy, Spicer said big capital – and specifically Anglo – were looking at ways to partner with black businessmen. There was no official government BEE policy during the first years of democracy, and the first big empowerment deals – Anglo unbundling its shares in JCI (see chapter 16), the establishment of New Africa Investments Limited (NAIL) (see chapter 18) and the emergence of Real Africa Holdings (see chapter 9) – were all private initiatives. These deals were concluded by lending empowerment partners capital to enable them to acquire an asset, with the empowerment partner later paying back the loan.

The most famous unbundling and empowerment scheme of the

time was Anglo's disposal of its assets in JCI, an old mining company in which it had the majority holding. The idea was to spin off JCI's most valuable assets into Anglo American Platinum, and two other companies: JCI, which was to hold various industrial assets, and Johnnic, which held media assets including the *Sunday Times* and its sister titles. But Anglo, although stating during the unbundling announcement that JCI was being broken up with the express purpose to help black empowerment, remained resolute that it was going to sell the assets at nothing less than market value.

But Anglo deals that worked well, said Spicer, were JCI and Johnnic, the latter of which was attractive because it held media ownership in Times Media (which included the *Sunday Times*, the *Financial Mail* and *Business Day*). And, he added, 'Some of those were able to merge with similar new opportunities, including telecoms, with the Vodafone and Vodacom deal; also, Cable & Wireless with MTN was very significant. Within and among black entrepreneurs, some of those early movers were able to move with a lot of determination.'[30]

Other successful deals included Sanlam, 'when they spun out Metropolitan, because the customer base at Metropolitan was primarily lower-income blacks, and that then became one of the anchors of NAIL. It was an asset that could be built and developed. And on the board of NAIL then were people like Dikgang Moseneke, later deputy chief justice, Cyril Ramaphosa, and Franklin Sonn, an academic and later South Africa's ambassador in the United States. That created direct black ownership.'[31]

Still, while big capital breathed a sigh of relief that South Africa hadn't been transformed into an African socialist experiment and started to retreat into the background, those years weren't easy for black entrepreneurs, Manuel said. 'It was an unbelievably difficult environment because people had different kinds of experiences. Motlana, for example, was a doctor – a very competent doctor with a large practice that had Soweto's great and the good as patients. He was a political figure, being part of Soweto's civics and a member of the Committee of Ten, and he had a presence.

'Standing right close by his side was a guy called Jonty Sandler [executive director of NAIL]. Jonty had a lot more business experience and savvy and supported these guys to go forward.

'Then there was Moseneke, who had come out of practice and moved into NAIL and was then to accumulate wealth until he was called to the Constitutional Court. Franklin [Sonn] was there for a while, had to preserve his shares in some way, but moved on to become the ambassador to Washington, DC.

'And of course, Cyril, who went into NAIL after he concluded his work as chairperson of the Constitutional Assembly in mid-1996. So, there were different moves, but all of them gave hope that it could be done.'[32]

But not only was progress not fast enough, largely, it simply didn't work, said Jürgen Kögl. He explained that this first generation of empowerment deals created a narrow band of super-rich and connected businessmen, and also that assets often very quickly returned to white owners. 'Because once these black shareholders got their cut of a business in the form of shares and equity, and they needed cash, who did they sell to? They sold to white business. Because blacks didn't have money and couldn't acquire those shares.'[33]

This is where the sticky issue of 'once empowered, always empowered' arose – shouldn't those corporates have been obliged to get new black partners if their old ones sold their shares? But, said Kögl, 'corporate South Africa said, "Well, we've done our BEE and if the black guys sell their shares back to white guys, what can we do?"' That's not how it was meant to work, he said. 'The black folks should have been selling their stuff to black folks on a concessional basis [at cheaper than market price], but they didn't.'[34]

And there were other inequities with which the new black businessmen had to contend, said Kögl. One of these was the introduction of capital gains tax for the first time in the country's history. 'Where white South Africans during the previous hundred years of capital formation were never taxed on capital gains, the black guys were taxed right up front.'[35]

Another was that corporates insisted on market-related pricing. 'In other words, if you wanted to buy something out of the JCI stable – whether it was Steenberg Golf Estate or whatever, a property-related business or some such – it had to be acquired at market-related prices. But the whole history of South African capitalism is littered with concessions and free licences.' Citing the examples of previously free fishing licences, and free rights to intellectual property such as educational material and telephone books, Kögl said, 'So, unlike white folks who had concessions ... none of that was applicable to black folks. That all came about when black people were put in possession of capital-formation projects, and then they were taxed and had to pay all these fees.'[36]

In initiating empowerment, and endorsing it, big business was to create a monster, according to Michael Spicer. 'How do you short-circuit the wealth-creation process ... because, left to itself, it evolves over decades and over generations, but politically there is no time for that, so you must have some artificial interventions. There's no play-book [and] in the end, the process consumes itself.

'Handouts and free empowerment kill off enterprise in both the existing economy and among the recipients of the largesse. It doesn't provide a base for entrepreneurial activity. It's like all subsidies. They become addicted to the subsidy, and by definition [of BEE] you don't really need to do anything because you're always going to be getting things free, or by virtue of your connections, so you don't have to understand the business or do anything.

'And all you get is an increasing clamour for more and more, and those who are still outside the magic circle wanting to get into the magic circle. It creates an insatiable demand for free tickets to the ball.'[37]

16

The new Randlord:

CYRIL RAMAPHOSA

'You will have enough money to be incorruptible.'

– Nthato Motlana to Cyril Ramaphosa in 1995,
persuading him to leave politics and go into business.[1]

On Sunday 14 April 1996, the secretary-general of the ANC, Cyril
Ramaphosa, stood on Nelson Mandela's left, and Nthato Motlana,
the executive chairman of NAIL, on the statesman's right, and
listened as the president read a prepared statement to the assembled
media in Cape Town. 'After thorough discussion between myself and
other senior members of the ANC, it has been decided that Comrade Cyril Ramaphosa … will be taking up a senior position in the
private sector.'[2] Although he would resign as a member of parliament,
Ramaphosa would remain a member of the NEC and secretary-
general of the ANC.

Ramaphosa had been deeply embedded and involved in the shaping
of the new political order after the unbanning of the ANC in 1990
and the subsequent democratic elections in 1994. But it was Mbeki
who became the clear favourite to succeed Mandela when the new
head of state appointed him as the first executive deputy president.

The announcement nevertheless came as a shock to many.

But did he jump or was he pushed? A 'shift' in power in government had, noted one source, fed concerns about 'a new culture and style of politics emerging', and that capable people were being shunted from the political frontline – people like Ramaphosa.[3] He had steadily been elbowed out of contention by a ruthless Thabo Mbeki following the ascendance of the exile grouping in the ANC after democracy, inside cabinet and in the NEC, and the effective sidelining of senior leaders of the UDF and other internal resistance movements.

Ramaphosa, who was 43 at the time of Mandela's announcement, looked decidedly deflated at the head of state's words. He'd had designs on the position of minister of finance but he toed Mandela's line. 'There is an overconcentration of capable people in parliament and cabinet. We need more black people at a senior level to begin to transform the economy, and I want to play a role,' he said.[4]

Ramaphosa was to move to NAIL, which was jostling to acquire Anglo's share in Johnnic, the industrial group that held interests in, among others, mining and media. But NAIL had been battling to get the finance needed to buy Anglo's share, which the company had said it would let go at market-related prices.

His appointment as deputy chairman of NAIL, and in charge of the company's attempts to secure a mining business from Anglo, seemingly was the culmination of a cunning plan by Motlana, set in motion in 1995. Motlana wanted to build a 'black Anglo American Corporation' and wanted NAIL to be led by 'trusted and credible African leaders', and Ramaphosa had reportedly expressed his willingness to join the company.[5] Motlana's argument was that even if Ramaphosa did have political ambitions, he was 10 years younger than Mbeki and could afford to sit out for a decade. He could return later as a wealthy man, Motlana pointed out.[6]

Ramaphosa said it is not 'entirely true' that he was pushed from politics; going into business was his choice, he said. He said that he approached Mandela and the ANC with a proposal and was granted permission to move to business, citing his 'entrepreneurial spirit ... surging to the fore'. He wanted to play a role in the empowerment project.[7]

He denied that he'd been positioning himself to challenge Thabo Mbeki and said that he accepted Mbeki's leadership. 'It became a lot easier to then say: why don't I go to another frontier? The business frontier.'[8]

On 24 February 1995, a year before Mandela's announcement that Ramaphosa would leave politics, Anglo had announced that it planned to unbundle Johannesburg Consolidated Investments (JCI) and put some of its interests up for sale. The company's interests in base metals, ferrochrome and gold would fall under JCI; Anglo's platinum interests would move to the newly formed Anglo American Platinum (Amplats); and a third entity, Johnnic, would hold JCI's interests in South African Breweries, Toyota, Times Media and Premier Foods.[9] Anglo said it would sell 35 per cent stakes in Johnnic and JCI to black investors, and retain about 12 per cent in each company.

JCI carried deep significance. It had grown to become one of the most successful and powerful mining and investment houses in the country. Now, just as Anglo had given Afrikaners a foothold in the mining industry in 1963 after it sold some mining assets cheaply to Afrikaner industrialists to form what was to later become Gencor,[10] it was hoped that Anglo's empowerment deal with JCI could do the same for blacks.

For Nthato Motlana, it was important to take charge of a mining operation, given the country's history and the enormous influence mining had had on politics, apartheid and shaping modern South Africa.[11]

Ramaphosa, meanwhile, given his background as the founder-secretary of the National Union of Mineworkers (NUM), had always harboured a desire to run a mining house – and run it well.[12] The activist turned politician, who was born in Johannesburg in 1952, grew up in Soweto. In 1972 he registered at the University of the

North and became involved in student politics; in 1974, he was detained for 11 months; and in June 1976, following the unrest in Soweto, he was detained for a further six months. In 1982, armed with a BProc degree, he joined the Council of Unions of South Africa (Cusa) as an advisor in the legal department; in the same year he became the first secretary of the NUM, in which capacity he worked closely with Cosatu. In 1990, he coordinated arrangements for the release of Nelson Mandela and the subsequent welcome rallies, and he was elected secretary-general of the ANC in 1991, heading up the negotiations commissions for the party and participating in Codesa.

Initially, the bid for Johnnic was led by the National Empowerment Consortium, consisting of a host of divergent interest groups, the largest being the pension funds of unions including the NUM, Numsa, the Food and Allied Workers Union, the South African Commercial, Catering and Allied Workers Union, and the South African Railways and Harbour Workers Union.[13] Alongside them there were various other small black businesses and groupings – a disparate group if ever there was one.

Then Motlana's NAIL indicated its interest in joining the group. NAIL possessed more financial muscle than any other of the consortium partners and was able to call the shots in negotiations.

Saki Macozoma, an ANC politician turned businessman who watched the deal closely, said it was clear that the fractious nature of the consortium was problematic – it was, he said, 'a group of misfits', 'not made up by people who saw eye to eye or had a common vision'. 'And then you got … egos and different styles of doing business, and one of the lessons I took from [my observations] was never to get into a consortium where I'm going to spend half the night in debates with supposed partners. It's a waste of time and energy.'[14]

The consortium, with Ramaphosa at the helm, finally clinched the deal in November 1996, buying a 35 per cent stake in Johnnic for R2.6 billion[15] – market price, as insisted on by Anglo, for a company with a market capitalisation of R8.5 billion.[16] Spicer described it as an 'important symbolic deal' to open up the racially exclusive economy.[17]

Johnnic had significant, if not controlling, stakes in some of the country's biggest companies, including South African Breweries, Toyota, MTN, and major media assets such as the *Sunday Times*, *Business Day* and *Financial Mail*. Ramaphosa became non-executive chairman of the Johnnic board, giving him broad strategic influence in the organisation.

The big prize, however, was the part of the original business that housed the company's mining interests – JCI. For this, NAIL – and Ramaphosa – were up against big-talking and flamboyant Robben Islander Mzi Khumalo, who put together a well-financed consortium to outbid Motlana's outfit.

Anglo, stating that it wanted to empower a broad base of black interests, and not just recycle the same names, opted to sell the 35 per cent stake to Khumalo's Africa Mining Group after it was able to pay 50c per share more than NAIL.[18] The purchase – R2.9 billion at R54.50 a share – included ownership of the country's then top gold mine, Western Areas.[19]

It would turn out to be a disaster for Khumalo, believed to have been made a billionaire out of this and a range of other empowerment deals, before losing almost all of it. Kögl, who advised Khumalo on the deal, said he 'completely overpaid' and was a victim of the structuring of the deals at the time.[20]

He brought in mining magnate Brett Kebble as a financier. As Spicer put it, 'He had to get the money in the market, and the only person who was prepared to help finance that was Brett Kebble, as opposed to the institutions, because everybody knew he overpaid for that stake.'[21]

Khumalo had financed the deal in the hope that an increase in the gold price would help him to pay back his debt – but the gold price tanked. Kebble ran the show at JCI from 1997 until his death – in extremely suspicious circumstances – in 2005, during which time he forced Khumalo out of the company.

Spicer said Khumalo suffered because, initially, no one really knew how to finance empowerment deals. 'The first phase was you did this on a debt basis, and you hoped that there would be capital appreciation and it would be sufficient to pay it off. Well, markets don't always play ball and so some people lost money. Some succeeded, and a lot of it depended on the timing. Mzi Khumalo got into gold with JCI at exactly the wrong time and he lost money. Patrice Motsepe got into gold at exactly the right time and built up African Rainbow Minerals very successfully. Some deals succeeded, and some didn't.'[22]

Godsell was, however, critical of both the approach by established business in the 1990s, and the recipients of BEE deals, and said no real transfer of wealth took place – and that, in fact, only a narrow band of connected individuals were enriched. 'White business made blacks owners of assets, never requiring them to pay for the assets. The enlightened people gave the assets away, so that [the black recipients] at least weren't debt-encumbered, but that was rare. The unenlightened people financed this alleged transfer of ownership through debt, which, particularly in the mining sector, was a very high-risk thing to do, because, in the end, the value of shares in a mining company are almost completely dependent on the commodity price cycles.'[23]

That form of ownership was 'phoney', Godsell said, because it was achieved without risk to the owners. 'And it means that owners can't do the central thing they have to in a market economy, and that is live through the bad times as well as the good, and invest in the growth of the business. I mean, how often do you think Cyril Ramaphosa has put his hand in his pocket to invest in businesses that he owns?'[24]

Ramaphosa might have lost out on running a mining house but his long slog in business was only just beginning, and Johnnic was his first taste of how difficult the business environment could be. Dubbed 'the new Randlord' by some of the foreign press,[25] he started out at the company with Johnnic in possession of some serious firepower. Its portfolio consisted of a 43.2 per cent interest in Omni Media, which controlled the *Sunday Times*, among other important media assets, 13.7 per cent in South African Breweries, 27.8 per cent in food and beverages outfit the Premier Group, 26.4 per cent in Toyota South Africa, and ownership of properties including Gallagher Estate in Midrand.

Immediately, under Ramaphosa's leadership, the company disposed of its interest in Toyota, and set out on a path to unbundle its other non-core assets. In 1998, less than two years after the empowerment transaction, Johnnic stated that it was going to focus on transforming from a 'passive industrial conglomerate' into a telecommunications, media and entertainment company – and the following year it sold its stakes in SA Breweries and Premier, and took control of Times Media Limited. Across two transactions in 1998 and 1999, it increased its shareholding in MTN to a sizeable 47.4 per cent.

Its major shareholders were representative of old capital supporting new, with Old Mutual holding 13 per cent of the company, and investors like the Public Investment Corporation, Rand Merchant Bank, Metropolitan, Coronation, Liberty and Sanlam all owning a slice between 1998 and 2004.[26]

Johnnic had become a big, big player. And 'Chairman Cyril', as Spicer referred to him, was leading the company. Following his transfer to business from politics, Ramaphosa was co-opted onto the boards of a range of companies, including MTN and Times Media Limited (as non-executive chair in both cases), and South African Breweries, Bidvest and Alexander Forbes.

His time at NAIL, however, came to an acrimonious end and he left with his whole support staff in 1999 after a fallout with executive director Jonty Sandler.[27] In 2001 he established Millennium Consolidated Investments (MCI) to house his personal investments and business interests, and within a year MCI became Alexander Forbes's empowerment partner, with MCI taking a 30 per cent stake in the business.[28] MCI's name was changed to Shanduka (meaning 'change') in 2004.[29]

Around the turn of the century Johnnic had spun off almost all of the assets it received as lobola from Anglo, with its major properties now being represented by its stake in MTN, its media titles and some gaming interests.

In 2003, it sold off its most attractive asset, MTN, which frustrated observers who believed the company was never geared to nor focused on obtaining control through majority shareholding. The unbundling 'left a sour taste in many mouths because it created wealth for only some of the company's shareholders'.[30] And in 2005 it lost control of subsidiary Johncom, which housed its share of titles like the *Sunday Times*.

In that same year Ramaphosa took Johnnic into a battle that would lead to the company's ultimate demise and his eventual departure from it. After it had been dramatically whittled down over the preceding nine years, Johnnic's most promising stake was the 19 per cent it held in a company called Tsogo Investment Holdings. Tsogo held a controlling 51 per cent shareholding in Tsogo Sun, a money-spinning gaming company, which owned, among other properties, Montecasino in Fourways, Johannesburg.[31] But another company, Hosken Consolidated Investments (HCI), led by former unionists Johnny Copelyn and Marcel Golding, and born out of the investment vehicles of the South African Clothing and Textile Workers' Union and the NUM, was dead keen on acquiring all of Tsogo.

What followed was one of the most dramatic and protracted boardroom battles since the dawn of democracy, as HCI (which owned 32 per cent of Tsogo Investment Holdings) tried to gain control of Tsogo by engineering a takeover of Johnnic.

Ramaphosa led the resistance when he got a whiff of HCI's hostile bid, and shareholders mostly went along with his directives.

When Copelyn and Golding's nominations to the Johnnic board were rejected, they resorted to more aggressive tactics, which included a 'technical deal' that robbed Johnnic of its empowerment status.[32] Ramaphosa refused to do a deal throughout. 'Frankly speaking, I didn't have skin in the game,' he said, apparently referring to the fact that his own money wasn't invested in Johnnic. 'I just happened to be there when the skirmishes took place.'[33]

But the end seemed inevitable. 'A Johnnic watcher, who declined to be named, pointed out that HCI's takeover "cannot be stopped". He noted that the takeover would be good, as Johnnic had a tendency to take an excruciatingly long time to make decisions,' reported the *Mail & Guardian*, inferring that the company was slow and inefficient.[34]

After the Competition Tribunal rejected an application by Johnnic to prevent HCI's takeover, the writing was on the wall. HCI gained control in December 2005, and in January 2006 Copelyn installed himself as chair of Johnnic. Ramaphosa, alongside a slew of other directors, resigned.

Ramaphosa's biographer Anthony Butler said the demise of Johnnic 'came to represent the disappointed hopes of the first era of black empowerment' in that it had been expected that the company would become the premier black company of its era.[35] But it was never 'real empowerment', Ramaphosa said later. 'The banks were empowered, the advisors were empowered, the merchant bankers, the lawyers and the accountants were all empowered [but] the very people who were meant to be empowered were not empowered ... They ended up walking away with zero.'[36]

Moving swiftly on, Ramaphosa devoted all his energy to Shanduka, the holding investment company he'd founded in 2001, and to his various directorships.

Shanduka became primarily focused on the financial services sector, taking stakes in companies including Alexander Forbes (as mentioned earlier) and Liberty (and later owning the South African McDonald's franchise). Its biggest coup, however, was when it took 40 per cent of Saki Macozoma's consortium when Standard Bank did its big empowerment deal. So Shanduka ended up with 1.2 per cent ownership of Standard Bank, and Macozoma's Safika with 1.8 per cent, in a deal worth R5.5 billion.[37]

In 2011 China's sovereign wealth fund, the China Investment Corporation, acquired a 25 per cent stake in Shanduka, buying the equity held by Old Mutual and Investec. This was at a time when China was making serious overtures to Africa, and after the country's then-deputy premier, Xi Jinping, had paid a state visit to the country. 'This partnership will allow us to jointly explore future investment opportunities in South Africa and other parts of Africa,' Ramaphosa said at the time.[38]

But Jürgen Kögl, who advised Alexander Forbes during the company's deal with Shanduka, and who had seen Ramaphosa operate up close, said the Chinese investment in Shanduka was purely for political and strategic reasons. 'The argument was that Ramaphosa could one day become deputy president, or even president, and that investing in him was a good decision. And the Chinese ambassador, who was a friend, asked my advice and I told him it won't be a good financial investment. And he came back to me and said the leadership in Beijing didn't want to insult anybody, especially not a future deputy president, and they decided to pay "carry value", in other words, the cost of the investment that Standard Bank had incurred – so the share price plus the money they paid to acquire a stake in Shanduka.'[39]

Views on Ramaphosa's prowess as businessman differed. Former colleagues described him as 'a good person to work for' who built 'a stronger team at Shanduka than at comparable companies'. Others, however, said that he was prone to dithering, and was someone who preferred 'discussion to decision'.[40] Kögl agreed that he was a reluctant decision-maker. 'As long as the income was there, he was a happy businessman.'[41] It was to become a hallmark of his presidency: an inability to take difficult decisions, an unwillingness to make enemies in service of principle, and a lack of conviction.

While Ramaphosa was, in effect, exiled from politics for 16 years, between 1996 and 2012, he was able to amass a fortune arguably unmatched by anyone making the transition from politics to commerce. He became a figure much sought after by big capital as it attempted to offload non-core assets to the emerging black indus-trialist class, and was, as mentioned, co-opted to the boards of some of the biggest companies in the country, with his seniority and influence in the governing ANC a prized asset.

Although it's difficult to assess the value of Ramaphosa's wealth because Shanduka never disclosed its financials, by 2007 the company acknowledged that it controlled assets worth more than R5 billion, and with Ramaphosa's stake in Shanduka amounting to 30 per cent, his value back then could already have surpassed R1 billion.[42]

After throwing his weight behind Jacob Zuma at the ANC's na-tional conference in 2012, when he was elected the party's deputy leader, becoming deputy president of the country in 2014, Shanduka was acquired by friend and dollar millionaire Phutuma Nhleko's investment firm Phembani.[43] Ramaphosa's profits from the transac-tion – in the region of $200 million, or R2.5 billion at the time[44] – were transferred into an independently managed trust; in line with the Executive Members' Ethics Act, he was to have no influence on how his wealth was managed.[45]

By 2015, Ramaphosa was regarded as the 42nd richest person in Africa, commanding a fortune of an estimated $450 million (about R6.8 billion).[46] His current worth is unknown.

Ramaphosa indulges in dealing in exotic game on his two farms, Phala Phala in the Waterberg in Limpopo, and Ntaba Nyoni near Badplaas in Mpumalanga; both are worth tens of millions of rands. He was the first South African to import long-horned Ankole cattle from Kenya, and auctions at the farms generate millions in income – something that was exploited by his enemies after a burglary in February 2020 that saw allegedly some $600 000 stolen from his Phala Phala estate, with his security detail and the police's presidential protection unit accused of trying to conceal the incident. His enemies sought to portray him as seeing himself as above the law, ignoring ex-change control regulations because he allegedly received payment for a game transaction in dollars, and abusing his position to hide the theft.

At the time of writing no criminality had been proven, and he remains arguably the most successful of all the new moneyed barons who emerged after the ANC's acquiescence to capitalism after 1994.

But he wasn't the only one.

17
Empowering the ANC:
VUSI KHANYILE

'I am told that at some stage ... there were questions about us, with people saying the ANC is struggling for resources, and what is Thebe doing? And I am further told that Madiba firmly said, "Thebe has nothing to do with you. Thebe has nothing to do with you or the ANC. Vusi will solve your problems. Leave Thebe alone."'

– Vusi Khanyile, on the opposition to the establishment
of Thebe Investment Corporation in 1992.[1]

The executive boardroom at Anglo American's head office at 44 Main Street, Johannesburg, was situated in the middle of the impressive building, on the second floor, just above the grand entrance hall with its triple-volume stained glass through which the sunlight streamed onto the marble floors inside.

The cornerstone of the building – symbolic of the might of capital – had been laid by Sir Ernest Oppenheimer in June 1938, 21 years after he'd founded the company. A significant feature on the Johannesburg skyline, it was situated just a stone's throw from Ferreirasdorp, where the first mining camp had been established half a century earlier.

Walking into the boardroom, with its 24-seater table and soft carpeting, on a bright winter's day in mid-1985, Vusi Khanyile was confronted by an all-white gathering. This was no surprise to the 35-year-old accounting graduate. While known to be 'liberal', the company was also, said Khanyile, 'very white'. 'But they did give me a scholarship to go and study [at the then University of the North (today the University of Limpopo)] ... I was locked up by the security police and expelled from university, and later Anglo enabled me to complete my studies overseas. And I was really grateful for that.'[2]

Khanyile recalls going for the interview for the Anglo scholarship. 'I was with students from Stellenbosch University, from UCT, from Wits, and they were in suits and ties. I was in my shabby jeans. I had never been prepared for that kind of thing. But it was a big turning point in my life. Anglo even then – let me pay credit to them – they had the capacity to use their financial resources to give a helping hand, as they did in my case and for many other people who were beneficiaries of the Anglo scholarships.'[3]

Khanyile finally got his honours degree in accounting from Birmingham University in 1982, after which he joined Anglo, working in the financial planning unit.

'As junior as I was, [on that day in mid-1985] my manager invited me to accompany him to a meeting of the executive committee. I think he wanted to give me exposure, and to show me that the reports I was working on, the reports I helped produce, were being put to use. I went along when he presented [and] I cannot fault his motive.'[4]

In the boardroom, the young number-cruncher found himself surrounded by white faces, and not only in the chairs around the table. 'I saw the pictures on the walls, all the leaders of Anglo over the years. I saw the history of South Africa in front of my eyes, and I said [to myself], "I cannot aspire to be in this room. I would first need to lose my soul to be in this room – my future belongs somewhere else." It was their attempt at inclusion, but for me, my political antennae just came up and I said, "That's not me."'[5]

When he left the meeting that day, he said, 'It was very clear to me

189

that my entrepreneurial aspiration would have to find another channel, not that channel.'[6]

Shortly after that, Khanyile, taking inspiration from Soweto entrepreneurs like Richard Maponya and Nthato Motlana, founded the Sizwe Finance Trust and opened his first office in the suburb of Jabulani in Soweto.

The purpose of Sizwe was to stimulate and support other businesses, and to try and obtain finance for emerging entrepreneurs – but Khanyile also believed that business should have a social conscience: it should invest back into the community. In this, Anglo influenced his thinking, he said. 'The different mines and the various companies in Anglo were compelled to contribute a certain percentage of their post-tax profits to the Chairman's Fund, which was used to support various causes in the country. This included the scholarship I won.'[7]

Leaving the embrace of Anglo was tough for Khanyile, who had to brave the almost impossible environment for an aspiring black businessman in PW Botha's security state. 'Literally a month or two after I had started, the country was plunged into a state of emergency. I thought, *Oh goodness, what have I just done!* I now have responsibility for staff, I pay rent and I had a young family that I was trying to provide for.'[8]

Describing the situation under apartheid, Khanyile noted, 'South Africa had a political marketplace and an economic marketplace, and the former regulated the latter. And it did that by introducing laws and regulations. But the political marketplace wasn't free, because you couldn't exchange and sell goods and services to the political consumer, like the ideas of democracy. And the people who weren't allowed to play in the economic marketplace were the same people who weren't allowed to play in the political marketplace. Black people could not be participants in either of the markets.'[9]

So, like many other South African blacks at the time, Khanyile wore another hat in addition to those of father and businessman – that of activist. 'And then of course I was incarcerated, I was detained, like many other activists at the time.' When he was released, he said, it became very clear to him that 'you can't build a business when you are fighting, at the same time, for liberation. And I took a decision to shut down the business.'[10]

His dream of 'entrepreneurial expression' didn't die, however – it was simply deferred, he said.[11] And as the political marketplace was starting to normalise – even before 1994, Khanyile said – he started to investigate the idea of a different kind of business, one that worked 'in the broader interests of society'.

There had been some successes in Soweto business – with Maponya someone that Khanyile and others admired – but he believed that there was still something lacking. 'There was no black business that operated as the representative of a collective or represented collective aspirations. There was no business whose success bore witness to what we promised as the liberators. And it was in that context, with the normalisation of the political market, and after I felt I had made my contribution, that I decided my role is in the economic marketplace. But I also knew you couldn't just pursue financial success without taking into account the welfare of community and society.'[12]

After the ANC was unbanned in 1990, Vusi Khanyile was drafted into the organisation's treasury department, helping to oversee the returning liberation movement's finances. He worked in the office of Thomas Nkobi, then the treasurer-general.

It was following the ANC's first national conference after its unbanning, in June 1991, that the organisation started feeling a cash crunch: the collapse of communism and the subsequent drying up of funds meant the ANC was never flush with money. Khanyile said it was Walter Sisulu, part of the ANC's big three, alongside Nelson Mandela and Oliver Tambo, who signalled the urgency of the ANC's situation. 'During the conference, I was minding my own business when I walked past a canteen where Sisulu was sitting and drinking a cup of tea. He called me over. I sat down and he proceeded to ask questions about how we'd paid for the conference. I shared with him what I knew (about the funding of the conference), and explained the sources of historic financial support for the ANC. And he said that in 1959, when he was secretary-general of the ANC, every penny that was spent on that year's conference had come from members, and that our greatest fundraiser was Chief Albert Luthuli, who went from community to community to raise funds,' said Khanyile.[13]

So moves had to be made to secure the financial future of the party. It was clear that there was going to be an election fairly soon, and the ANC had to have resources at its disposal in order to launch a proper election campaign. And beyond that, it was going to need money to ensure that the organisation was able to function nationwide.

Jürgen Kögl said he and Mzi Khumalo had managed the conference's finances, and done a good job. 'It was audited by Gill Marcus's father, Nate, who was an accountant in the treasurer-general's office. I think there was a discrepancy of something like R56,' he recalled proudly.[14] 'Mandela and Nkobi then asked us for a proposal to make the ANC financially sustainable.'

Kögl and Khumalo's plan was for the ANC to use 10 per cent of its annual membership income, augmented by contributions from a 'portfolio of donors', to establish a wealth fund. 'We submitted it to the high command and made a presentation at the old Shell House to Mandela, Nkobi, Tambo, Mbeki and Ramaphosa. We argued that the ANC should establish an investment fund similar to the Kuwait Investment Fund. We explained that the Kuwaitis took 10 per cent of their oil revenues and invested it with this fund, based in London. They used professional fund managers to build an investment portfolio to generate investment income that could be used by their government for whatever reason, outside yearly budget allocations.'[15]

They wanted the fund to be managed by a big investment company, such as Allan Gray or Sanlam or Old Mutual, said Kögl. 'It would have ensured that benefactors didn't get donor fatigue because the party goes back to them every four years or so. The ANC could have built this to show donors they could fund themselves.'[16]

But it wasn't implemented. Instead, said Kögl, 'It was work-shopped into a private equity thing.' Explaining why private equity was unsuitable, it's 'one of the riskiest investments you can do', he said. 'You need to be very patient, and have a long view, when you invest in a non-listed start-up company.'[17]

The 'private equity thing' to which Kögl disdainfully refers was the Thebe Investment Corporation, the first post-apartheid black-owned investment firm, established in 1992 with R100 000 in capital. And who better to lead this private investment firm than a former senior officer in the ANC's treasury department?

Vusi Khanyile said he was partly motivated to take the job by the conversation he'd had with Walter Sisulu at the ANC's 1991 confer-ence, when the party elder had explained to him how important it was for the organisation to be financially independent and accountable to its members. Thebe was established to ensure exactly that, with its major shareholder the ANC through an entity called the Batho Batho Trust.

And, of course, there was his continued belief, at the time, that while black capital clearly had to operate in an environment where the rules had long ago been established, 'We couldn't only be a business that was there to make money; we had to be one that declared we're part of a collective and we represent collective aspirations. Our success must bear witness to that promise.'[18]

For Thebe to be the ANC's representative in the world of busi-ness, 'We had to follow an approach of enlightened interests' – an echo of Spicer and big capital's earlier version of 'enlightened self-interest' – 'where our leaders had an enlightened view of society. We wanted to establish a firm where the owner wasn't Khanyile or [some other person], but a firm that represented communal aspirations, where the value created belongs to the community.'[19]

Who was the 'community' that represented broad aspirations and who was to benefit from Thebe's success? It was the ANC, Khanyile said.

The big question was who would represent that community in the company. 'We could think of no better than Nelson Mandela, Walter Sisulu and [theologian and the leading Afrikaner anti-apartheid activist] Beyers Naudé. They were the first trustees of Batho Batho Trust, the majority shareholder of Thebe Investment Corporation, which was registered in the same year and 'set up in tandem' with the Batho Batho Trust.[20]

Khanyile said that while the support of these ANC stalwarts was crucial in helping Thebe survive, they did not advance the company's commercial interests. 'It is 100 per cent true that their involvement was significant. I felt at the time that if it's a trust, [and it was to be] the foundation and the owner of the business, it must play a critical role in supporting the business and ensuring that there was an ethical framework for the business. And we could not get better custodians,' said Khanyile.

Mandela, Sisulu and Naudé had to give direction where Thebe's dividends were to be paid. Many will disagree with him, but according to Khanyile there has always been 'complete separation between company and trust'.[21]

Mandela, in particular, was very supportive of Thebe's endeavours – and came in handy, politically, when some opposition arose to the company's establishment. Khanyile said 'comrades' started questioning Thebe's purpose, and some accused them of 'bringing capitalism by the back door into the people's camp'. Khanyile said he felt 'judged' by this. 'I felt misunderstood by my own comrades, my colleagues, by people I respected. It was painful. It was lonely. So, they [Mandela, Sisulu and Naudé] came in very handy then. They understood that separation, I would say between capital and politics, and I think they saw the dangers of that. And here I refer to the separation between Thebe and the trust, and the trust and the political organisation.'[22]

Thebe's first offices were in a building on the corner of Market and Eloff streets in the Johannesburg city centre, and Khanyile re-membered watching 20 000 rampaging Inkatha impis marching past on their way to the ANC's headquarters at Shell House in 1994, in protest against the looming election. Nineteen people were killed when ANC security guards opened fire on the protestors.[23]

Khanyile said the ANC understood the importance of financial accountability in the early years after its return from exile, and tried to bring in the necessary skills – but that it was difficult. Apart from Khanyile, there was a dearth of suitably qualified professionals to appoint. So when Thebe was established, it had to look hard for suitable employees. 'We looked among our own members, but skills were rare, and our growth was limited by the skills of our members. I think we [could count] on two hands the number of black chartered accountants in the country at the time. Black people had just not been given the opportunity to qualify. I think you are aware that the first black CA was in Umtata after the Transkei became independent. It's only in the Transkei that he was able to get a firm of auditors to give him articleship so that he could qualify.'[24]

Khanyile said the 'catalytic moment for Thebe' was when it was able to corral money to invest in SA Express, which was launched in 1994, one of the first small, regional airlines in the country, with Thebe owning 51 per cent of the company. Back then, nobody else was 'playing in that space' of regional airline operators. 'The business concept for a secondary aviation industry did not exist in South Africa at the time,' Khanyile said. 'We were able to mobilise R500 million from development finance institutions internationally, because we identified that the sector was going to start expanding. And we established a business that employed 400 people – we created 400 jobs that did not exist before we started.'[25]

'When that airline started, for the launch flight, we had the children of the black Nobel [peace] prize winners in the world [on board] – we had the son of Martin Luther King [who won the prize in 1964], we had the daughter of Albert Luthuli [1960], we had the daughter of Bishop Tutu [1984]. We dubbed it the peace flight.'[26]

This, he said, was a turning point for Thebe. 'We were able to import technology and equipment from abroad, and the development capital that came in to start this business became our track record. Two years later, on the [basis] of that track record, we were able to raise capital in South Africa and we actually flew, we really grew. We helped create an industry that did not exist at the time.'

Initially, the Batho Batho Trust was Thebe's sole shareholder. The trust deed documents state Batho Batho was set up to support 'democracy and socioeconomic transformation' and 'the institutional viability and self-sustainability of historically black organisations'.[27]

Nonetheless, the intention was for Batho Batho 'to receive dividends' on behalf of the ANC.[28] This is according to internal party documents held at the University of Fort Hare that were sealed by the party shortly after the *Sunday Times* reported on their existence in 2010. The documents also state that 'the area that the trust covers must be defined in extremely narrow terms, such that any profits received are donated to the ANC'.[29] Legally and technically, though, there is no link between the party and the Batho Batho Trust, with the latter established 'to support the efforts of historically disadvantaged South Africans', according to company information on Thebe's website.

Batho Batho was 'an understanding shareholder' and in it 'for the long run', said Khanyile. '[The shareholder] understood the importance of keeping the experiment, this baby [Thebe], alive. Therefore, ultimate control was very important. The controlling shareholder of our business drove a transformation agenda, understood transformation and was committed to it as part of a long-term project. The Batho Batho Trust have always been the controlling shareholder.'[30]

The trust's shareholding has been diluted over the years, although in 2022 at almost 47 per cent it remained Thebe's largest shareholder by a long distance. Almost 40 per cent is held by a management and employees' scheme, and almost 10 per cent by Sanlam (incidentally one of the very first empowerment players in 1992).

Despite there being no official relationship between Batho Batho and the ANC, energy minister Gwede Mantashe has acknowledged that Batho Batho is the ANC's investment vehicle into Thebe. Mantashe, who was the ANC's secretary-general between 2007 and 2017, has direct knowledge of the ANC's sources of funding.

When in 2022 the disclosure report of the Independent Electoral Commission (IEC) revealed that the trust had donated R15 million to the ANC, Mantashe brushed off criticism that that ANC was benefiting from government's policy decisions. In response to 'energy experts and environmental activists who have accused him of favouring the fossil fuel industry and failing to recognise the need to create a sustainable energy future' and the accusation that 'the ANC profits from international oil giant Shell's exploration effort appear to cast light on Mantashe's position', the energy minister explained that the ANC had to have 'access to finances so that it survives'. Mantashe clarified, 'They [Batho Batho Trust] didn't give a gift to the ANC; it pays dividends because the ANC is an investor at Thebe.'[31]

Mantashe explained, 'Thebe is an old company. It was formed in 1992 and ANC invested, because the ANC had foresight that the international funding was going to dry up, therefore they had to invest somewhere, and they invested in Thebe.'[32]

Similarly, a decade previously, when Thebe's partnership with Shell first became known, Kenny Fihla, who was then chair of Batho Batho, said, 'We make no bones about the fact that we donate to the ANC – precisely because the trust was established by the president of the ANC at the time [Mandela].'[33]

In that same year – 2012 – it was also revealed that the Trust was part of a consortium that received financing in the form of loans from two state entities, the Industrial Development Corporation and the Public Investment Corporation, to buy a BEE stake in Capitec, then one of the fastest-growing banks in the country.[34] Apart from Batho Batho, a range of ANC-connected individuals stood to gain from the investment, including the life partner of Kgalema Motlanthe – a former ANC deputy president, and head of state for the eight months between September 2008 and May 2009 – the wife of a later mayor of Johannesburg, Parks Tau, and others. The loans were later paid off after the consortium sold 'just enough' equity to settle its debt, with the rest – almost R1 billion in shareholding – set to benefit the consortium, including Batho Batho and, through it, the ANC.[35] The chair of Capitec's board at the time was Michiel le Roux from Stellenbosch, one of the founders of the company, who later became one of the country's wealthiest men.

Thebe Investment Corporation has invested in various ventures since its establishment, ranging from car rental to mining to book publishing, with the firm's net asset value reaching R1 billion in 1998, six years after it was registered. It bought a 30 per cent stake in Nasou and Via Afrika, Naspers's education business, in 1997, and was the empowerment partner of economist Dawie Roodt's Efficient Group, a financial services firm, acquiring a 25.1 per cent stake in 2008.

One of the company's most visible partnerships was with Shell South Africa in 2008, when it bought a 25 per cent shareholding in the oil giant's local refinery business. It went into renewable energy in 2014, winning bids for wind and solar projects. In 2017, it acquired a quarter ownership of businessman Mike Teke's Seriti Resources, which in 2017 took ownership of Anglo's New Vaal, New Denmark and Kriel collieries.[36] Teke is a big player in the energy industry.

Thebe has had some serious support from big capital over the years, with Old Mutual, Investec, Sanlam and Absa at various stages holding up to 15 per cent equity in the business. And although Batho Batho has reduced its shareholding in Thebe over the years, it remains the controlling shareholder. In 1998 the Trust sold 26 per cent of the 100 per cent it held in Thebe to Old Mutual, Fedsure and Sanlam. Absa took ownership of 15.65 per cent of Thebe in 2007 after buying out Old Mutual and Investec.[37]

They didn't see risk in trying to establish a new business, Khanyile said. 'If I look back now, I say how stupid. We were not scared of anything. And I say we give it a good shot. If it works, it works. If it doesn't work, we can say we did try to create a company that is different from others.'[38]

Khanyile, describing himself as 'a rural boy' – he was born in 1950 in Mooi River, an agricultural town in what was then Natal – points out that in the African context, wealth is represented by cattle. 'You have young men who look after the herd, the family herd, but [then you also have] a royal herd, and you have other people who look after the royal herd, for the nation is their home. And I said the Maponyas are the royal family. They have got their own family herds. This is a communal herd.

'We want to show that to prove that it's possible to have a business that succeeds and does common good. But if it doesn't work, we walk away, because we actually have no money of our own that's at risk. All that we were risking was our time and our energies and risking our families in the process. But if it doesn't work, we'll go away and do something else.'[39]

Khanyile, who retired from Thebe in 2018 to go farming in Limpopo and Mpumalanga, said Thebe's approach to business and capitalism was underpinned by 'patriotism'. The company was established to support and invest in 'community organisations'. And he said it was chastening to hear his comrades dismiss the idea in the early years. 'When I travelled in southern Africa it was scary to hear comrades say you can't be black and in business. If you are African and in business it was disgraceful, the only people who could be in business could be non-Africans ... because you can't be in business and be patriotic and fighting for liberation. And it was difficult for people to back us. Investors asked, Vusi, how much of the business do you own? And I replied, I own nothing. And the question was, how does that work? What motivates management and the board? We didn't own the business, the Trust did. And we could walk away at any moment. And I answered these questions by explaining that this business can make a difference in society.'[40]

Thebe, Khanyile said, was established 'as a new enterprise working for the common good, and for broader society.'[41] It was Kwame Nkrumah, Khanyile said, who argued that 'seek ye first the political kingdom and everything else shall be given unto you, which means first attain the levers of political power. Once you have those, you can legislate.'[42]

And he believed it was thanks to Thebe that other black firms emerged soon after its own founding. 'Nothing breeds success like success. And soon after us, NAIL and Real Africa Holdings were established. And Thebe wasn't the only game in town any more.'[43]

18

From Robben Island to the boardroom:
SAKI MACOZOMA

'Everyone wanted to be an Anglo or a Rembrandt or
an AngloVaal, and this mentality also found its way
into empowerment companies, who also tended
to move towards conglomeration.'

– Saki Macozoma, former Robben Island prisoner,
and now in control of assets worth billions of rands.[1]

Born in the eastern Cape in 1957, Saki Macozoma grew up in a politi-
cised home. He was sent to Robben Island in 1977 after leading student
protests in Port Elizabeth following the 1976 Soweto Uprising. He
spent five years on the island, befriending Nelson Mandela and other
struggle leaders, before he was released in 1982.

Macozoma completed his BA through Unisa and won a scholarship to study journalism and economics at Boston University
in the US. He returned to South Africa in 1986. He joined the
ANC after its unbanning in 1990, becoming a spokesperson and being elected to the NEC in 1991. 'Somewhere in 1992' he decided
to engineer his financial independence from politics. 'I knew
I couldn't depend on politics for my personal survival, and made a

conscious decision to try something other than politics,' he said.[2]

He joined South African Breweries soon after as a business development manager and remained at the company until he was elected to parliament as an ANC MP in April 1994.

By the time Macozoma started work at SA Breweries, big capital had started to engineer empowerment deals in advance of the democratic transition. In May 1993, exactly a year before Mandela was sworn in as head of state, Sanlam concluded the first big empowerment transaction when it sold 10 per cent of Metropolitan Life to a consortium called Methold (Metropolitan Holdings) led by Soweto doctor Nthato Motlana.[3] Methold, which soon afterwards changed its name to New Africa Investments Limited (NAIL) in order to establish its own identity, bought the 10 per cent share for R137 million, funded by the Industrial Development Corporation, a state-owned development finance institution.[4]

Motlana said, 'We cannot accept guilt offerings or handouts. At the same time, our goal is not a gradual bottom-up approach to economic advancement. We cannot wait decades to participate fully and effectively in the economic future of South Africa. Through New Africa Investments Limited (NAIL) we seek to gain a strong foothold in the economy.'[5]

Motlana, who was active in resistance politics throughout the 1980s, was Mandela's personal physician during his incarceration on Robben Island and remained his doctor following his release. In the late 1970s, Motlana had led a group of doctors to form the first black-owned chemicals company called Africhem, then he formed Kwacha, the company that established both Lesedi Clinic in Soweto, the first black-owned private hospital in the country, and Sizwe Medical Aid Scheme, the first such scheme owned and operated by blacks.

The Sanlam/Metropolitan Life deal, widely accepted as the start of BEE, introduced a period in which a whole wave of 'first generation' BEE deals were concluded – many, if not most, with black businessmen who were intimately linked to or came out of the ANC. Trevor

Manuel said the Sanlam BEE deal was one of the more successful arrangements of the early years of empowerment. 'And it was because the customer base at Metropolitan ... was primarily lower-income blacks. It then became one of the anchors of NAIL, and it was an asset that they built on and developed further.'[6]

Sanlam's foray into BEE was led by its strategic investment vehicle, Sankorp. Grietjie Verhoef, a professor of accounting, economic and business history at the University of Johannesburg, said Sankorp understood the 'emotional frustration' of blacks and compared it to Afrikaners' exclusion from the mainstream economy during the first half of the twentieth century. 'Sankorp argued that it could make a unique contribution to facilitate effective black participation in the South African economy by forming alliances with black people and utilising their purchasing power to enhance black participation and ownership in the economy. Sankorp was primarily interested in business alliances from which both Sankorp and its partners could benefit.'[7]

Methold – and later NAIL – was controlled by a complicated hierarchical ownership scheme with Motlana at the top as executive chair, Dikgang Moseneke as a deputy executive chairman, and 11 of the 16 board members being black. The 'beauty of the scheme was that [Motlana] maintained control without injecting any more capital into Corporate Africa, the entity that held 55 per cent of equity in NAIL'.[8] The company was listed on the JSE in August 1994 and two months later was valued at R785 million; it controlled assets of R7 billion.

Verhoef said the deal was successful because Sanlam/Sankorp realised value for its own shareholders, while at the same time it committed to NAIL over the long term in transferring skills and developed a template for future empowerment deals. 'The contribution of Sankorp to BEE was the establishment of the principle of transferring control over factors of production through sound business transactions as the only justifiable mechanism of transferring investment and managerial skills to business partners.'[9]

Cyril Ramaphosa joined the board in 1996 as one of three

executive deputy chairs and was appointed to lead the company's bid to acquire Johnnic from Anglo (see chapter 16).[10]

Saki Macozoma, an alumnus of Robben Island, where he'd spent five years incarcerated in the 1970s, had been in parliament for less than two years in April 1996 when Stella Sigcau, then minister of public enterprises, asked him to move to Transnet as deputy managing director. Macozoma made the move, and took over as managing director of the state's freight parastatal in September that year.

It was during his stint there that Macozoma learnt the ropes, and started forming relationships with established – 'white' – business. 'I was thrown into the deep end, but I don't think I would have taken the job had I not taken the gap year with SAB. You can go to a business school and hopefully it gives you the tools to understand what you're dealing with, but it doesn't give you the intelligence – intuitive intelligence and the social intelligence – to drive a complex organisation. I was at Transnet for five years, [during which I] restructured SAA [the airline fell under Transnet at the time], built a new balance sheet for it and resolved a problematic pension fund issue.

'And then while I was there, I worked with a lot of businesspeople like Conrad Strauss [Standard Bank chairman until 2000], Derek Cooper [Standard Bank board member], Gerhard van Niekerk [managing director of Old Mutual until 2000] and others who, in a way, helped me understand the world I was now in. And they, especially the Standard Bank guys, found me interesting enough to invite me onto the board of Standard Bank, which I joined in 1997. And I was there until 2014, mostly as deputy chairman of the group, and as chairman of Liberty and Stanlib.'[11]

Macozoma continued to serve on the ANC's NEC as well as on its subcommittee on economic transformation, a body that, until the ANC's unravelling started to accelerate in 2022, exerted strong influence on South African economic policy.

Around 1997, Macozoma said, there were significant debates

in the committee about reparations by business to black and disadvantaged South Africans, as well as the future shape of black
economic empowerment, a concept that at that point had not yet been
formalised into official policy. Debates were also taking place elsewhere
as to how business should atone for its apartheid sins, with various
proposals floated. Professor Sampie Terreblanche, a leftist academic
from Stellenbosch, advocated a wealth tax to help create social stability, reconciliation and economic growth. Stephen Mulholland, editor
of *Business Day*, proposed a central fund into which capital could pour
one per cent of its market capitalisation. But Bob Tucker from the
Banking Council of South Africa advocated against a reparation fund,
and said individuals and business should be encouraged to contribute
to general reconstruction and development.[12]

It was during this time that 'the politics of business' became important to Macozoma. He said there were varying views inside the
liberation movement, and similar divergent views on the business side.
'I heard the views from Fabcos and Nafcoc, and also on the NEC side.
And then, because I was managing director at Transnet, I heard other
views from people like Cooper and Strauss.'[13] Being in charge of a
large state-owned company at the same time as he sat on the board of
Standard Bank meant that he was coming into contact with leading
businessmen.

To Macozoma, big capital had historically been unresponsive to
the politics of the day, and post-1994 seemed wary and suspicious of
the new order. 'My observation was that business, except for the two
big conglomerates at the top – Anglo and the Ruperts – did not have
an understanding of how to build a new society. You couldn't build big
businesses in a society that was governed as it was under apartheid. It
can only thrive if society thrives. But it appeared to me that some of
the business leaders were happy to commit class suicide rather than
find friends in the black community who shared their ideas and who
could make common cause with them about how business could be
conducted and how South Africa should be governed.'[14]

Macozoma founded a dinner club in 1997 to bring together white business leaders and prominent black leaders to discuss matters like reparation and empowerment. 'And I decided to organise black business from the position I held at Transnet so that we could have these discussions, because you can't try to solve the political problem and leave the economic problem as a festering sore.' There was a lot of space for private business to 'self-correct', he said, even though there was no official BEE policy as yet. 'I told business leaders that they must not wait for legislation to do something, because if they don't and government enacts BEE, the state could overreach. Better to understand the importance of it and do it on your own and on your own terms.'[15]

White and black didn't know each other, and there remained massive distrust on all sides of the equation. He said many black businessmen were entering the business world from politics – himself included – and new companies started appearing, like NAIL and Thebe. Macozoma distinguishes between the old-order white business environment, and 'young leaders' like Michael Spicer and Jacko Maree, Standard Bank deputy chair and chief executive, and Rick Menell, chair of AngloVaal – 'leaders who were enthusiastic about a new relationship between white and black businesspeople'.[16]

Still, while black partners gained significant shareholding in companies during the first wave of empowerment deals, they didn't take ownership and had no say in the direction of those companies. The empowerment debate was centred around blacks obtaining shareholding, or blacks obtaining operational control.[17]

Macozoma explains that a fair amount of cynicism underpinned many empowerment deals, with white business unwilling to let black shareholders or executives have too much power or say over companies. 'There were business leaders who didn't want "clever blacks" in their boardrooms, to quote Zuma. These deals were sub-optimal for themselves, for their country and for society, because they wanted to bring people who were weak and who could be pliant. The problem with somebody who's pliant is that when you need them, they won't be there to defend this system, because [empowerment] needed defending.'

Macozoma credits the Urban Foundation (see chapter 15) as a milestone on the way to the normalisation of black participation in the mainstream economy. It was Harry Oppenheimer and Anton Rupert who helped 'muscle' people into accepting that urban blacks were there to stay, he said. 'It was them who said that, despite the apartheid government saying that Transkei will exist forever, and that they'll dump the people of Soweto there, it was not going to happen. With the establishment of the Urban Foundation they said ... people had to accept the reality and they had to deal with the urban African. And this was contrary to the government that buried its head in the sand. The Urban Foundation developed a group of black people who became familiar with business. And then later, when companies including SAB and IBM started opening positions for blacks, and integrating their operations, it enhanced the process even further. So, the black businessmen involved in those first empowerment deals had some exposure and some experience.'[18]

Reparations by big capital 'for undue gains occasioned by apartheid'[19] was also a hot topic among members of Macozoma's dinner club. 'The mining industry is the best example of this, because it was based on cheap labour delivered and enforced by the state. But how do you quantify reparations? Companies change form and change ownership; they get acquired by other companies.'

That was when the idea of a business-wide response to the injustices of the past was mooted, and the idea of the Business Trust was born. Michael Spicer confirmed that 'a lot of money' was raised to capitalise the Business Trust: 'We quickly raised R1 billion ... and in those days R1 billion was real money.'[20]

Said Theuns Eloff, 'Government initially said, "Thanks, we'll take the money," but we said no way. Government could tell us what its priorities were, but we'd execute it privately.'[21]

Eight ministers sat on the board of the Trust, however, 'and we devised the turnaround for the tourism sector, which was identified as an area with growth'. Macozoma was appointed as chair of SA Tourism, with Michael Spicer as his deputy.

'The Business Trust is quite an important, forgotten and unmentioned effort by business to ensure collective action. It lasted more than a decade, and eventually Zuma killed it,' said Macozoma.[22]

The former Transnet CEO was appointed to the board of NAIL in 1997. By 1999 the company had started to list badly and was considered unfocused and in need of leadership. Motlana and Jonty Sandler, a savvy businessman who'd established himself as Motlana's principal advisor, were forced out of the company after a corporate governance scandal in which four directors wanted to transfer shares in a subsidiary, African Merchant Bank, to themselves.[23] They walked away with golden handshakes of R50 million each – a huge haul but much less than the R250 million they'd wanted to leave the company.[24]

Macozoma took over as chief executive in mid-2001, succeeding Moseneke. Zwelakhe Sisulu, son of Walter and a former group chief executive officer of the South African Broadcasting Corporation, took over as non-executive chair.[25] Safika, a black investment company founded by Moss Ngoasheng and Vuli Cuba, and of which Macozoma would later become executive chair, took a 20 per cent holding in NAIL and eventually became the majority shareholder. At the time Macozoma, Ngoasheng and Cuba each held a 20 per cent stake in the company, with Standard Bank in charge of another 20 per cent and the rest owned by a range of smaller shareholders.

But Macozoma, like many analysts, became frustrated with NAIL's lack of operational focus and led a process of asset disposal before he left the company in 2004, unbundling its interests, which by then were mostly concentrated in the media industry, including radio stations like Jacaranda FM, Kfm 94.5 and production house Urban Brew.[26] It was the end for black business's most audacious project since the advent of democracy.

Describing NAIL as 'a project of its time', Macozoma said it followed the established norms of conglomeration, like most South African companies of the period. 'You buy this and buy this, and in the end – because there was an element of fronting [in which companies use black involvement to satisfy legal requirements], if you like – companies like NAIL ended up with two per cent here, one per cent there, half a per cent there, and then when it's all put together, they looked like this big conglomerate.'[27]

But NAIL had no control of the destiny of the companies in which it owned shares, Macozoma said, 'and in the end, that is why we dismembered it. Because there is no point in us having a percentage of [for example] Metropolitan if you have no influence on policy, you have no influence on direction, you have no influence on anything. And yet, *they* benefit from saying they are part of the NAIL group.'[28]

It wasn't a complete waste of time and resources, however, and Macozoma mentions that cellular communications company MTN grew out of NAIL. 'NAIL had majority control and built that company up to the point where it could go on its own.' While he conceded that 'many things could have been done better, I think it's important to recognise that some good companies came out of a company like NAIL, and the others that were operating at the time.'[29]

Macozoma left the boards of Standard Bank and Liberty in May 2014 to devote his energy to Safika, which became the BEE partner of Standard and a number of other companies. He has led the expansion of the company into various sectors, particularly mining, where its majority shareholding in Ntsimbintle Holdings, owner of lucrative manganese operations in the Northern Cape, has been very profitable. The company, which also invests in financial services, agriculture and property, has also expanded to Australia. Macozoma and Ngoasheng remain the controlling shareholders at Safika and are in charge of assets worth billions of rands.

Macozoma ascribed his success to BEE; he said that if there wasn't an effort to empower black businesspeople, he wouldn't have achieved what he did. 'People like to denigrate BEE and say BEE people are those chosen by the ANC. But the majority of black people who went into business did so [under] their own steam. But what could have been done differently?'[30]

Empowerment was never meant to – nor could it – solve South Africa's economic problems. During South Africa's most successful years, between 1994 and 2008, it was led by Mandela and Mbeki, and the ANC was stronger and more policy coherent, Macozoma said. And although he said he didn't think that his children and grand-children would need empowerment to the same degree that he did, he also didn't think it would come to an end. He ascribed this partly to 'the incompetence of the state', but said that 'it will [also] be difficult politically to do so'.

Economic marginalisation decades after the end of apartheid is driven by the collapse of the education system, he pointed out. 'Are we focusing enough on education, because surely that is the key, basic numeracy and literacy? I don't think we are.'

The entire concept of empowerment needs to be completely rethought, he said. 'The idea that all you need to do, which the RET forces are saying, is to rob white people of all their wealth and all their companies and what have you, and give it to a group of black people, is ridiculous.'[31]

19

The suitcase man:

PATRICE MOTSEPE

'What makes you think you are going to make
money where Anglo has not?'

– Harry Oppenheimer to Patrice Motsepe after he
took control of seven of AngloGold's shafts in 1997.[1]

In 1997, Anglo's gold division handed over seven underperforming gold-producing shafts to Patrice Motsepe's young mining company, African Rainbow Minerals (ARM). Motsepe, then just 35 years old, had no experience, almost no money, and was aiming to make good where the mighty AngloGold could not. And after flattening the mines' management structures, revamping operating hours and streamlining the workforce, ARM did make money – a lot of it. Motsepe was able to repay Anglo the $8.2 million loan to purchase the mines within three years.

Motsepe has since moved way beyond mining, and now commands a business empire stretching from financial services to sport and philanthropy, and is widely recognised as one of South Africa's most upstanding and respected business leaders. He's also part of one of the most powerful families in the country. His brother-in-law is

President Cyril Ramaphosa, who is married to Tshepo Motsepe, a medical doctor who trained at Harvard. His other sister, Bridgette, is a mining magnate in her own right and is married to Jeff Radebe, an ANC stalwart and longtime cabinet minister who's served under every president since 1994. This network has over the years given him access to the most influential individuals in the land and has ensured that he remains within earshot of the country's decision-makers.

He has also, over the years, been a generous benefactor to the governing party, donating millions of rands at fundraisers and national conferences. But, interestingly, he has forged an extremely close relationship with historic big capital. His big break, as noted above, was thanks to Anglo American, the colossus that dominated South African mining and the economy for eighty years and more. And thanks to Sanlam, the financial services and insurance giant that was formed as Afrikaners' original empowerment vehicle after the Anglo-Boer War, Motsepe has been able to construct an investment holding company consisting of a range of interests that analysts regard as one of South Africa's best-run organisations.

Motsepe, thanks to some shrewd investments and clever management, is credited with having created broad-based wealth for black shareholders over the course of many years – something that, critics of BEE like economist Moeletsi Mbeki maintain, is an exception to the norm of enriching only a few politically connected cronies.[2]

Patrice Motsepe, named after Congolese freedom fighter Patrice Lumumba, was born in Soweto on 28 January 1962 to Augustine and Kay Motsepe. The family was moved to the apartheid homeland of Ga-Rankuwa at Hammanskraal, north of Pretoria, where Motsepe's father ran a couple of businesses, including a corner shop, some eateries and a beer hall.[3]

Motsepe spent time behind the counter from age 6, and learnt valuable lessons from his father, he said. 'People don't know that there were very successful black businessmen in the years of apartheid. Whenever my father made a profit, he always ploughed it back into the store.'[4]

Augustine Motsepe sent his children to a Catholic boarding school in Aliwal North, where they learnt to speak fluent Afrikaans – a language Motsepe 'speaks better than an Afrikaans speaker'.[5] After completing high school in Ga-Rankuwa, he enrolled at the University of Swaziland, before obtaining a law degree at the University of the Witwatersrand. He joined the prestigious firm of Bowman Gilfillan (later Bowmans) in 1988, during the years of political upheaval and violence ahead of the ANC's unbanning in 1990.

He was seconded to US firm McGuireWoods, in Richmond, Virginia, where he immersed himself in mining and law. Two years later, in 1993, he became a partner at Bowman Gilfillan, specialising in mining law. In this way, he came to understand what made some mines succeed and others fail, and saw that the successful ones were small and lean, with no corporate overheads.[6] He also believed in the free market system, something to which many in the ANC were hostile. In the 1990s, when the debate around nationalising mines in line with the Freedom Charter was swirling, he cautioned against it, noting that 'the Freedom Charter doesn't discourage private enterprise'. 'My comrades would call me a black capitalist,' he conceded, but at the same time he pointed out that nationalised state mines had failed in South America and elsewhere in Africa.[7]

In 1994, he decided to go out on his own. Democracy had arrived, and although there were some empowerment deals around – like the NAIL/Sanlam deal, and Anglo/Johnnic (see chapters 16 and 18) – black economic empowerment wasn't yet policy or law. But opportunities were starting to open up, and Motsepe launched his first company, Future Mining. 'For nine months I couldn't even afford an office. They used to call me the suitcase man because I worked from a briefcase,' he said.[8] And he took a 'radical' approach to his employees' payment structure. Instead of R1 000 per month, he offered R750 – but he added an incentive scheme that could double this.

Run from the boot of his car, Future Mining provided contracting services to mines. This included low-level jobs like sweeping shafts for gold dust, and other menial work. The company's first big contract was at an Anglo mine in Orkney, on the western side of the Witwatersrand gold reef.

In 1997 Motsepe moved up a gear. The gold price was falling and the rand was stable. That's when Bobby Godsell, AngloGold's chief executive, was looking to offload struggling shafts or close down some of them altogether. But at the same time, he was looking to empower black mining leaders. 'I was seeking to create black capitalists out of people who had no capital,' he said.[9]

Godsell handed over the seven shafts to ARM, formed in 1997, with the understanding that it would pay Anglo from future profits – a hell of a gamble. Harry Oppenheimer was sceptical about Motsepe's ability to succeed, and NUM boss James Motlatsi was equally so; he said that Motsepe 'wanted me to support the deal, but I said it will be embarrassing to black people if Patrice cannot make money out of it'.[10]

Motsepe, drawing from lessons learnt about bloated corporates and unproductive workforces, revamped the mines' operations. He relocated his office to Orkney, ensured that his miners worked more hours than under the previous dispensation, and reduced the work-force by a third.[11] He turned the mines' fortunes around, paid back Anglo and became profitable. ARM made profits of R30 million within six months and increased productivity by 39 per cent.[12]

In 2002 ARM went into partnership with Harmony Gold, then the fourth-largest gold producer in the country, buying more under-performing Anglo shafts in the Free State for R2.2 billion.[13] These marginal mines became jackpots for the joint venture: named Free Gold, they generated R400 million in turnover in their first quarter.[14]

ARM was listed on the JSE in 2002, and Motsepe expanded his mining interests, branching out into platinum and coal.

By the turn of the century, the government had started to implement statutory sectoral charters to force empowerment on South African business. This meant that every sector – mining, financial services and other economic sectors – had to comply with minimum black participation and ownership. These proposals came off the back of a government-appointed BEE Commission, led by Cyril Ramaphosa, then one of the biggest empowerment players in the country (and, of course, Motsepe's brother-in-law). The commission was formed in 1998 and finalised its report in 2000, recommending various interventions 'to help people join the new South Africa'.[15] Spicer said that the mining proposals, which some players like the ANC demanded should be as high as 50 per cent, caused havoc with share prices.[16]

Motsepe, with ARM, was by then perfectly placed as a tried empowerment partner in the mining industry, but the financial services sector charter, which was due to kick in during 2004, posed challenges for companies like Sanlam, the company that a decade before, in 1993, had concluded the first notable empowerment deal with Nthato Motlana's NAIL, before developing and executing empowerment schemes became mandatory.

In 2003 Motsepe formed a consortium, Ubuntu-Botho Investments, to launch a bid as Sanlam's empowerment partner, in which his own family trust held the majority share. Motsepe invested R200 million of his own money, which meant that the consortium's debt was significantly reduced. In 2004, Ubuntu-Botho bought eight per cent of Sanlam's issued shareholding, borrowing R1.1 billion to clinch the transaction.

The fit between the Afrikaans Sanlam and the Afrikaans-speaking Tswana from Hammanskraal couldn't have worked better. The consortium bought the shares at R7.65 per share, and when the deal matured a decade later, Sanlam was trading at R52 per share. Ubuntu-Botho – unlike many other empowerment consortia before it, like NAIL and Johnnic – was able to repay its debt and expand its ownership. In 2008 Motsepe became a dollar billionaire – the first black African on *Forbes*'s list of billionaires.

By the end of 2013, Ubuntu-Botho's equity stake in Sanlam had grown to 14 per cent, and Motsepe was chair of the board.

Sanlam readily acknowledged that the partnership was as profitable for it as it was for Motsepe. 'The deal was structured so that it was a partnership from the outset, whereby if Ubuntu-Botho helped us grow, it could make more money,' Sanlam CEO Johan van Zyl said in 2014. 'We set it up as a business arrangement and I think that is the key part. Today people look at it as a big empowerment deal because you can call it that, but in my view we entered into a business partnership, which was good for both of us. The more they helped us, the more they benefited, and that has worked very well.'[17]

In 2015, Motsepe signed a 10-year deal with Sanlam, agreeing to remain a core shareholder for a decade.[18]

The following year, Motsepe made his big play to give effect to his dream of a globally competitive African finance and investment house. He launched African Rainbow Capital (ARC), wholly owned by Ubuntu-Botho Investments, and pulled the best and the brightest to his new venture, luring Van Zyl as well as senior executives Johan van der Merwe and Machiel Reyneke, previously CEO and chief financial officer of Sanlam Investments, respectively. Motsepe's big-picture vision was complemented by the proven investment track record of 'the two Johans', and today ARC boasts an impressive investment portfolio.

Pundits laud the company for the way it's managed, and the diversity of its investments and performance, calling it a 'rare creature ... a cash-flush black economic empowerment group'[19] and 'a beacon of hope' helping to dispel state capture cynicism. 'ARC ticks all the boxes. It has committed own capital of R10 billion and is based on the partnership principle. Its aim is long-term growth for shareholders, and it is a diversified business, which minimises risk. Most importantly, Motsepe and Van Zyl have a proven track record.'[20]

Successful in fulfilling his 'main aim' of creating 'companies that are globally competitive', Motsepe appeared on *Forbes*'s top 100 living business minds in the world in 2017, alongside leaders like Warren

Buffett, Bill Gates and Mark Zuckerberg.[21] And almost 30 years after the arrival of democracy and the normalisation of relations in the country, Motsepe has become one of the three wealthiest people in South Africa, having built a fortune believed to be in the range of $2.5 billion, or R49.9 billion, which puts him in the league of Nicky Oppenheimer ($8.5 billion, or R142.6 billion) and Johann Rupert ($7.8 billion, R130.8 billion),[22] the other two giants of South African industry and commerce.[23]

Motsepe has never been overtly politically active. He has never campaigned for the ANC and is not considered a political animal. But he moves in senior ANC circles and has been one of the most significant donors to the party. And in 2010, a year after Zuma became president, he donated R10 million to Zuma's foundation,[24] run by Dudu Myeni, who the Zondo Commission subsequently recommended be prosecuted for her role in state capture.

In 2012, Motsepe's ARM was the biggest donor to the ANC, 'as he had been in previous years', according to the party's head of fundraising at its national conference in Mangaung, where Motsepe's brother-in-law Ramaphosa made his return to national politics after his exile to the business world. At a lavish gala dinner ahead of the conference, Motsepe was seated next to then president Jacob Zuma, a place that had been secured after a 'competitive bidding process'.[25]

And in 2021, Motsepe, alongside Ramaphosa, donated R6 million to the ANC immediately ahead of the municipal elections during a time when the governing party was unable to pay salaries or print election posters. ARM gave the party R5.8 million, while Ramaphosa – the leader of the ANC – made two payments, of R166 000 and R200 000.[26]

But Motsepe has started to spread his largesse wider than the ANC. According to declarations to the IEC made by political parties in accordance with the law, in 2021 Harmony Gold also donated money to the Democratic Alliance (R2.1 million), the Economic Freedom

Fighters (R1 million), the Inkatha Freedom Party (R343 000) and the Freedom Front Plus (R242 000).[27]

And despite moving in the most influential of ANC and government circles, Motsepe has also declared his aversion to doing business with government. 'I have never liked it and it's even worse now, now that [I've] got relatives in government,' he said in 2022. 'It is an absolute … headache.'[28]

Motsepe is known for his benevolence, and announced in 2013 that he would donate half of the wealth he generated to the Motsepe Foundation, joining other billionaires like Bill Gates, who also donated half his fortune to a charitable and philanthropic foundation. 'I decided quite some time ago to give at least half the funds generated by our family assets to uplift poor and other disadvantaged and marginalised South Africans but was also duty bound and committed to ensuring that it would be done in a way that protects the interests and retains the confidence of our shareholders and investors.'[29] And during the Covid-19 pandemic Motsepe joined Nicky Oppenheimer and Johann Rupert in pledging R1 billion to help small businesses recover from the devastating effects of the virus. [30]

A great lover of sport, Motsepe is the owner of soccer club Mamelodi Sundowns, and was elected president of the Confederation of African Football (CAF) in March 2021, which has become a passion. But he's not only a soccer lover. In 2019 he bought 37 per cent of the Blue Bulls Company, which controls the Pretoria-based rugby team. The other largest shareholder in the Bulls? Rupert, who also owns 37 per cent.[31]

Motsepe is an enigma.

Conclusion

When Gavin Relly and his colleagues flew to Lusaka in September 1985, they were light years removed from the country that Motsepe and others came to inhabit. The South Africa almost 40 years on from that visit is a completely different place, freed from racial segregation and discriminatory laws, an open society moving in step with a globalised world.

But the ANC as a governing party has also been transformed: from an organisation focused on political liberation, underpinned by socialist economic ideals, to a failing party of government, characterised by predatory political elites completely enamoured with the excesses of capitalism.

The road the country has had to travel over the last four decades has been arduous and painful, with deep-set structural and fundamental problems that contribute to a weak economy, which in turn has led to embedded inequality and poverty, and serial and enormous unemployment.

Empowerment has faced deep criticism, with many arguing that BEE has over the years, and despite tinkering at the edges, not managed to change the structure of the South African economy, and has failed to transfer wealth to a broad enough foundation of black and excluded South Africans. It was always the same people who benefited, critics say, with Motsepe, Ramaphosa, Macozoma, Mzi Khumalo and Tokyo Sexwale names that were often recycled in empowerment transactions, which were sometimes nothing more than paper transactions.[1]

Almost all of these moguls have become extremely wealthy at one point or another, with almost every single one attaining billionaire status. Macozoma has seemingly not reached those heights, although he controls assets worth billions through his Safika Holdings, while Khumalo lost his status years ago.

Sexwale, who once headed the mighty Mvelaphanda Group, and who was invested in a range of industries, including mining, became a billionaire thanks to his business interests. He was worth R2 billion in 2014, according to a report by wealth managers New World Wealth – the third richest black South African behind Motsepe and Ramaphosa.[2]

Sexwale – similar to other new billionaires and millionaires – exploited his ties to the ANC. He was a Robben Island prisoner alongside Nelson Mandela, with whom he maintained a close bond, and became the first premier of the new Gauteng province in 1994. He left politics three years later – a year after Ramaphosa did the same – after apparently growing tired of 'the plots and counter-plots', but denying that he was pushed out by Thabo Mbeki. And he was praised for his leadership, with critics saying Gauteng 'thrived' under him and that his mistakes 'were few'.[3]

He remained close to Mandela, donated shares in his company to the statesman's children, and paid for his 85th birthday party.[4] When he was touted as a possible strategic investor in state-owned telecoms giant Telkom, his 'political connections and sway' were said to be to his advantage.[5]

He established Mvelaphanda Holdings in 1998, and, like Macozoma and Ramaphosa with Standard Bank, and Motsepe with Sanlam, Sexwale was the beneficiary of a major BEE deal when his Batho Bonke consortium became Absa's BEE partner in 2004. Mvelaphanda's biggest assets became the 10 per cent it held in Absa, as well as the 10 per cent in giant construction company Group Five. It also controlled Mvelaphanda Resources, one of the country's biggest black-owned mining houses. Like other empowerment companies, Mvelaphanda tended towards conglomeration, holding assets in energy, hotels, transportation, telecommunications, property, health and financial services.

Apart from serving on 43 boards of directors by the time he was appointed to Jacob Zuma's cabinet, Sexwale served as advisor to international bank JP Morgan Chase, and on the council of the Brookings Institution, an American think-tank.

Big capital in South Africa, founded by a mining industrial complex and dominant in the economy since the end of the nineteenth century, knew it had to influence the transition in order to survive it, and did so by investing in relationships, processes and projects during the late 1980s and early 1990s. In this way, it managed to shift the ANC's worldview from one historically marinated in Marxism and socialism, to one embracing private enterprise and private enrichment. And it had to let the black majority into the boardroom and show them the delights and possibilities that came with wealth and accumulation, for so long the preserve of the white Randlords and financial kings of Johannesburg.

Before his death in 2022, Michael Spicer, the Anglo executive who played such a pivotal role for big capital in engaging the ANC and liberation movement, defended big business's actions before, during and after the transition. He said that capital had clearly had to do something in order to bring black South Africans into the fold, both as a measure to defend itself and also as a way of evening out the playing field. But the system, he believed, no longer functioned. 'It has now become a sort of an expectation that there's a free give-away for everybody, and frankly there's a lot of greed involved, and a lot of the individuals think that the minimum you should make in one hit is a couple of hundred million.' Lamenting that this has killed any entrepreneurial spirit – 'why would you do that if you just get equity free, gratis … why start and go through all the pain of growing your business if you're going to get a cut of big businesses? – he said BEE 'has become entitlement'. 'The big debating point is do you have growth through empowerment or empowerment through growth? Putting the cart before the horse is one of the reasons why this economy has not grown.'[6]

There's no doubt that a huge amount of capital that would otherwise have been invested in new productive enterprise has gone into BEE, he said. This is 'simply reshuffling the deck of existing assets. And it's become a cost to existing shareholders, and they've absorbed it, but it's one of the many things that has made South Africa less competitive.'[7]

Godsell said the big tragedy in South Africa is the fact that an economic transition did not accompany the political transition, because even though ownership might have been created for some black businessmen, it didn't come with any risk. And Godsell said this doesn't represent real ownership. 'If you're on the board of a company as a political declaration, for a company to have your name on its letterhead, it's not real economic inclusion. Because if you're not involved in making the tough choices, then you're not an economic partner.' As he saw it, 'Business is about risk and reward. If you take away the risks, you effectively take away the rewards.'[8]

Big capital helped South Africa make the political transition possible, but the country has been unable to take advantage of the provenance bestowed on it after 1994. Business has struggled to define its relationship with the ANC government, while the political elite, despite enjoying the fruits of the market, have remained antagonistic towards capital.

A corrupt, weakened and misfiring ANC government has over the last decade done enormous damage to the economy and the country's prospects. 'The ANC's endless psycho-drama is far more important to them than economic matters. They're locked into this incredibly slow minuet of factions and counter-factions,' Spicer said, making the obvious observation that 'for the country, really, these aren't the most important issues at all'. 'This is a remarkably resilient country and economy, but in the last decade or more, we've probably gone beyond what we can handle. The country and economy are no longer able to absorb the levels of mistakes and corruption and bad governance. It's taken its toll.'[9]

To create a new South Africa on the foundation of a racist, apartheid society, with an evil system of economic exclusion, was always going to be difficult. But now it is proving impossible. Saki Macozoma said the ANC have 'squandered the opportunity' to rebuild the country. 'It gives me great pain,' he said.[10]

In discussions about the economy generally and the early years of democracy in particular, Trevor Manuel repeatedly returned to the issue of trust: it had to be built from scratch, it had to be earned from international investors and the markets, it had to be established between the new government and the SARB. Trust in the political leadership, and ensuring stable economic policies and predictability, were at the centre of what Manuel and those in the economic cluster – including Mbeki – were trying to do.

Manuel, clearly disillusioned with the organisation to whose ideals he devoted his life, said the only way to achieve economic growth and inclusion now is to make sure that all the levers of power work together. 'Then you can achieve success. But it does mean that you need to be tough, you need to have the ability to stand up to people and to have difficult discussions. Some of the hardest battles I had were with friends about how to get support for the public finance management decisions we had to take. And if you controlled that, how you could generate support in the broader economy. It worked, and the biggest transformation came when jobs were created in the early 2000s, [and] perhaps more importantly in 2005 and 2006. But the ANC didn't like it, so in 2007 it needed to get rid of Thabo Mbeki and bring down the house.'[11]

All of those battles – on what is needed to achieve economic growth, how to structure the state and the economy, transformation and the role of big capital – need to be fought again.

And trust in government, by investors and business? 'All of that's gone,' said Manuel. 'All of that is gone.'[12]

223

References

Adams, S. 6 March 2008. 'The prince of mines'. Forbes. https://www.forbes.com/forbes/2008/0324/088.html?sh=2c953e8b3afe

ANC policy documents. 31 May 1992. 'Ready to Govern: ANC policy guidelines for a democratic South Africa'. African National Congress. https://www.anc1912.org.za/policy-documents-1992-ready-to-govern-anc-policy-guidelines-for-a-democratic-south-africa/

Areff, A. 25 June 2022. 'Motsepe hates doing business with govt, especially when "you've got relatives" there'. Fin24. https://www.news24.com/fin24/companies/motsepe-hates-doing-business-with-govt-especially-when-youve-got-relatives-there-20220625

Associated Press. 14 March 1987. 'Commission investigates funding for ANC Ad'. AP News. https://apnews.com/article/0a7e50c432a325dc02fac2c1c76a2774

Associated Press. 8 August 1987. 'Standard Chartered to leave South Africa'. The New York Times. https://www.nytimes.com/1987/08/08/business/standard-chartered-set-to-leave-south-africa.html

Associated Press. 14 April 1996. 'Ramaphosa Changes Post'. YouTube. https://www.youtube.com/watch?v=usyEhjEE6mo

Bähr, J and Kopper, C. 2016. *Munich Re: The company history, 1880–1980*. CH Beck. https://www.munichre.com/content/dam/munichre/contentlounge/website-pieces/documents/Munich-Re-The-Company-History.pdf/_jcr_content/renditions/original./Munich-Re-The-Company-History.pdf

Barnard, N. 2015. *Geheime revolusie: Memoires van 'n spioenbaas*. Tafelberg

Block, D and Soggot, M. 7 May 1999. 'Forced to take R50m and leave'. Mail & Guardian. https://mg.co.za/article/1999-05-07-forced-to-take-r50m-and-leave/

Bloom, AH. 17 September 1985. 'Notes of a meeting at Mfuwe Game Lodge, 13 September 1985'. https://atom.lib.uct.ac.za/uploads/r/

university-of-cape-town-libraries-special-collections/2/9/4/294cf72
dea83f0548db6e6a3c8af2ab9aa4ba880db41dfd148161ddbb2c1d4dc/
BCS604.pdf

Bosch, M. 9 June 2008. 'S.Africa's Sexwale: from freedom fighter to
tycoon'. Reuters. https://www.reuters.com/article/safrica-sexwale-
idUSL0980888220080609

Bridge, S and Moses, A. 16 July 2004. 'Ramaphosa's BEE bonanza'.
IOL. https://www.iol.co.za/news/south-africa/ramaphosas-bee-
bonanza-217325

Bruce, N. 1985. 'The rand and the cash crisis'. *Leadership*, 4(3)

Butler, A. 2019. *Cyril Ramaphosa: The road to presidential power*. Jacana
Publishers

Camdessus, M. 2000. *Looking to the Future: The IMF in Africa*. The
International Monetary Fund

Chatham House. 29 October 1985. 'Oliver Tambo: The future of South
Africa: The ANC view'. https://www.chathamhouse.org/events/all/
members-event-research-event/webinar-african-liberation-historical-
and-contemporary

Chikanga, K. 15 August 2004. 'Millennium now called Shanduka'. IOL.
https://www.iol.co.za/business-report/companies/millennium-now-
called-shanduka-757023

Cowell, A. 17 August 1985. 'Botha Speech: 2 Signals'. *The New York Times*

Cranston, S. 21 May 2015. 'Empowerment: A new giant rising?'
BusinessLive. https://www.businesslive.co.za/archive/2015-05-21-
empowerment-a-new-giant-rising/

Cranston, S. 7 September 2017. 'ARC: All you need to know about
JSE's newest entrant'. https://www.businesslive.co.za/fm/money-
andinvesting/2017-09-07-arc-all-you-need-to-know-about-jses-
newestentrant/

Daley, S. 14 April 1996. 'Key Mandela aide to join group promoting
investment by blacks'. The New York Times. https://www.nytimes.
com/1996/04/14/world/key-mandela-aide-to-join-group-
promoting-investment-by-blacks.html

Davies, R. 2021. *Towards a New Deal: A political economy of the times of my
life*. Jonathan Ball Publishers

Davis, G. 19 April 1996. 'How Cyril was edged out by Thabo'. Mail &
Guardian. https://mg.co.za/article/1996-04-19-how-cyril-was-
edged-out-by-thabo/

Department of Finance. N.d. 'Growth, Employment and Redistribution: A Macroeconomic strategy'. National Treasury. http://www.treasury. gov.za/publications/other/gear/chapters.pdf

Department of Information and Publicity. 12 March 1996. 'Statement on the South Africa Foundation Document, "Growth for all"'. Hartford Web Publishing. http://www.hartford-hwp.com/archives/37a/024.html

Derby, R. 25 April 2018. 'Still a long way to go for meaningful BEE'. BusinessLive. https://www.businesslive.co.za/bd/opinion/ columnists/2019-04-25-ron-derby-still-a-long-way-to-go-for- meaningful-bee/

De Villiers, R and Stemmet, J. 2020. *Prisoner 913: The release of Nelson Mandela*. Tafelberg

Duke, L. 1 November 1996. 'Blacks buy into South African industry'. The Washington Post. https://www.washingtonpost.com/archive/ politics/1996/11/01/blacks-buy-into-s-african-industry/9281be8f- 42bc-4335-a5c5-7a84b8ad73f4/

Du Toit, P. 2019. *The Stellenbosch Mafia*. Jonathan Ball Publishers

Ellis, S. 2012. *External Mission: The ANC in exile, 1960-1990*. Jonathan Ball Publishers

Eloff, T. 14 December 1997. 'The Consultative Business Movement, 1988–1994'. Submission to the Truth and Reconciliation Commission. (Provided by Eloff.)

Eloff, T. May 2015. 'The importance of process in the South African peace and constitutional negotiations'. Practitioner notes no 3. Centre for Mediation in Africa. University of Pretoria https://www.up.ac. za/media/shared/237/Practitioner%20Notes/practitioner-notes- journal-03.zp61397.pdf

Engineering News. 12 December 2001. 'Motsepe speaks in global news magazine'. https://www.engineeringnews.co.za/article/motsepe- speaks-in-global-news-magazine-2001-12-12

Esterhuyse, W. 2012. *Eindstryd: Geheime gesprekke en die einde van apartheid*. Tafelberg

Evans, J. 4 March 2022. 'Mantashe says ANC had "foresight" to invest in Shell-affiliated Batho-Batho Trust to get R15-million payout'. Daily Maverick. https://www.dailymaverick.co.za/article/2022-03-04- mantashe-says-anc-had-foresight-to-invest-in-shell-affiliated-batho- batho-trust-to-get-r15-million-payout/

Forbes. Nd. 'World's Billionaires List: The richest in 2022'. https://www.forbes.com/billionaires/

Forbes. 18 November 2015. 'Cyril Ramaphosa'. https://www.forbes.com/profile/cyril-ramaphosa/?sh=65df628124fe

Gerber, J. 23 February 2022. 'Party funding: Several parties benefit from Patrice Motsepe's deep pockets'. News24. https://www.news24.com/news24/southafrica/news/party-funding-several-parties-benefit-from-patrice-motsepes-deep-pockets-20220223

Gevisser, M. 11 October 1996. 'Cyril Ramaphosa, deputy chairman of New Africa Investments, Ltd.'. *Mail & Guardian*

Gevisser, M. 2007. *Thabo Mbeki: The dream deferred.* Jonathan Ball Publishers

Giliomee, H. 2003. *The Afrikaners: A biography of a people.* Tafelberg Publishers

Giliomee, H. May 2008. 'Great expectations: Pres. PW Botha's Rubicon speech of 1985'. *New Contree Journal,* 55

Giliomee, H. 2012. *Die Laaste Afrikanerleiers: 'n Opperste toets van mag.* Tafelberg

Gqubule, D. April 2021. 'Black Economic Empowerment Transactions in South Africa after 1994'. Working paper. Southern Centre of Inequality Studies, University of the Witwatersrand. https://www.wits.ac.za/media/wits-university/faculties-and-schools/commerce-law-and-management/research-entities/scis/documents/BEE%20Transactions%20in%20SA%20after%201994.pdf

Green, P. 2009. *Trevor Manuel: 'n Lewensverhaal.* Tafelberg

Hancock, WK. 1962. *Smuts: The Sanguine Years, 1870–1919.* Cambridge University Press

Hartley, R. 2017. *Ramaphosa: The man who would be king.* Jonathan Ball Publishers

Heunis, J. 2007. *Die Binnekring: Terugblikke op die laaste dae van blanke regering.* Jonathan Ball Publishers

I-Net Bridge. 30 January 2013. 'Patrice Motsepe donates half his wealth'. BusinessTech. https://businesstech.co.za/news/trending/30852/patrice-motsepe-donates-half-his-wealth/

IOL. 25 July 2004. 'The real tale of Nail's black empowerment still to be told'. https://www.iol.co.za/business-report/economy/the-real-tale-of-nails-black-empowerment-still-to-be-told-756164

IOL. 26 July 2004. 'Macozoma makes a mint on Nail shares'. https://www.iol.co.za/business-report/companies/macozoma-makes-a-mint-on-nail-shares-756186

ITWeb. 18 September 2002. 'Alexander Forbes and Millennium Consolidated Investments in empowerment deal'. https://www.itweb.co.za/content/kLgB17eJGnPM59N4

Jeffery, A. 18 January 2013. 'BEE is flawed and should be scrapped'. Mail & Guardian. https://webcache.googleusercontent.com/search?q=cache:kFwVualihV0J:https://mg.co.za/article/2013-01-18-bee-is-flawed-and-should-be-scrapped/+&cd=5&hl=en&ct=clnk&gl=za

Joffe, H. 20 January 1989. 'Exit Ball just as he entered: without speeches'. Weekly Mail. https://mg.co.za/article/1989-01-20-00-exit-ball-just-as-he-entered-without-speeches/

Johnnic Holdings Annual Report. 2004. https://www.sec.gov/Archives/edgar/vprr/0404/04045720.pdf

Jordan, B. 8 April 2012. 'ANC trust stands to gain from fracking'. Sunday Times. https://www.timeslive.co.za/sunday-times/lifestyle/2012-04-08-anc-trust-stands-to-gain-from-fracking/

Lelyveld, J. 11 April 1982. 'The many faces of Barlow Rand Ltd'. The New York Times. https://www.nytimes.com/1982/04/11/business/the-many-faces-of-barlow-rand-ltd.html

Mabanga, T. 8 July 2005. 'Clash of the titans'. Mail & Guardian. https://mg.co.za/article/2005-07-08-clash-of-the-titans/

Mail & Guardian. 28 February 1997. 'Khumalo's coup'. https://mg.co.za/article/1997-02-28-khumalos-coup/

Mail & Guardian. 12 December 1997. 'Farewell to the first premier of Gauteng'. https://mg.co.za/article/1997-12-12-farewell-to-the-first-premier-of-gauteng/

Mandela, N. 23 May 1990. Address at Options for Building an Economic Future Conference convened by the Consultative Business Movement attended by South African business executives. http://www.mandela.gov.za/mandela_speeches/1990/900523_econ.htm Accessed 23 June 2022.

Mbeki, T. 1984. 'The Fatton Thesis: A rejoinder'. *Canadian Journal of African Studies*, 18(3)

McGregor, A, Rose, R and Cranston, S. 23 January 2009. 'The new economic elite'. BusinessLive. https://www.businesslive.co.za/archive/2009-01-23-the-new-economic-elite/

Miller, J. 2016. *An African Volk: The apartheid regime and the search for survival*. Oxford University Press

Mining Weekly. 29 November 2002. 'The Free State golden handshake: The turnaround specialist and the leader of tomorrow'. https://www.miningweekly.com/article/the-free-state-golden-handshake-the-turnaround-specialist-and-the-leader-of-tomorrow-2002-11-29/

Mittner, M. 21 April 2016. 'Investor's Notebook: ARC is a beacon of hope'. BusinessLive. https://www.businesslive.co.za/archive/2016-04-21-investors-notebook-arc-is-a-beacon-of-hope2/

Moseneke, D. 2016. *My Own Liberator: A memoir*. Picador Africa

Mtongana, L. 24 September 2017. 'Motsepe: I never aimed for Forbes list'. BusinessLive. https://www.businesslive.co.za/bt/business-and-economy/2017-09-23-motsepe-i-never-aimed-for-forbes-list/

Murray, H. 1985. 'Gavin Relly in conversation with Hugh Murray'. *Leadership*, 4(3)

Myre, G. 18 January 1989. 'Casino head admits bribery in latest corruption scandal'. Associated Press. https://apnews.com/article/d12ac16d3311e0158d67080ef52842d8

Nattrass, N. 1994. 'South Africa: The economic restructuring agenda – a critique of the MERG report'. *Third World Quarterly*, 15(2). https://www.tandfonline.com/doi/pdf/10.1080/01436599408420376?needAccess=true

Nattrass, N and Seekings, J. 2011. 'The economy and poverty in the twentieth century'. Ross, R, Mager, AK and Nasson, B (eds). *The Cambridge History of South Africa, Volume 2, 1885–1994*. Cambridge University Press

Ndzamela, P. 20 March 2014. 'Ubuntu-Botho/Sanlam BEE deal'. BusinessLive. https://www.businesslive.co.za/archive/2014-03-20-ubuntu-bothosanlam-bee-deal/

Nelson Mandela Foundation. N.d. Address by State President PW Botha, 15 August 1985. O'Malley Archive. https://omalley.nelsonmandela.org/omalley/index.php/site/q/03lv01538/04lv01600/05lv01638/06lv01639.htm

News24. 14 May 2002. 'Motsepe: From briefcase to big board'. https://www.news24.com/News24/Motsepe-From-briefcase-to-big-board-20020514

News24. 21 September 2014. '"Broke" Judy claims Tokyo spends R2m a month. https://www.news24.com/News24/Broke-Judy-claims-Tokyo-blows-R2m-a-month-20140921

Njilo, N. 18 November 2021. 'Ramaphosa and Motsepe donated over R6m to ANC ahead of election, says IEC'. BusinessLive. https://www.businesslive.co.za/bd/politics/2021-11-18-ramaphosa-and-motsepe-donated-over-r6m-to-anc-ahead-of-election-says-iec/

Nsehe, M. 2 June 2015. 'South African deputy president to earn at least $200 million from sale of investment firm'. Forbes. https://www.forbes.com/sites/mfonobongnsehe/2015/06/02/south-african-deputy-president-to-earn-at-least-200-million-from-sale-of-investment-firm/?sh=2a1b79b01493

Omarjee, L. 2 April 2020. 'Donations, loans & pledges: What you need to know about those billions aimed at fighting Covid-19'. Fin24. https://www.news24.com/fin24/economy/south-africa/donations-loans-pledges-what-you-need-to-know-about-those-billions-aimed-at-fighting-covid-19-20200402-2

Open Secrets. 16 October 2017. 'Declassified: Apartheid profits – Tiny Rowland, a very British spy?' Daily Maverick. https://www.dailymaverick.co.za/article/2017-10-16-declassified-apartheid-profits-tiny-rowland-a-very-british-spy/

Our Constitution. October 1989. 'Events leading up to the signing of the Harare Declaration'. https://ourconstitution.constitutionhill.org.za/the-harare-declaration-october-1989/

Padayachee, V and Van Niekerk, R. 2019. *Shadow of Liberation: Contestation and compromise in the economic and social policy of the ANC, 1943–1996.* Wits University Press

Papenfus, T. 2011. *Pik Botha en Sy Tyd*. Litera Publikasies

Parliamentary Monitoring Group. 13 September 2000. 'Black Economic Empowerment Commission: briefing by Cyril Ramaphosa & Lott Ndlovu'. https://pmg.org.za/committee-meeting/191/

Paton, C. 16 December 2012. 'Motsepe centre stage at ANC's Mangaung gala dinner'. BusinessLive. https://www.businesslive.co.za/archive/2012-12-16-motsepe-centre-stage-at-ancs-mangaung-gala-dinner-/

Phembani. 19 August 2015. 'Phembani finalises large merger with Shanduka after receiving approval from Competition Tribunal'. https://www.phembani.com/index.php/2015/08/19/pembani-

finalises-large-merger-with-shanduka-after-receiving-approval-
from-competition-tribunal/

Phillips, N. 2004. 'The funding of black economic empowerment in South
Africa'. Master's degree thesis. University of Stellenbosch. http://
scholar.sun.ac.za/handle/10019.1/16411

Pottinger, B. 1988. *The Imperial Presidency: PW Botha, the first 10 years*.
Southern Book Publishers

Reuters. 22 December 2011. 'China's CIC takes stake in S. Africa's
Shanduka'. https://www.reuters.com/article/ozabs-shanduaka-cic-
20111222-idAFJOE7BL02720111222

Robinson, S. 17 April 2005. 'South Africa: The New Rand Lords'. Time.
http://content.time.com/time/subscriber/article/0,33009,1050314,00.
html

Rumney, R. 26 May 1995. 'Black buyer for Johnnic'. Mail & Guardian.
https://mg.co.za/article/1995-05-26-black-buyer-for-johnnic/

Rynhart, G and Wielenga, C. 1 March 2021. 'Business deserves thanks for
role in averting SA civil war'. Business Day. https://www.businesslive.
co.za/bd/opinion/2021-03-01-business-deserves-thanks-for-role-in-
averting-sa-civil-war/#

Sachs, M. 2021. 'Fiscal Dimensions of South Africa's Crisis'. Public
Economic Project. Southern Centre for Inequality Studies, University
of the Witwatersrand

Sake24. 3 May 2010. 'ANC owns major stake in Thebe'. News24. https://
www.news24.com/fin24/anc-owns-major-stake-in-thebe-20100503

Sampson, A. 1999. *Mandela: The authorised biography*. HarperCollins

Sampson, A. 2008. *The Anatomist*. Jonathan Ball Publishers

Sanlam Investments. N.d. Our empowerment journey. https://www.
sanlaminvestments.com/about/sustainableinvesting/Pages/
empowerment-journey.aspx

SAPA. 2 October 2010. 'Patrice Motsepe donates R10m to Zuma's
foundation'. Mail & Guardian. https://mg.co.za/article/2010-10-02-
patrice-motsepe-donates-r10m-to-zumas-foundation/

Savage, M. 2014. 'Trekking Outward: A chronology of meetings between
South Africans and the ANC in exile, 1983–2000'. University of Cape
Town. https://atom.lib.uct.ac.za/index.php/za-uct-bc-s-bcs604

Simpson, T. 2021. *History of South Africa: From 1902 to the present*.
Penguin Books

South African History Online. Nd. '19 die at Shell House massacre'.
  https://www.sahistory.org.za/dated-event/19-die-shell-house-
  massacre
South African Institute of Race Relations. 2017. 'South Africa Survey
  2018'.
Spaarwater, M. 2012. *A Spook's Progress: From making war to making peace.*
  Zebra Press
Sparks, A. 2003. *Beyond the Miracle: Inside the New South Africa.* Jonathan
  Ball Publishers
Spicer, M. April 2016. 'The Business-Government relationship: What has
  gone wrong?' *Journal of the Helen Suzman Foundation*, Issue 78
Tambo, A. 2014. *Oliver Tambo Speaks.* Kwela Books
Thebe Investment Corporation. N.d. Thebe's timeline of historic
  milestones. https://www.thebe.co.za/history/
The Bulls. N.d. 'Vodacom Bulls latest signing … Patrice Motsepe'.
  https://thebulls.co.za/news/vodacom-bulls-latest-signing-patrice-
  motsepe
The Economist. 5 June 1997. 'The new Randlord'. https://www.
  economist.com/business/1997/06/05/the-new-randlord
The Freedom Charter. 26 June 1995. African National Congress. https://
  www.anc1912.org.za/the-freedom-charter-2/
The Presidency. 26 November 2014. 'Deputy President Cyril Ramaphosa
  acts to address potential conflicts of interest'. https://www.
  thepresidency.gov.za/press-statements/deputy-president-cyril-
  ramaphosa-acts-address-potential-conflicts-interest
Timse, T, Mckune, C and Brummer, S. 28 September 2012. 'ANC stands
  to benefit from R1bn Capitec bank bonanza'. Mail & Guardian.
  https://mg.co.za/article/2012-09-28-anc-stands-to-benefit-from-
  r1bn-capitec-bank-bonanza/
Truth and Reconciliation Commission of South Africa Report. 1998.
  Volume 4. https://www.justice.gov.za/TRC/report/finalreport/
  Volume%204.pdf
Turok, B. 2003. *Nothing But the Truth.* Jonathan Ball Publishers
Van Zyl Slabbert, F. 2006. *Duskant die Geskiedenis: 'n Persoonlike terugblik
  op die politieke oorgang in Suid-Afrika.* Jonathan Ball Publishers &
  Tafelberg
Verhoef, G. 1 June 2003. '"The invisible hand": The roots of black
  economic empowerment, Sankorp and societal change in South

Africa, 1985–2000'. *Journal for Contemporary History*, 28(1).

Waldmeir, P. 1998. *Anatomy of a Miracle: The end of apartheid and the birth of the New South Africa*. Rutgers University Press

Walton, EH. 1912. *The Inner History of the National Convention of South Africa*. Maskew Miller

Welsh, D. 2009. *The Rise and Fall of Apartheid*. Jonathan Ball Publishers

Interviews

Doug Band, 12 April 2022

Jeremy Cronin, 23 March 2021

Theuns Eloff, 1 April 2022

Bobby Godsell, 4 May 2022

Vusi Khanyile, 6 and 19 April 2022

Martin Kingston, 12 April 2022

Jürgen Kögl, 7, 11 and 26 April 2022, 25 and 28 May 2022, and 9 and 22 June 2022

Saki Macozoma, 4 May 2022

Trevor Manuel, 2, 5 and 29 March 2021, and 3 May 2022

Jay Naidoo, 9 May 2022

Michael Spicer, 5 and 18 March 2021

Clem Sunter, 5 April 2022

Notes

Introduction

1 Nattrass, N and Seekings, J. 2011. 'The economy and poverty in the twentieth century'. Ross, R, Mager, AK and Nasson, B (eds). *The Cambridge History of South Africa, Volume 2, 1885–1994*. Cambridge University Press.
2 Author's interview with Michael Spicer, 18 March 2021.
3 Author's interview with Michael Spicer, 5 March 2021.
4 Ibid.
5 Author's interview with Saki Macozoma, 4 May 2022.
6 Author's interview with Trevor Manuel, 29 March 2021.
7 Author's interview with Bobby Godsell, 4 May 2022.
8 Ibid.
9 Author's interview with Jay Naidoo, 9 May 2022.
10 Ibid.
11 Ibid.
12 Author's interview with Michael Spicer, 5 March 2021.
13 Author's interview with Jay Naidoo, 9 May 2022.
14 Author's interview with Michael Spicer, 5 March 2021.
15 Author's interview with Trevor Manuel, 29 March 2021.

Chapter I

1 Author's interview with Michael Spicer, 5 March 2021.
2 Bloom, AH. 17 September 1985. 'Notes of a meeting at Mfuwe Game Lodge, 13 September 1985'. https://atom.lib.uct.ac.za/uploads/r/university-of-cape-town-libraries-special-collections/2/9/4/294cf72 dea83f0548db6e6a3c8af2ab9aa4ba880db41dfd148161ddbb2c1d4dc/BCS604.pdf. Accessed 21 June 2022.
3 Ibid. Accessed 20 June 2022.
4 The frontline states were a loose coalition of African countries from

the 1960s to the early 1990s committed to ending apartheid and white minority rule in South Africa and Rhodesia; they included Angola, Botswana, Lesotho, Mozambique, Tanzania, Zambia and Zimbabwe.

5   Miller, J. 2016. *An African Volk: The apartheid regime and the search for survival.* Oxford University Press.

6   Author's interview with Michael Spicer, 18 March 2021.

7   Bloom, AH. 17 September 1985. 'Notes of a meeting at Mfuwe Game Lodge, 13 September 1985'. https://atom.lib.uct.ac.za/uploads/r/ university-of-cape-town-libraries-special-collections/2/9/4/294cf72 dea83f0548db6e6a3c8af2ab9aa4ba880db41dfd148161ddbb2c1d4dc/ BCS604.pdf. Accessed 21 June 2022.

8   Hancock, WK. 1962. *Smuts: The Sanguine Years, 1870–1919.* Cambridge University Press; and Walton, EH. 1912. *The Inner History of the National Convention of South Africa.* Maskew Miller.

9   Bloom, AH. 17 September 1985. 'Notes of a meeting at Mfuwe Game Lodge, 13 September 1985'. https://atom.lib.uct.ac.za/uploads/r/ university-of-cape-town-libraries-special-collections/2/9/4/294cf72 dea83f0548db6e6a3c8af2ab9aa4ba880db41dfd148161ddbb2c1d4dc/ BCS604.pdf. Accessed 21 June 2022.

10 Ibid.

11 Ibid.

12 Ibid.

13 Ibid.

14 Ibid.

15 Author's interview with Michael Spicer, 18 March 2021.

16 Author's interview with Trevor Manuel, 2 March 2021.

17 Author's interview with Michael Spicer, 5 March 2021.

18 Ibid.

19 Giliomee, H. May 2008. 'Great expectations: Pres. PW Botha's Rubicon speech of 1985'. *New Contree Journal*, 55.

20 Welsh, D. 2009. *The Rise and Fall of Apartheid.* Jonathan Ball Publishers.

21 Author's interview with Michael Spicer, 5 March 2021.

22 Murray, H. 1985. 'Gavin Relly in conversation with Hugh Murray'. *Leadership*, 4(3).

23 Author's interview with Clem Sunter, 5 April 2022.

24 Author's interview with Michael Spicer, 5 March 2021.

25 Author's interview with Clem Sunter, 5 April 2022.

26 Murray, H. 1985. 'Gavin Relly in conversation with Hugh Murray'. *Leadership*, 4(3).
27 Author's interview with Martin Kingston, 12 April 2022.
28 Author's interview with Doug Band, 12 April 2022.
29 Sampson, A. 2008. *The Anatomist*. Jonathan Ball Publishers.
30 Author's interview with Michael Spicer, 5 March 2021.
31 Ibid.
32 The Freedom Charter. 26 June 1995. African National Congress. https://www.anc1912.org.za/the-freedom-charter-2/. Accessed 22 June 2022.
33 Author's interview with Michael Spicer, 18 March 2021.
34 Truth and Reconciliation Commission Final Report. 1998. Volume 4, Chapter 2. https://www.justice.gov.za/TRC/report/. Accessed 12 August 2022.
35 Nattrass, N and Seekings, J. 2011. 'The economy and poverty in the twentieth century'. Ross, R, Mager, AK and Nasson, B (eds). *The Cambridge History of South Africa, Volume 2, 1885–1994*. Cambridge University Press.
36 Ibid.
37 Ibid.
38 McGregor, A, Rose, R and Cranston, S. 23 January 2009. 'The new economic elite'. BusinessLive. https://www.businesslive.co.za/archive/2009-01-23-the-new-economic-elite/. Accessed 12 August 2022.
39 Author's interview with Michael Spicer, 18 March 2021.

Chapter 2

1 Author's interview with Jay Naidoo, 9 May 2022.
2 Simpson, T. 2021. *History of South Africa: From 1902 to the present*. Penguin Books.
3 Pottinger, B. 1988. *The Imperial Presidency: PW Botha, the first 10 years*. Southern Book Publishers.
4 Simpson, T. 2021. *History of South Africa: From 1902 to the present*. Penguin Books.
5 Pottinger, B. 1988. *The Imperial Presidency: PW Botha, the first 10 years*. Southern Book Publishers.
6 Simpson, T. 2021. *History of South Africa: From 1902 to the present*. Penguin Books.

7   Pottinger, B. 1988. *The Imperial Presidency: PW Botha, the first 10 years*. Southern Book Publishers.

8   Simpson, T. 2021. *History of South Africa: From 1902 to the present*. Penguin Books.

9   Pottinger, B. 1988. *The Imperial Presidency: PW Botha, the first 10 years*. Southern Book Publishers.

10 A state of emergency is usually resorted to when the welfare of a nation is severely threatened by war, invasion, insurrection or natural disaster. The states of emergency gave the president the ability to rule by decree, to increase the powers of the defence force and the police, and to restrict and censor any reportage of political unrest.

11 Tambo, A. 2014. *Oliver Tambo Speaks*. Kwela Books.

12 Pottinger, B. 1988. *The Imperial Presidency: PW Botha, the first 10 years*. Southern Book Publishers.

13 Author's interview with Jay Naidoo, 9 May 2022.

14 Ibid.

15 Author's interview with Michael Spicer, 5 March 2021.

16 Author's interview with Jay Naidoo, 9 May 2022.

17 Author's interview with Clem Sunter, 5 April 2022.

18 Author's interview with Doug Band, 12 April 2022.

19 Author's interview with Michael Spicer, 5 March 2021.

20 Ibid.

21 Author's interview with Clem Sunter, 5 April 2022.

22 Author's interview with Michael Spicer, 5 March 2021.

23 Author's interview with Clem Sunter, 5 April 2022.

24 Ibid.

25 Ibid.

26 Ibid.

27 Ibid.

28 Ibid.

29 Author's interview with Michael Spicer, 18 March 2021.

30 Author's interview with Michael Spicer, 5 March 2021.

31 Ibid.

32 Author's interview with Clem Sunter, 5 April 2022.

33 Ibid.

34 Ibid.

35 Ibid.

36 Ibid.

37 Ibid.

38 Author's interview with Michael Spicer, 5 March 2021.
39 Author's interview with Clem Sunter, 5 April 2022.

Chapter 3

1 Author's interview with Doug Band, 12 April 2022.
2 Author's interview with Michael Spicer, 5 March 2021.
3 Papenfus, T. 2011. *Pik Botha en Sy Tyd*. Litera Publikasies.
4 Giliomee, H. May 2008. 'Great expectations: Pres. PW Botha's Rubicon speech of 1985'. *New Contree Journal*, 55.
5 Heunis, J. 2007. *Die Binnekring: Terugblikke op die laaste dae van blanke regering*. Jonathan Ball Publishers.
6 Nelson Mandela Foundation. N.d. Address by State President PW Botha, 15 August 1985. O'Malley Archive. https://omalley. nelsonmandela.org/omalley/index.php/site/q/03lv01538/04lv01600/ 05lv01638/06lv01639.htm. Accessed 20 June 2022.
7 Cowell, A. 17 August 1985. 'Botha Speech: 2 Signals'. *The New York Times*.
8 Giliomee, H. May 2008. 'Great expectations: Pres. PW Botha's Rubicon speech of 1985'. *New Contree Journal*, 55.
9 Sampson, A. 2008. *The Anatomist*. Jonathan Ball Publishers.
10 Ibid.
11 The financial rand was a parallel currency used to lock in foreign investment and discourage disinvestment. The currency was cheaper than the commercial rand. Investors therefore could buy rands cheaply, but when they wanted to sell, it was also at a rate cheaper than the main currency.
12 Bruce, N. 1985. 'The rand and the cash crisis'. *Leadership*, 4(3).
13 Author's interview with Doug Band, 12 April 2022.
14 Ibid.
15 Murray, H. 1985. 'Gavin Relly in conversation with Hugh Murray'. *Leadership*, 4(3).
16 Welsh, D. 2009. *The Rise and Fall of Apartheid*. Jonathan Ball Publishers.
17 Murray, H. 1985. 'Gavin Relly in conversation with Hugh Murray'. *Leadership*, 4(3).
18 Author's interview with Michael Spicer, 18 March 2021.
19 Gevisser, M. 2007. *Thabo Mbeki: The dream deferred*. Jonathan Ball Publishers.

20 Murray, H. 1985. 'Gavin Relly in conversation with Hugh Murray'. *Leadership*, 4(3).

21 Author's interview with Michael Spicer, 5 March 2021.

22 Author's interview with Trevor Manuel, 3 May 2022.

23 Author's interview with Michael Spicer, 5 March 2021.

24 Ibid.

25 Giliomee, H. 2003. *The Afrikaners: A biography of a people*. Tafelberg Publishers.

26 Ibid.

27 Author's interview with Martin Kingston, 12 April 2022.

28 Giliomee, H. 2003. *The Afrikaners: A biography of a people*. Tafelberg Publishers.

29 Author's interview with Doug Band, 12 April 2022.

30 Simpson, T. 2021. *History of South Africa: From 1902 to the present*. Penguin Books.

31 Author's interview with Trevor Manuel, 2 March 2021.

32 Author's interview with Doug Band, 12 April 2022.

33 Nattrass, N and Seekings, J. 2011. 'The economy and poverty in the twentieth century'. Ross, R, Mager, AK and Nasson, B (eds). *The Cambridge History of South Africa, Volume 2, 1885–1994*. Cambridge University Press.

Chapter 4

1 Author's interview with Martin Kingston, 12 April 2022.

2 Ellis, S. 2012. *External Mission: The ANC in exile, 1960–1990*. Jonathan Ball Publishers.

3 Waldmeir, P. 1998. *Anatomy of a Miracle: The end of apartheid and the birth of the New South Africa*. Rutgers University Press.

4 Rynhart, G and Wielenga, C. 1 March 2021. 'Business deserves thanks for role in averting SA civil war'. Business Day. https://www.businesslive.co.za/bd/opinion/2021-03-01-business-deserves-thanks-for-role-in-averting-sa-civil-war/#. Accessed 21 June 2022.

5 Author's interview with Trevor Manuel, 2 March 2021.

6 Savage, M. 2014. 'Trekking Outward: A chronology of meetings between South Africans and the ANC in exile, 1983–2000'. University of Cape Town. https://atom.lib.uct.ac.za/index.php/za-uct-bc-s-bcs604. Accessed 12 August 2022.

7 Ibid.

8 Sampson, A. 2008. *The Anatomist*. Jonathan Ball Publishers.
9 Chatham House. 29 October 1985. 'Oliver Tambo: The future of South Africa: The ANC view'. https://www.chathamhouse. org/events/all/members-event-research-event/webinar-african-liberation-historical-and-contemporary. Accessed 21 June 2022.
10 Sampson, A. 2008. *The Anatomist*. Jonathan Ball Publishers.
11 Ibid.
12 Savage, M. 2014. 'Trekking Outward: A chronology of meetings between South Africans and the ANC in exile, 1983–2000'. University of Cape Town. https://atom.lib.uct.ac.za/index.php/za-uct-bc-s-bcs604. Accessed 12 August 2022.
13 Author's interview with Theuns Eloff, 1 April 2022.
14 Esterhuyse, W. 2012. *Eindstryd: Geheime gesprekke en die einde van apartheid*. Tafelberg.
15 Author's interview with Jürgen Kögl, 11 April 2022.
16 Spaarwater, M. 2012. *A Spook's Progress: From making war to making peace*. Zebra Press.
17 Ellis, S. 2012. *External Mission: The ANC in exile, 1960–1990*. Jonathan Ball Publishers.
18 Ibid.
19 Ibid.
20 Ibid.
21 Padayachee, V and Van Niekerk, R. 2019. *Shadow of Liberation: Contestation and compromise in the economic and social policy of the ANC, 1943–1996*. Wits University Press.
22 Ibid.
23 Ellis, S. 2012. *External Mission: The ANC in exile, 1960-1990*. Jonathan Ball Publishers.
24 Padayachee, V and Van Niekerk, R. 2019. *Shadow of Liberation: Contestation and compromise in the economic and social policy of the ANC, 1943–1996*. Wits University Press.
25 Gevisser, M. 2007. *Thabo Mbeki: The dream deferred*. Jonathan Ball Publishers.
26 Ibid.
27 Mbeki, T. 1984. 'The Fatton Thesis: A rejoinder'. *Canadian Journal of African Studies*, 18(3).
28 Author's interview with Michael Spicer, 18 March 2021.
29 Relayed to the author by Jürgen Kögl on 25 August 2022.

30 Padayachee, V and Van Niekerk, R. 2019. *Shadow of Liberation: Contestation and compromise in the economic and social policy of the ANC, 1943–1996.* Wits University Press.

31 Author's interview with Martin Kingston, 12 April 2022.

32 Padayachee, V and Van Niekerk, R. 2019. *Shadow of Liberation: Contestation and compromise in the economic and social policy of the ANC, 1943–1996.* Wits University Press.

33 Ibid.

34 Author's interview with Martin Kingston, 12 April 2022.

35 Author's interview with Trevor Manuel, 2 March 2021.

36 Author's interview with Jay Naidoo, 9 May 2022.

37 Author's interview with Doug Band, 12 April 2022.

38 Author's interview with Michael Spicer, 5 March 2021.

Chapter 5

1 Lelyveld, J. 11 April 1982. 'The many faces of Barlow Rand Ltd'. The New York Times. https://www.nytimes.com/1982/04/11/business/the-many-faces-of-barlow-rand-ltd.html. Accessed 21 June 2022.

2 Author's interview with Theuns Eloff, 1 April 2022.

3 Ibid.

4 Author's interview with Michael Spicer, 18 March 2021.

5 Author's interview with Theuns Eloff, 1 April 2022.

6 Lelyveld, J. 11 April 1982. 'The many faces of Barlow Rand Ltd'. The New York Times. https://www.nytimes.com/1982/04/11/business/the-many-faces-of-barlow-rand-ltd.html. Accessed 21 June 2022.

7 Ibid.

8 Eloff, T. 14 December 1997. 'The Consultative Business Movement, 1988–1994'. Submission to the Truth and Reconciliation Commission. (Provided by Eloff.)

9 Joffe, H. 20 January 1989. 'Exit Ball just as he entered: without speeches'. Weekly Mail. https://mg.co.za/article/1989-01-20-00-exit-ball-just-as-he-entered-without-speeches/. Accessed 21 June 2022.

10 Associated Press. 14 March 1987. 'Commission investigates funding for ANC Ad'. AP News. https://apnews.com/article/0a7e50c432a325dc02fac2c1c76a2774. Accessed 21 June 2022.

11 Ibid.

12 Joffe, H. 20 January 1989. 'Exit Ball just as he entered: without speeches'. Weekly Mail. https://mg.co.za/article/1989-01-20-00-exit-

ball-just-as-he-entered-without-speeches/. Accessed 21 June 2022.

13 Anton Mostert was the judge who headed the commission of inquiry into the so-called 'information scandal' in 1977 and found that senior government minister Connie Mulder and secretary of information Eschel Rhoodie were involved in corruption, with the knowledge of prime minister John Vorster. It led to Vorster's removal and signalled Botha's takeover of the NP and government.

14 Eloff, T. 14 December 1997. 'The Consultative Business Movement, 1988–1994'. Submission to the Truth and Reconciliation Commission. (Provided by Eloff.)

15 Ibid.

16 Author's interview with Martin Kingston, 12 April 2022.

17 Eloff, T. 14 December 1997. 'The Consultative Business Movement, 1988–1994'. Submission to the Truth and Reconciliation Commission. (Provided by Eloff.)

18 Ibid.

19 Ibid.

20 Ibid.

21 Ibid.

22 Ibid.

23 Ibid.

24 Author's interview with Michael Spicer, 5 March 2021.

25 Eloff, T. 14 December 1997. 'The Consultative Business Movement, 1988–1994'. Submission to the Truth and Reconciliation Commission. (Provided by Eloff.)

26 Ibid.

27 Author's interview with Michael Spicer, 18 March 2021.

28 Author's interview with Theuns Eloff, 1 April 2022.

29 Ibid.

30 Ibid.

31 Author's interview with Jürgen Kögl, 11 April 2022.

32 Author's interview with Theuns Eloff, 1 April 2022.

33 Ibid.

34 Ibid.

35 Joffe, H. 20 January 1989. 'Exit Ball just as he entered: without speeches'. Weekly Mail. https://mg.co.za/article/1989-01-20-00-exit-ball-just-as-he-entered-without-speeches/. Accessed 22 June 2022.

Chapter 6

1 Author's interview with Michael Spicer, 18 March 2021.
2 De Villiers, R and Stemmet, J. 2020. *Prisoner 913: The release of Nelson Mandela.* Tafelberg.
3 Barnard, N. 2015. *Geheime revolusie: Memoires van 'n spioenbaas.* Tafelberg.
4 Author's interview with Jürgen Kögl, 11 April 2022.
5 Ibid.
6 Ibid.
7 Ibid.
8 Ellis, S. 2012. *External Mission: The ANC in exile, 1960–1990.* Jonathan Ball Publishers.
9 Ibid.
10 Author's interview with Clem Sunter, 5 April 2022.
11 Author's interview with Michael Spicer, 18 March 2021.
12 Our Constitution. October 1989. 'Events leading up to the signing of the Harare Declaration'. https://ourconstitution.constitutionhill.org.za/the-harare-declaration-october-1989/. Accessed 22 June 2022.
13 Ibid.
14 Giliomee, H. 2012. *Die Laaste Afrikanerleiers: 'n Opperste toets van mag.* Tafelberg.
15 Author's interview with Doug Band, 12 April 2022.
16 Author's interview with Theuns Eloff, 1 April 2022.
17 Ibid.
18 Giliomee, H. 2012. *Die Laaste Afrikanerleiers: 'n Opperste toets van mag.* Tafelberg.
19 Author's interview with Michael Spicer, 18 March 2021.
20 Waldmeir, P. 1998. *Anatomy of a Miracle: The end of apartheid and the birth of the New South Africa.* Rutgers University Press.
21 Ibid.
22 Associated Press. 8 August 1987. 'Standard Chartered to leave South Africa'. The New York Times. https://www.nytimes.com/1987/08/08/business/standard-chartered-set-to-leave-south-africa.html. Accessed 22 June 2022.
23 Author's interview with Trevor Manuel, 2 March 2021.
24 Ibid.

Chapter 7

1 Author's interview with Jürgen Kögl, 11 April 2022.
2 Author's interview with Jürgen Kögl, 7 April 2022.
3 Author's interview with Jürgen Kögl, 11 April 2022.
4 Ibid.
5 Ibid.
6 Gevisser, M. 2007. *Thabo Mbeki: The dream deferred.* Jonathan Ball Publishers.
7 Author's interview with Jürgen Kögl, 11 April 2022.
8 Ellis, S. 2012. *External Mission: The ANC in exile, 1960–1990.* Jonathan Ball Publishers.
9 Author's interview with Michael Spicer, 5 March 2021.
10 Author's interview with Trevor Manuel, 2 March 2021.
11 Ibid.
12 Author's interview with Jeremy Cronin, 23 March 2021.
13 Author's interview with Michael Spicer, 5 March 2021.
14 Ibid.
15 Author's interview with Jürgen Kögl, 11 April 2022.
16 Gevisser, M. 2007. *Thabo Mbeki: The dream deferred.* Jonathan Ball Publishers.
17 Ibid.
18 Author's interview with Jürgen Kögl, 11 April 2022.
19 Author's interview with Trevor Manuel, 29 March 2021.
20 Author's interview with Theuns Eloff, 1 April 2022.
21 Author's interview with Michael Spicer, 18 March 2021.
22 Author's interview with Jürgen Kögl, 11 April 2022.
23 Sanlam lent seed capital to help establish another Afrikaner behemoth, the Ruperts' Rembrandt, later Remgro. Du Toit, P. 2019. *The Stellenbosch Mafia.* Jonathan Ball Publishers.
24 Giliomee, H. 2003. *The Afrikaners: A biography of a people.* Tafelberg Publishers.
25 Phillips, N. 2004. 'The funding of black economic empowerment in South Africa'. Master's degree thesis. University of Stellenbosch. http://scholar.sun.ac.za/handle/10019.1/16411. Accessed 12 August 2022.
26 Author's interview with Trevor Manuel, 2 March 2021.
27 Ibid.

28 Bähr, J and Kopper, C. 2016. *Munich Re: The company history, 1880–1980*. CH Beck. https://www.munichre.com/content/dam/munichre/contentlounge/website-pieces/documents/Munich-Re-The-Company-History.pdf/_jcr_content/renditions/original./Munich-Re-The-Company-History.pdf. Accessed 22 June 2022.
29 Author's interview with Jürgen Kögl, 11 April 2022.
30 Ibid.
31 Myre, G. 18 January 1989. 'Casino head admits bribery in latest corruption scandal'. Associated Press. https://apnews.com/article/d12ac16d3311e0158d67080ef52842d8. Accessed 12 August 2022.
32 Author's interview with Jay Naidoo, 9 May 2022.
33 Author's interview with Theuns Eloff, 1 April 2022.
34 Author's interview with Trevor Manuel, 2 March 2021.
35 Ibid.

Chapter 8

1   Address by Nelson Mandela at Options for Building an Economic Future Conference convened by the Consultative Business Movement attended by South African business executives. 23 May 1990. http://www.mandela.gov.za/mandela_speeches/1990/900523_econ.htm. Accessed 23 June 2022.
2   Author's interview with Michael Spicer, 5 March 2021.
3   Author's interview with Jay Naidoo, 9 May 2022.
4   Author's interview with Martin Kingston, 12 April 2022.
5   Author's interview with Jeremy Cronin, 23 March 2021.
6   Ibid.
7   Ibid.
8   Author's interview with Theuns Eloff, 1 April 2022.
9   Author's interview with Michael Spicer, 5 March 2021.
10 Ibid.
11 Author's interview with Doug Band, 12 April 2022.
12 Ibid.
13 Author's interview with Trevor Manuel, 5 March 2022.
14 Author's interview with Trevor Manuel, 2 March 2021.
15 Quoting Shakespeare is an Mbeki trademark, and Gevisser confirmed the speech was written by him. Address by Nelson Mandela at Options for Building an Economic Future Conference convened by the Consultative Business Movement attended by South African

business executives. 23 May 1990. http://www.mandela.gov.za/
mandela_speeches/1990/900523_econ.htm. Accessed 23 June 2022.

16 Address by Nelson Mandela at Options for Building an Economic
Future Conference convened by the Consultative Business Movement
attended by South African business executives. 23 May 1990. http://
www.mandela.gov.za/mandela_speeches/1990/900523_econ.htm.
Accessed 23 June 2022.

17 Ibid.

18 *Workers Hammer*, date unknown, 1990.

19 Author's interview with Michael Spicer, 5 March 2021.

20 Ibid.

21 Author's interview with Jay Naidoo, 9 May 2022.

22 Ibid.

23 Padayachee, V and Van Niekerk, R. 2019. *Shadow of Liberation:
Contestation and compromise in the economic and social policy of the ANC,
1943–1996.* Wits University Press.

24 Author's interview with Jay Naidoo, 9 May 2022.

25 Ibid.

26 Ibid.

27 Ibid.

28 The Freedom Charter. 26 June 1995. African National Congress.
https://www.anc1912.org.za/the-freedom-charter-2/. Accessed 23
June 2022.

29 This decision-making body of the ANC today consists of over 100
members, including the 'top six' – the president, the deputy president,
the national chair, the secretary-general, the deputy secretary-general
and the treasurer-general.

30 Author's interview with Jay Naidoo, 9 May 2022.

31 Ibid.

32 Ibid.

33 Ibid.

34 Ibid.

35 Ibid.

Chapter 9

1 Author's interview with Jay Naidoo, 9 May 2022.

2 Author's interview with Vusi Khanyile, 19 April 2022.

3 Padayachee, V and Van Niekerk, R. 2019. *Shadow of Liberation:*

Contestation and compromise in the economic and social policy of the ANC, 1943–1996. Wits University Press.
4 Ibid.
5 Author's interview with Jürgen Kögl, 7 April 2022.
6 Author's interview with Michael Spicer, 5 March 2021.
7 Author's interview with Trevor Manuel, 29 March 2021.
8 Ibid.
9 Ibid.
10 Ibid.
11 Author's interview with Michael Spicer, 18 March 2021.
12 Ibid.
13 Author's interview with Michael Spicer, 5 March 2021.
14 Author's interview with Theuns Eloff, 1 April 2022.
15 Ibid.
16 Author's interview with Jeremy Cronin, 23 March 2021.
17 Author's interview with Michael Spicer, 18 March 2021.
18 Author's interview with Bobby Godsell, 4 May 2022.
19 Ibid.
20 Ibid.
21 Spicer, M. April 2016. 'The Business-Government relationship: What has gone wrong?' *Journal of the Helen Suzman Foundation*, Issue 78.
22 Author's interview with Trevor Manuel, 3 May 2022.
23 Ibid.
24 Open Secrets. 16 October 2017. 'Declassified: Apartheid profits – Tiny Rowland, a very British spy?' Daily Maverick. https://www.dailymaverick.co.za/article/2017-10-16-declassified-apartheid-profits-tiny-rowland-a-very-british-spy/. Accessed 23 June 2022.
25 Ibid.
26 Author's communication with Jürgen Kögl, 28 May 2022.
27 Van Zyl Slabbert, F. 2006. *Duskant die Geskiedenis: 'n Persoonlike terugblik op die politieke oorgang in Suid-Afrika.* Jonathan Ball Publishers & Tafelberg.
28 Ibid.
29 Author's interview with Jürgen Kögl, 11 April 2022.
30 Author's interview with Doug Band, 12 April 2022.
31 Author's interview with Michael Spicer, 18 March 2021.
32 Ibid.
33 Author's interview with Michael Spicer, 5 March 2021.

34 Gevisser, M 2007. *Thabo Mbeki: The dream deferred.* Jonathan Ball Publishers.

35 Interview with Jürgen Kögl, 11 April 2022.

36 Author's interview with Doug Band, 12 April 2022.

37 Ibid.

38 Ibid.

Chapter 10

1 Author's interview with Trevor Manuel, 5 March 2021.

2 Author's interview with Jay Naidoo, 9 May 2022.

3 Eloff, T. May 2015. 'The importance of process in the South African peace and constitutional negotiations'. Practitioner notes no 3. Centre for Mediation in Africa. University of Pretoria https://www.up.ac. za/media/shared/237/Practitioner%20Notes/practitioner-notes-journal-03.zp61397.pdf. Accessed 27 June 2022.

4 Author's interview with Theuns Eloff, 1 April 2022.

5 Ibid.

6 Author's interview with Jay Naidoo, 9 May 2022.

7 Author's interview with Theuns Eloff, 1 April 2022.

8 Author's interview with Jay Naidoo, 9 May 2022.

9 Author's interview with Michael Spicer, 5 March 2021.

10 Eloff, T. May 2015. 'The importance of process in the South African peace and constitutional negotiations'. Practitioner notes no 3. Centre for Mediation in Africa. University of Pretoria https://www.up.ac. za/media/shared/237/Practitioner%20Notes/practitioner-notes-journal-03.zp61397.pdf. Accessed 27 June 2022.

11 Author's interview with Theuns Eloff, 1 April 2022.

12 Author's interview with Trevor Manuel, 3 May 2022.

13 Author's interview with Jay Naidoo, 9 May 2022.

14 Ibid.

15 Ibid.

16 Author's interview with Theuns Eloff, 1 April 2022.

17 Ibid.

18 Ibid.

19 ANC policy documents. 31 May 1992. 'Ready to Govern: ANC policy guidelines for a democratic South Africa'. African National Congress. https://www.anc1912.org.za/policy-documents-1992-ready-to-

govern-anc-policy-guidelines-for-a-democratic-south-africa/.
Accessed 27 June 2022.

20 Author's interview with Trevor Manuel, 5 March 2021.
21 Ibid.
22 Ibid.
23 Ibid.
24 Ibid.
25 Ibid.
26 Ibid.
27 Padayachee, V and Van Niekerk, R. 2019. *Shadow of Liberation:
   Contestation and compromise in the economic and social policy of the ANC,
   1943–1996.* Wits University Press.
28 Ibid.
29 Author's interview with Michael Spicer, 18 March 2021.
30 Ibid.
31 Author's interview with Jay Naidoo, 9 May 2022.
32 Ibid.
33 Ibid.
34 Ibid.
35 Ibid.
36 Ibid.
37 Ibid.
38 Truth and Reconciliation Commission of South Africa Report.
   1998. Volume 4. https://www.justice.gov.za/TRC/report/finalreport/
   Volume%204.pdf. Accessed 10 July 2022.
39 Ibid.
40 Ibid.
41 Ibid.
42 Ibid.

Chapter II

1 Author's interview with Jeremy Cronin, 23 March 2021.
2 ANC policy documents. 31 May 1992. 'Ready to Govern: ANC policy
   guidelines for a democratic South Africa'. African National Congress.
   https://www.anc1912.org.za/policy-documents-1992-ready-to-
   govern-anc-policy-guidelines-for-a-democratic-south-africa/.
   Accessed 27 June 2022.
3 Author's interview with Trevor Manuel, 29 March 2021.

4   Ibid.
5   Ibid.
6   Ibid.
7   Ibid.
8   Author's interview with Jeremy Cronin, 23 March 2021.
9   Author's interview with Jay Naidoo, 9 May 2022.
10 Author's interview with Jeremy Cronin, 23 March 2021.
11 Author's interview with Michael Spicer, 18 March 2021.
12 Padayachee, V and Van Niekerk, R. 2019. *Shadow of Liberation: Contestation and compromise in the economic and social policy of the ANC, 1943–1996.* Wits University Press.
13 Ibid.
14 Ibid.
15 Ibid.
16 Ibid.
17 Ibid.
18 Ibid.
19 Author's interview with Trevor Manuel, 29 March 2021.
20 Ibid.
21 Padayachee, V and Van Niekerk, R. 2019. *Shadow of Liberation: Contestation and compromise in the economic and social policy of the ANC, 1943–1996.* Wits University Press.
22 Author's interview with Trevor Manuel, 5 March 2021.
23 Author's interview with Michael Spicer, 5 March 2021.
24 Nattrass, N. 1994. 'South Africa: The economic restructuring agenda – a critique of the MERG report'. *Third World Quarterly*, 15(2). https://www.tandfonline.com/doi/pdf/10.1080/01436599408420376?needAccess=true. Accessed 19 July 2022.
25 Padayachee, V and Van Niekerk, R. 2019. *Shadow of Liberation: Contestation and compromise in the economic and social policy of the ANC, 1943–1996.* Wits University Press.
26 Author's interview with Trevor Manuel, 5 March 2021.
27 Ibid.
28 Padayachee, V and Van Niekerk, R. 2019. *Shadow of Liberation: Contestation and compromise in the economic and social policy of the ANC, 1943–1996.* Wits University Press.
29 Author's interview with Michael Spicer, 5 March 2021.

30 Nattrass, N. 1994. 'South Africa: The economic restructuring agenda –
   a critique of the MERG report'. *Third World Quarterly*, 15(2). https://
   www.tandfonline.com/doi/pdf/10.1080/01436599408420376?
   needAccess=true. Accessed 19 July 2022.
31 Author's interview with Michael Spicer, 18 March 2021.
32 Interview with Jay Naidoo, 9 May 2022.
33 Ibid.
34 Author's interview with Trevor Manuel, 5 March 2021.
35 Ibid.
36 Ibid.
37 Author's interview with Jeremy Cronin, 23 March 2021.
38 Author's interview with Michael Spicer, 18 March 2021.
39 Ibid.
40 Author's interview with Jay Naidoo, 9 May 2022.
41 Ibid.
42 Ibid.
43 Ibid.

Chapter 12

1   Author's interview with Martin Kingston, 12 April 2022.
2   Author's interview with Trevor Manuel, 5 March 2021.
3   Ibid.
4   Ibid.
5   Author's interview with Jay Naidoo, 9 May 2022.
6   Ibid.
7   South African Institute of Race Relations. 2017. 'South Africa Survey
    2018'.
8   Ibid.
9   Ibid.
10 Ibid.
11 Ibid.
12 Ibid.
13 Ibid.
14 Ibid.
15 Ibid.
16 Ibid.
17 Nattrass, N and Seekings, J. 2011. 'The economy and poverty in the
    twentieth century'. Ross, R, Mager, AK and Nasson, B (eds). *The*

Cambridge History of South Africa, Volume 2, 1885–1994. Cambridge University Press.
18 Author's interview with Martin Kingston, 12 April 2022.
19 Author's interview with Jürgen Kögl, 26 April 2022.
20 Author's interview with Trevor Manuel, 3 May 2022.
21 Sparks, A. 2003. *Beyond the Miracle: Inside the New South Africa.* Jonathan Ball Publishers.
22 Ibid.
23 Author's interview with Michael Spicer, 5 March 2021.
24 Ibid.
25 Author's interview with Martin Kingston, 12 April 2022.
26 Ibid.
27 Ibid.
28 Ibid.
29 Author's interview with Trevor Manuel, 3 May 2022.
30 Ibid.
31 Ibid.
32 Ibid.
33 Sparks, A. 2003. *Beyond the Miracle: Inside the New South Africa.* Jonathan Ball Publishers.
34 Sampson, A. 1999. *Mandela: The authorised biography.* HarperCollins.
35 Author's interview with Jeremy Cronin, 23 March 2021.
36 Ibid.
37 Author's interview with Jay Naidoo, 9 May 2022.
38 Author's interview with Jeremy Cronin, 23 March 2021.
39 Author's interview with Jay Naidoo, 9 May 2022.
40 Author's interview with Trevor Manuel, 5 March 2021.
41 Ibid.
42 Ibid.
43 Author's interview with Trevor Manuel, 3 May 2022.
44 Ibid.
45 Ibid.
46 Author's interview with Michael Spicer, 5 March 2021.
47 Author's interview with Trevor Manuel, 3 May 2022.

Chapter 13

1 Author's interview with Jay Naidoo, 9 May 2022.
2 Author's interview with Trevor Manuel, 29 March 2021.

3 Ibid.

4 Green, P. 2009. *Trevor Manuel: 'n Lewensverhaal.* Tafelberg.

5 Ibid.

6 Author's interview with Martin Kingston, 12 April 2022.

7 Author's interview with Doug Band, 12 April 2022.

8 Author's interview with Jay Naidoo, 9 May 2022.

9 Author's interview with Trevor Manuel, 29 March 2021.

10 Ibid.

11 Author's interview with Jay Naidoo, 9 May 2022.

12 Ibid.

13 Ibid.

14 Author's interview with Michael Spicer, 5 March 2021.

15 Author's interview with Jay Naidoo, 9 May 2022.

16 Ibid.

17 Author's interview with Trevor Manuel, 29 March 2021.

18 Sparks, A. 2003. *Beyond the Miracle: Inside the New South Africa.* Jonathan Ball Publishers.

19 Department of Information and Publicity. 12 March 1996. 'Statement on the South Africa Foundation Document, "Growth for all"'. Hartford Web Publishing. http://www.hartford-hwp.com/archives/37a/024.html. Accessed 28 June 2022.

20 Author's interview with Michael Spicer, 18 March 2021.

21 Ibid.

22 Author's interview with Theuns Eloff, 1 April 2022.

23 Eloff, T. 14 December 1997. 'The Consultative Business Movement, 1988–1994'. Submission to the Truth and Reconciliation Commission. (Provided by Eloff.)

24 Author's interview with Theuns Eloff, 1 April 2022.

25 Ibid.

26 Author's interview with Michael Spicer, 18 March 2021.

27 Author's interview with Theuns Eloff, 1 April 2022.

28 Author's interview with Doug Band, 12 April 2022.

29 Ibid.

30 Ibid.

31 Besides Roux and Abedian, the following individuals were part of the GEAR policy drafting team: Andrew Donaldson (department of finance), Alan Hirsch (department of trade and industry), Guy Mhone (department of labour), Brian Kahn (University of Cape Town), Ben

Smit and Servaas van der Berg (University of Stellenbosch), Stephen
Gelb (University of Durban-Westville), Daleen Smal and Ernie van
der Merwe (SARB), Ian Goldin and Dirk van Seventer (Development
Bank of Southern Africa), and Luiz Pereira da Silva and Richard
Ketley (World Bank).

32 Author's interview with Trevor Manuel, 29 March 2021.
33 Ibid.
34 Green, P. 2009. *Trevor Manuel: 'n Lewensverhaal.* Tafelberg.
35 Author's interview with Trevor Manuel, 29 March 2021.
36 Green, P. 2009. *Trevor Manuel: 'n Lewensverhaal.* Tafelberg.

Chapter 14

1 Author's interview with Trevor Manuel, 29 March 2021.
2 Department of Finance. N.d. 'Growth, Employment and
Redistribution: A Macroeconomic strategy'. National Treasury. http://
www.treasury.gov.za/publications/other/gear/chapters.pdf. Accessed
13 August 2022.
3 Ibid.
4 Sachs, M. 2021. 'Fiscal Dimensions of South Africa's Crisis'. Public
Economic Project. Southern Centre for Inequality Studies, University
of the Witwatersrand.
5 Ibid.
6 Ibid.
7 Camdessus, M. 2000. *Looking to the Future: The IMF in Africa.* The
International Monetary Fund.
8 Author's interview with Michael Spicer, 18 March 2021.
9 Ibid.
10 Padayachee, V and Van Niekerk, R. 2019. *Shadow of Liberation:
Contestation and compromise in the economic and social policy of the ANC,
1943–1996.* Wits University Press.
11 Ibid.
12 Turok, B. 2003. *Nothing But the Truth.* Jonathan Ball Publishers.
13 Author's interview with Jay Naidoo, 9 May 2022.
14 Author's interview with Jeremy Cronin, 23 March 2021.
15 Ibid.
16 Davies, R. 2021. *Towards a New Deal: A political economy of the times of
my life.* Jonathan Ball Publishers.
17 Author's interview with Trevor Manuel, 29 March 2021.

18 Camdessus, M. 2000. *Looking to the Future: The IMF in Africa.* The International Monetary Fund.
19 Ibid.
20 Green, P. 2009. *Trevor Manuel: 'n Lewensverhaal.* Tafelberg.
21 Author's interview with Trevor Manuel, 29 March 2021.
22 Padayachee, V and Van Niekerk, R. 2019. *Shadow of Liberation: Contestation and compromise in the economic and social policy of the ANC, 1943–1996.* Wits University Press.
23 Gevisser, M. 2007. *Thabo Mbeki: The dream deferred.* Jonathan Ball Publishers.
24 Sampson, A. 1999. *Mandela: The authorised biography.* HarperCollins.
25 Author's interview with Jürgen Kögl, 11 April 2022.
26 Author's interview with Michael Spicer, 18 March 2021.
27 Author's interview with Trevor Manuel, 29 March 2021.
28 Author's interview with Michael Spicer, 5 March 2021.
29 Author's interview with Jay Naidoo, 9 May 2022.
30 Author's interview with Jeremy Cronin, 23 March 2021.
31 Author's interview with Trevor Manuel, 29 March 2021.
32 Ibid.
33 Green, P. 2009. *Trevor Manuel: 'n Lewensverhaal.* Tafelberg.
34 Author's interview with Trevor Manuel, 29 March 2021.
35 Ibid.
36 Ibid.
37 Ibid.

Chapter 15

1   Author's interview with Michael Spicer, 5 March 2021.
2   Author's interview with Bobby Godsell, 4 May 2022.
3   Ibid.
4   Ibid.
5   Author's interview with Trevor Manuel, 3 May 2022.
6   Ibid.
7   Author's interview with Bobby Godsell, 4 May 2022.
8   Author's interview with Trevor Manuel, 3 May 2022.
9   Author's interview with Jürgen Kögl, 25 May 2022.
10 Ibid.
11 Ibid.
12 Ibid.

13 Ibid.
14 Ibid.
15 Ibid.
16 Author's interview with Michael Spicer, 18 March 2021.
17 Author's interview with Jürgen Kögl, 25 May 2022.
18 Author's interview with Trevor Manuel, 3 May 2022.
19 Ibid.
20 Ibid.
21 Ibid.
22 Author's interview with Michael Spicer, 18 March 2021.
23 Ibid.
24 Ibid.
25 Author's interview with Michael Spicer, 5 March 2021.
26 Author's interview with Trevor Manuel, 3 May 2022.
27 Ibid.
28 Ibid.
29 Author's interview with Bobby Godsell, 4 May 2022.
30 Author's interview with Michael Spicer, 5 March 2021.
31 Ibid.
32 Author's interview with Trevor Manuel, 3 May 2022.
33 Author's interview with Jürgen Kögl, 25 May 2022.
34 Ibid.
35 Ibid.
36 Ibid.
37 Author's interview with Michael Spicer, 18 March 2021.

Chapter 16

1 Butler, A. 2019. *Cyril Ramaphosa: The road to presidential power*. Jacana Publishers.
2 Associated Press. 14 April 1996. 'Ramaphosa Changes Post'. YouTube. https://www.youtube.com/watch?v=usyEhjEE6mo. Accessed 15 July 2022.
3 Davis, G. 19 April 1996. 'How Cyril was edged out by Thabo'. Mail & Guardian. https://mg.co.za/article/1996-04-19-how-cyril-was-edged-out-by-thabo/. Accessed 15 July 2022.
4 Daley, S. 14 April 1996. 'Key Mandela aide to join group promoting investment by blacks'. The New York Times. https://www.nytimes.com/1996/04/14/world/key-mandela-aide-to-join-group-

promoting-investment-by-blacks.html. Accessed 15 July 2022.

5   Moseneke, D. 2016. *My Own Liberator: A memoir*. Picador Africa.

6   Butler, A. 2019. *Cyril Ramaphosa: The road to presidential power*. Jacana Publishers.

7   Hartley, R. 2017. *Ramaphosa: The man who would be king*. Jonathan Ball Publishers.

8   Ibid.

9   Gqubule, D. April 2021. 'Black Economic Empowerment Transactions in South Africa after 1994'. Working paper. Southern Centre of Inequality Studies, University of the Witwatersrand. https://www.wits.ac.za/media/wits-university/faculties-and-schools/commerce-law-and-management/research-entities/scis/documents/BEE%20Transactions%20in%20SA%20after%201994.pdf. Accessed 15 July 2022.

10 Harry Oppenheimer sold a large share of General Mining to Federale Mynbou (Fedmyn), an Afrikaner-controlled mining house; Fedmyn later obtained the majority shareholding and changed the company's name to Genmin. Giliomee, H. 2003. *The Afrikaners: A biography of a people*. Tafelberg Publishers.

11 Moseneke, D. 2016. *My Own Liberator: A memoir*. Picador Africa.

12 Butler, A. 2019. *Cyril Ramaphosa: The road to presidential power*. Jacana Publishers.

13 Rumney, R. 26 May 1995. 'Black buyer for Johnnic'. Mail & Guardian. https://mg.co.za/article/1995-05-26-black-buyer-for-johnnic/. Accessed 15 July 2022.

14 Author's interview with Saki Macozoma, 4 May 2022.

15 Gqubule, D. April 2021. 'Black Economic Empowerment Transactions in South Africa after 1994'. Working paper. Southern Centre of Inequality Studies, University of the Witwatersrand. https://www.wits.ac.za/media/wits-university/faculties-and-schools/commerce-law-and-management/research-entities/scis/documents/BEE%20Transactions%20in%20SA%20after%201994.pdf. Accessed 15 July 2022.

16 Butler, A. 2019. *Cyril Ramaphosa: The road to presidential power*. Jacana Publishers.

17 Duke, L. 1 November 1996. 'Blacks buy into South African industry'. The Washington Post. https://www.washingtonpost.com/archive/politics/1996/11/01/blacks-buy-into-s-african-industry/9281be8f-

42bc–4335–a5c5–7a84b8ad73f4/. Accessed 15 July 2022.

18 Butler, A. 2019. *Cyril Ramaphosa: The road to presidential power*. Jacana Publishers.

19 Mail & Guardian. 28 February 1997. 'Khumalo's coup'. https://mg.co.za/article/1997-02-28-khumalos-coup/. Accessed 15 July 2022.

20 Author's interview with Jürgen Kögl, 9 June 2022.

21 Author's interview with Michael Spicer, 5 March 2021.

22 Ibid.

23 Author's interview with Bobby Godsell, 4 May 2022.

24 Ibid.

25 The Economist. 5 June 1997. 'The new Randlord'. https://www.economist.com/business/1997/06/05/the-new-randlord. Accessed 15 July 2022; Robinson, S. 17 April 2005. 'South Africa: The New Rand Lords'. Time. http://content.time.com/time/subscriber/article/0,33009,1050314,00.html. Both accessed 15 July 2022.

26 Johnnic Holdings Annual Report. 2004. https://www.sec.gov/Archives/edgar/vprr/0404/04045720.pdf. Accessed 15 July 2022.

27 Moseneke, D. 2016. *My Own Liberator: A memoir*. Picador Africa.

28 ITWeb. 18 September 2002. 'Alexander Forbes and Millennium Consolidated Investments in empowerment deal'. https://www.itweb.co.za/content/kLgB17eJGnPM59N4. Accessed 15 July 2022.

29 Chikanga, K. 15 August 2004. 'Millennium now called Shanduka'. IOL. https://www.iol.co.za/business-report/companies/millennium-now-called-shanduka-757023. Accessed 14 August 2022.

30 Butler, A. 2019. *Cyril Ramaphosa: The road to presidential power*. Jacana Publishers.

31 Mabanga, T. 8 July 2005. 'Clash of the titans'. Mail & Guardian. https://mg.co.za/article/2005-07-08-clash-of-the-titans/. Accessed 15 July 2022.

32 Butler, A. 2019. Cyril *Ramaphosa: The road to presidential power*. Jacana Publishers.

33 Hartley, R. 2017. *Ramaphosa: The man who would be king*. Jonathan Ball Publishers.

34 Mabanga, T. 8 July 2005. 'Clash of the titans'. Mail & Guardian. https://mg.co.za/article/2005-07-08-clash-of-the-titans/. Accessed 15 July 2022.

35 Butler, A. 2019. Cyril *Ramaphosa: The road to presidential power*. Jacana Publishers.

36 Ibid.

37 Bridge, S and Moses, A. 16 July 2004. 'Ramaphosa's BEE bonanza'. IOL. https://www.iol.co.za/news/south-africa/ramaphosas-bee-bonanza-217325. Accessed 15 July 2022.

38 Reuters. 22 December 2011. 'China's CIC takes stake in S. Africa's Shanduka'. https://www.reuters.com/article/ozabs-shanduaka-cic-20111222-idAFJOE7BL02720111222. Accessed 15 July 2022.

39 Author's interview with Jürgen Kögl, 22 June 2022.

40 Butler, A. 2019. *Cyril Ramaphosa: The road to presidential power*. Jacana Publishers.

41 Author's interview with Jürgen Kögl, 22 June 2022.

42 Butler, A. 2019. *Cyril Ramaphosa: The road to presidential power*. Jacana Publishers.

43 Phembani. 19 August 2015. 'Phembani finalises large merger with Shanduka after receiving approval from Competition Tribunal'. https://www.phembani.com/index.php/2015/08/19/pembani-finalises-large-merger-with-shanduka-after-receiving-approval-from-competition-tribunal/. Accessed 14 August 2022.

44 Nsehe, M. 2 June 2015. 'South African deputy president to earn at least $200 million from sale of investment firm'. Forbes. https://www.forbes.com/sites/mfonobongnsehe/2015/06/02/south-african-deputy-president-to-earn-at-least-200-million-from-sale-of-investment-firm/?sh=2a1b79b01493. Accessed 14 August 2022.

45 The Presidency. 26 November 2014. 'Deputy President Cyril Ramaphosa acts to address potential conflicts of interest'. https://www.thepresidency.gov.za/press-statements/deputy-president-cyril-ramaphosa-acts-address-potential-conflicts-interest. Accessed 14 August 2022.

46 Forbes. 18 November 2015. 'Cyril Ramaphosa'. https://www.forbes.com/profile/cyril-ramaphosa/?sh=65df628124fe. Accessed 15 July 2022.

Chapter 17

1 Author's interview with Vusi Khanyile, 6 April 2022.

2 Author's interview with Vusi Khanyile, 19 April 2022.

3 Author's interview with Vusi Khanyile, 6 April 2022.

4 Author's interview with Vusi Khanyile, 19 April 2022.

5 Ibid.

6   Ibid.

7   Ibid.

8   Author's interview with Vusi Khanyile, 6 April 2022.

9   Ibid.

10 Ibid.

11 Ibid.

12 Ibid.

13 Author's interview with Vusi Khanyile, 19 April 2022.

14 Author's interview with Jürgen Kögl, 25 May 2022.

15 Ibid.

16 Ibid.

17 Ibid.

18 Author's interview with Vusi Khanyile, 19 April 2022.

19 Ibid.

20 Timse, T, Mckune, C and Brummer, S. 28 September 2012. 'ANC stands to benefit from R1bn Capitec bank bonanza'. Mail & Guardian. https://mg.co.za/article/2012-09-28-anc-stands-to-benefit-from-r1bn-capitec-bank-bonanza/. Accessed 6 July 2022.

21 Author's interview with Vusi Khanyile, 6 April 2022.

22 Ibid.

23 South African History Online. Nd. '19 die at Shell House massacre'. https://www.sahistory.org.za/dated-event/19-die-shell-house-massacre. Accessed 29 August 2022.

24 Author's interview with Vusi Khanyile, 6 April 2022.

25 Ibid.

26 Ibid.

27 Timse, T, Mckune, C and Brummer, S. 28 September 2012. 'ANC stands to benefit from R1bn Capitec bank bonanza'. Mail & Guardian. https://mg.co.za/article/2012-09-28-anc-stands-to-benefit-from-r1bn-capitec-bank-bonanza/. Accessed 6 July 2022.

28 This is according to a trove of party documents held at the University of Fort Hare – which were sealed by the party shortly after their existence was reported by the *Sunday Times* in 2010. Sake24. 3 May 2010. 'ANC owns major stake in Thebe'. News24. https://www.news24.com/fin24/anc-owns-major-stake-in-thebe-20100503. Accessed 6 July 2022.

29 Timse, T, Mckune, C and Brummer, S. 28 September 2012. 'ANC stands to benefit from R1bn Capitec bank bonanza'. Mail & Guardian.

https://mg.co.za/article/2012-09-28-anc-stands-to-benefit-from-r1bn-capitec-bank-bonanza/. Accessed 6 July 2022.

30 Author's interview with Vusi Khanyile, 19 April 2022.

31 Evans, J. 4 March 2022. 'Mantashe says ANC had "foresight" to invest in Shell-affiliated Batho-Batho Trust to get R15-million payout'. Daily Maverick. https://www.dailymaverick.co.za/article/2022-03-04-mantashe-says-anc-had-foresight-to-invest-in-shell-affiliated-batho-batho-trust-to-get-r15-million-payout/. Accessed 6 July 2022.

32 Ibid.

33 Jordan, B. 8 April 2012. 'ANC trust stands to gain from fracking'. Sunday Times. https://www.timeslive.co.za/sunday-times/lifestyle/2012-04-08-anc-trust-stands-to-gain-from-fracking/. Accessed 14 August 2022.

34 Timse, T, Mckune, C and Brummer, S. 28 September 2012. 'ANC stands to benefit from R1bn Capitec bank bonanza'. Mail & Guardian. https://mg.co.za/article/2012-09-28-anc-stands-to-benefit-from-r1bn-capitec-bank-bonanza/. Accessed 6 July 2022.

35 Ibid.

36 Thebe Investment Corporation. N.d. Thebe's timeline of historic milestones. https://www.thebe.co.za/history/. Accessed 14 August 2022.

37 Ibid.

38 Author's interview with Vusi Khanyile, 6 April 2022.

39 Ibid.

40 Ibid.

41 Author's interview with Vusi Khanyile, 19 April 2022.

42 Ibid.

43 Ibid.

Chapter 18

1 Author's interview with Saki Macozoma, 4 May 2022.

2 Ibid.

3 Sanlam Investments. N.d. Our empowerment journey. https://www.sanlaminvestments.com/about/sustainableinvesting/Pages/empowerment-journey.aspx. Accessed 10 July 2022.

4 Gqubule, D. April 2021. 'Black Economic Empowerment Transactions in South Africa after 1994'. Working paper. Southern Centre of Inequality Studies, University of the Witwatersrand.

https://www.wits.ac.za/media/wits-university/faculties-and-schools/
commerce-law-and-management/research-entities/scis/documents/
BEE%20Transactions%20in%20SA%20after%201994.pdf. Accessed
10 July 2022.

5   Verhoef, G. 1 June 2003. '"The invisible hand": The roots of black
economic empowerment, Sankorp and societal change in South
Africa, 1985–2000'. *Journal for Contemporary History*, 28(1).

6   Author's interview with Trevor Manuel, 3 May 2022.

7   Verhoef, G. 1 June 2003. '"The invisible hand": The roots of black
economic empowerment, Sankorp and societal change in South
Africa, 1985–2000'. *Journal for Contemporary History*, 28(1).

8   Ibid.

9   Ibid.

10   Gevisser, M. 11 October 1996. 'Cyril Ramaphosa, deputy chairman of
New Africa Investments, Ltd.' *Mail & Guardian*.

11   Author's interview with Saki Macozoma, 4 May 2022.

12   Truth and Reconciliation Commission of South Africa Report.
1998. Volume 4. https://www.justice.gov.za/TRC/report/finalreport/
Volume%204.pdf. Accessed 10 July 2022.

13   Author's interview with Saki Macozoma, 4 May 2022.

14   Ibid.

15   Ibid.

16   Ibid.

17   Phillips, N. 2004. 'The funding of black economic empowerment in
South Africa'. Master's degree thesis. University of Stellenbosch.

18   Author's interview with Saki Macozoma, 4 May 2022.

19   Ibid.

20   Author's interview with Michael Spicer, 18 March 2021.

21   Author's interview with Theuns Eloff, 1 April 2022.

22   Author's interview with Saki Macozoma, 4 May 2022.

23   IOL. 25 July 2004. 'The real tale of Nail's black empowerment still to
be told'. https://www.iol.co.za/business-report/economy/the-real-
tale-of-nails-black-empowerment-still-to-be-told-756164. Accessed
14 August 2022.

24   Block, D and Soggot, M. 7 May 1999. 'Forced to take R50m and
leave'. Mail & Guardian. https://mg.co.za/article/1999-05-07-forced-
to-take-r50m-and-leave/. Accessed 10 July 2022.

25   Author's interview with Saki Macozoma, 4 May 2022.

26 IOL. 26 July 2004. 'Macozoma makes a mint on Nail shares'. https://www.iol.co.za/business-report/companies/macozoma-makes-a-mint-on-nail-shares-756186. Accessed 10 July 2022.

27 Author's interview with Saki Macozoma, 4 May 2022.

28 Ibid.

29 Ibid.

30 Ibid.

31 Ibid.

Chapter 19

1 Adams, S. 6 March 2008. 'The prince of mines'. Forbes. https://www.forbes.com/forbes/2008/0324/088.html?sh=2c953e8b3afe. Accessed 16 July 2022.

2 Jeffery, A. 18 January 2013. 'BEE is flawed and should be scrapped'. Mail & Guardian. https://webcache.googleusercontent.com/search?q=cache:kFwVualihV0J:https://mg.co.za/article/2013-01-18-bee-is-flawed-and-should-be-scrapped/+&cd=5&hl=en&ct=clnk&gl=za. Accessed 16 July 2022.

3 Engineering News. 12 December 2001. 'Motsepe speaks in global news magazine'. https://www.engineeringnews.co.za/article/motsepe-speaks-in-global-news-magazine-2001-12-12. Accessed 14 August 2022.

4 Adams, S. 6 March 2008. 'The prince of mines'. Forbes. https://www.forbes.com/forbes/2008/0324/088.html?sh=2c953e8b3afe. Accessed 16 July 2022.

5 Anecdote shared by an acquaintance about an encounter with Motsepe in Afrikaans.

6 Adams, S. 6 March 2008. 'The prince of mines'. Forbes. https://www.forbes.com/forbes/2008/0324/088.html?sh=2c953e8b3afe. Accessed 16 July 2022.

7 Ibid.

8 Ibid.

9 Ibid.

10 Ibid.

11 Ibid.

12 Mining Weekly. 29 November 2002. 'The Free State golden handshake: The turnaround specialist and the leader of tomorrow'. https://www.miningweekly.com/article/the-free-state-golden-

handshake-the-turnaround-specialist-and-the-leader-of-
tomorrow-2002-11-29/. Accessed 16 July 2022.

13 News24. 14 May 2002. 'Motsepe: From briefcase to big board'.
https://www.news24.com/News24/Motsepe-From-briefcase-to-big-
board-20020514. Accessed 16 July 2022.

14 Mining Weekly. 29 November 2002. 'The Free State golden
handshake: The turnaround specialist and the leader of tomorrow'.
https://www.miningweekly.com/article/the-free-state-golden-
handshake-the-turnaround-specialist-and-the-leader-of-
tomorrow-2002-11-29/. Accessed 16 July 2022.

15 Parliamentary Monitoring Group. 13 September 2000. 'Black
Economic Empowerment Commission: briefing by Cyril Ramaphosa
& Lott Ndlovu'. https://pmg.org.za/committee-meeting/191/.
Accessed 14 August 2022.

16 Author's interview with Michael Spicer, 18 March 2021.

17 Ndzamela, P. 20 March 2014. 'Ubuntu-Botho/Sanlam BEE deal'.
BusinessLive. https://www.businesslive.co.za/archive/2014-03-20-
ubuntu-bothosanlam-bee-deal/. Accessed 16 July 2022.

18 Cranston, S. 21 May 2015. 'Empowerment: A new giant rising?'
BusinessLive. https://www.businesslive.co.za/archive/2015-05-21-
empowerment-a-new-giant-rising/. Accessed 16 July 2022.

19 Cranston, S. 7 September 2017. 'ARC: All you need to know about
JSE's newest entrant'. https://www.businesslive.co.za/fm/money-and-
investing/2017-09-07-arc-all-you-need-to-know-about-jses-newest-
entrant/. Accessed 16 July 2022.

20 Mittner, M. 21 April 2016. 'Investor's Notebook: ARC is a beacon of
hope'. BusinessLive. https://www.businesslive.co.za/archive/2016-04-
21-investors-notebook-arc-is-a-beacon-of-hope2/. Accessed 16 July
2022.

21 Mtongana, L. 24 September 2017. 'Motsepe: I never aimed for Forbes
list'. BusinessLive. https://www.businesslive.co.za/bt/business-and-
economy/2017-09-23-motsepe-i-never-aimed-for-forbes-list/.
Accessed 16 July 2022.

22 These amounts are against a ZAR/USD exchange rate of R16.78:$1,
on 6 August 2022.

23 Forbes. N.d. 'World's Billionaires List: The richest in 2022'. https://
www.forbes.com/billionaires/. Accessed 14 July 2022.

24 SAPA. 2 October 2010. 'Patrice Motsepe donates R10m to Zuma's

foundation'. Mail & Guardian. https://mg.co.za/article/2010-10-02-patrice-motsepe-donates-r10m-to-zumas-foundation/. Accessed 16 July 2022.

25 Paton, C. 16 December 2012. 'Motsepe centre stage at ANC's Mangaung gala dinner'. BusinessLive. https://www.businesslive.co.za/archive/2012-12-16-motsepe-centre-stage-at-ancs-mangaung-gala-dinner-/. Accessed 16 July 2022.

26 Njilo, N. 18 November 2021. 'Ramaphosa and Motsepe donated over R6m to ANC ahead of election, says IEC'. BusinessLive. https://www.businesslive.co.za/bd/politics/2021-11-18-ramaphosa-and-motsepe-donated-over-r6m-to-anc-ahead-of-election-says-iec/. Accessed 14 August 2022.

27 Gerber, J. 23 February 2022. 'Party funding: Several parties benefit from Patrice Motsepe's deep pockets'. News24. https://www.news24.com/news24/southafrica/news/party-funding-several-parties-benefit-from-patrice-motsepes-deep-pockets-20220223. Accessed 16 July 2022.

28 Areff, A. 25 June 2022. 'Motsepe hates doing business with govt, especially when "you've got relatives" there'. Fin24. https://www.news24.com/fin24/companies/motsepe-hates-doing-business-with-govt-especially-when-youve-got-relatives-there-20220625. Accessed 16 July 2022.

29 I-Net Bridge. 30 January 2013. 'Patrice Motsepe donates half his wealth'. BusinessTech. https://businesstech.co.za/news/trending/30852/patrice-motsepe-donates-half-his-wealth/. Accessed 14 August 2022.

30 Omarjee, L. 2 April 2020. 'Donations, loans & pledges: What you need to know about those billions aimed at fighting Covid-19'. Fin24. https://www.news24.com/fin24/economy/south-africa/donations-loans-pledges-what-you-need-to-know-about-those-billions-aimed-at-fighting-covid-19-20200402-2. Accessed 14 August 2022.

31 The Bulls. Nd. 'Vodacom Bulls latest signing ... Patrice Motsepe'. https://thebulls.co.za/news/vodacom-bulls-latest-signing-patrice-motsepe. Accessed 14 August 2022.

Conclusion

1 Derby, R. 25 April 2018. 'Still a long way to go for meaningful BEE'. BusinessLive. https://www.businesslive.co.za/bd/opinion/

columnists/2019-04-25-ron-derby-still-a-long-way-to-go-for-meaningful-bee/. Accessed 16 July 2022.

2   News24. 21 September 2014. '"Broke" Judy claims Tokyo spends R2m a month. https://www.news24.com/News24/Broke-Judy-claims-Tokyo-blows-R2m-a-month-20140921. Accessed 14 August 2022.

3   Mail & Guardian. 12 December 1997. 'Farewell to the first premier of Gauteng'. https://mg.co.za/article/1997-12-12-farewell-to-the-first-premier-of-gauteng/. Accessed 14 August 2022.

4   Bosch, M. 9 June 2008. 'S.Africa's Sexwale: from freedom fighter to tycoon'. Reuters. https://www.reuters.com/article/safrica-sexwale-idUSL0980888220080609. Accessed 14 August 2022.

5   Ibid.

6   Author's interview with Michael Spicer, 5 March 2021.

7   Ibid.

8   Author's interview with Bobby Godsell, 4 May 2022.

9   Author's interviews with Michael Spicer, 5 March and 18 March 2021.

10 Author's interview with Saki Macozoma, 4 May 2022.

11 Author's interview with Trevor Manuel, 29 March 2021.

12 Ibid.

Acknowledgements

Thank you to Eugene Ashton, Annie Olivier, Jeremy Boraine and the production staff at Jonathan Ball Publishers who worked hard to launch and execute this project. It's our third book together, and it certainly was the toughest. They offered me fantastic support, including logistics, which gave me space to write.

This book would not have been possible without the support of News24's editor-in-chief, Adriaan Basson, who knows how difficult writing is.

Appreciation should also go to my employer, Media24, which, under the leadership of Ishmet Davidson, continues to support journalism in the best way possible – by creating a prosperous and stable working environment.

I deeply appreciate everyone I interviewed for this book, without whom it would almost certainly have not been possible, and specifically Michael Spicer, who gave generously of his time before his untimely death in early 2022 and provided much of the impetus to tell this story.

This book covers a vast period consisting of layer upon layer of political, economic and social history and events told from different perspectives. Mistakes, imperfections and wrongful interpretations are mine.

Index

Page numbers in italics indicate photo captions

About the author

Pieter du Toit is a journalist with News24, where he is assistant editor for investigations.

The ANC Billionaires is his third book with Jonathan Ball Publishers. *Enemy of the People* appeared in 2017, which he co-authored with Adriaan Basson, and *The Stellenbosch Mafia* was published in 2019. Both previous books were bestsellers, with *The Stellenbosch Mafia* occupying the number one spot on the Nielsen South Africa chart in the first week of its release.

After attending school and university in Stellenbosch, he went on to work for various titles at Media24, including as a crime reporter in Pretoria, parliamentary correspondent in Cape Town and news editor in Johannesburg. He lives in Johannesburg with his family.